D0312860

THE RISE
AND FALL
OF
CHARLES LINDBERGH

ALSO BY CANDACE FLEMING

Young Adult

*The Family Romanov: Murder, Rebellion,
and the Fall of Imperial Russia*

Fatal Throne: The Wives of Henry VIII Tell All

The Lincolns: A Scrapbook Look at Abraham and Mary

Middle-Grade

*Amelia Lost: The Life and Disappearance
of Amelia Earhart*

Ben Franklin's in My Bathroom!

Eleanor Roosevelt's in My Garage!

The Fabled Fifth Graders of Aesop Elementary School

The Fabled Fourth Graders of Aesop Elementary School

*The Great and Only Barnum: The Tremendous, Stupendous
Life of Showman P. T. Barnum*

Strongheart: Wonder Dog of the Silver Screen

Younger Readers

*The Amazing Collection of Joey Cornell: Based on the
Childhood of a Great American Artist*

Clever Jack Takes the Cake

Imogene's Last Stand

Oh, No!

THE RISE
AND FALL
OF
CHARLES
LINDBERGH

CANDACE FLEMING

schwartz & wade books · new york

QUOTATIONS IN THIS BOOK

You will notice that some of the quotations in this book are in present tense. This is how Charles Lindbergh wrote them himself. Often, when recording past events in his journals or memoirs, he recalled them as if they were happening in real time, allowing his readers to get inside his head during actual moments of inspiration, decision, or debate. In these instances, I have chosen to italicize his thoughts rather than placing them within quotation marks. It should be noted that none of the internal dialogue found in these pages has been invented. All of it comes directly from Lindbergh's firsthand accounts. The liberal use of both his and Anne Lindbergh's real words to reveal their thoughts and feelings, observations and conversations will, I hope, allow readers to form a deeper connection with them.

Text copyright © 2020 by Candace Fleming
Jacket photographs courtesy of Underwood Archives/Archive Photos/Getty Images and
Yuko Yamada/Moment/Getty Images

All rights reserved. Published in the United States by Schwartz & Wade Books, an imprint of
Random House Children's Books, a division of Penguin Random House LLC, New York.

Schwartz & Wade Books and the colophon are trademarks of Penguin Random House LLC.

Visit us on the Web! GetUnderlined.com

Educators and librarians, for a variety of teaching tools, visit us at
RHTeachersLibrarians.com

Library of Congress Cataloging-in-Publication Data
Names: Fleming, Candace, author.
Title: The rise and fall of Charles Lindbergh / by Candace Fleming.
Description: First edition. | New York City: Schwartz & Wade Books, [2020] |
Audience: Ages: 12+. | Audience: Grades: 9–12.
Identifiers: LCCN 2019014659 | ISBN 978-0-525-64654-9 (hardcover) |
ISBN 978-0-525-64655-6 (hardcover library b
Subjects: LCSH: Lindbergh, Charles A. (Charles
Air pilots—United States—Bio
Classification: LCC TL540.L5 F56 2020 | DDC 629.13092 [B]—dc23

The text of this book is set in 10.4-point Cheltenham ITC Pro.
Book design by Stephanie Moss

Printed in the United States of America
10 9 8 7 6 5 4 3 2 1
First Edition

CONTENTS

THE RISE

PART ONE: GROWING UP

"A sound individual is produced by a sound life stream."

PART TWO: AIRBORNE

"I tasted a wine of the gods."

PART THREE: NEW YORK TO PARIS

"The greatest feat of a solitary man in the records of the human race."

PART FOUR: COPILOT

"[He] has swept out of sight all the other men I have ever known . . . my world—my little embroidery beribboned world is smashed."

PART FIVE: KIDNAPPED

"He was twenty months old, blond, blue-eyed, and just beginning to talk."

PART SIX: BLOWN OFF COURSE

"We are starting all over again—no ties, no hopes, no plans."

THE FALL

PART SEVEN: LOSING ALTITUDE

"Hitler, I am beginning to feel, is . . . a visionary who really wants the best for his country."

PART EIGHT: AMERICA FIRST

"We [must] band together to preserve that most priceless possession, our inheritance of European blood . . . against . . . dilution by foreign races."

CONTENTS

ACKNOWLEDGMENTS

This book would never have taken flight without the dedication and generosity of so many librarians, archivists, and historians who answered questions, combed through documents, and dug out photographs. I need to thank several of them in particular: Matthew Schaefer, head archivist at the Herbert Hoover Presidential Library and Museum in West Branch, Iowa; Dennis Northcutt, associate archivist at the Missouri History Museum Library and Research Center; the entire staff of the Yale University Library, who oversee the Charles Augustus Lindbergh Papers housed there; the archival staff at the National Air and Space Museum, especially Elizabeth Borja; and the reference librarians at the Minnesota Historical Society. I am particularly grateful to Mark W. Falzini, author, Lindbergh kidnapping expert, and archivist in charge of the largest collection of documents pertaining to the case, housed at the New Jersey State Museum, for opening my eyes to the complexities of the case, as well as for fact-checking the manuscript. I also owe a huge debt to Susan A. Brewer, Professor Emeritus of History, University of Wisconsin–Stevens Point and author of *Why America Fights: Patriotism and War Propaganda from the Philippines to Iraq*. Not only did she read and comment on the completed manuscript, she emailed and called to discuss those Gordian knots in history and find solutions for its telling, not because she had to, but because she cared.

Friends, too, have made a vast contribution to this book. What would I have done without Katrin Tiernan, who sacrificed her summer days (and at times, her sanity) to translate the German text of *Das Doppelleben des Charles A. Lindbergh* into English? Thanks, too,

ACKNOWLEDGMENTS

to the talented and insightful women of my writers group—Penny Blubaugh, Stephanie Hemphill, and Barbara Rosenstock—for their sharp eyes and smart comments.

For the writing—the actual crafting of this story—I need to thank first and foremost my editor, Anne Schwartz. As always, she pushed me to make the story better with her piercing questions and brilliant suggestions. In Anne, I have found not simply an editor but a writing coach, a sounding board, and a good friend. I would be remiss not to thank designers Rachael Cole and Stephanie Moss for once again creating a gorgeous book; Anne-Marie Varga, editorial assistant at Schwartz & Wade for fielding my many requests; copy editors Barbara Perris, Alison Kolani, and Colleen Fellingham for their close and careful read; Adrienne Waintraub and Lisa Nadel for their unwavering support of my books; Ethan Ellenberg, my literary agent, for his always-wise counsel; and last, but never least, my shoulder to lean on, provider of diagrams, maps, and takeout, Eric Rohmann.

THE RALLY

THE STREETS AROUND NEW YORK CITY'S Madison Square Garden swarmed with America First rally-goers—thirty thousand in all—shouting, stabbing the air with their signs. The staunchest Firsters had begun lining up before dawn in hopes of getting a front-row seat. Others had come straight from work on that Friday afternoon. Although everyone had a ticket, not everyone would get inside. The Garden's cavernous arena wasn't big enough to hold all the movement's supporters. Those who didn't manage to get through the door would have to listen from the street via loudspeakers set up for that purpose. Tuned in to a local radio station, the speakers blasted a selection of news and music meant to entertain. But the noise merely whipped the crowd into an even greater frenzy.

So did the sudden appearance of a group of protesters. Led by a young woman with short dark hair, they marched back and forth, carrying signs that read AID TO FRANCE and MAINTAIN THE BRITISH BLOCKADE.

A sullen murmur of disapproval seemed to come from everywhere in the crowd, like low growls of thunder. A fist of men separated themselves from the other Firsters and pushed close to the protesters.

"Get out of here or we'll kill you!" yelled one of the men.

"Nazis!" a protester retorted.

The men lunged. After wrestling away the protesters' signs, the Firsters ripped them to shreds, while the mob hurled insults.

Policemen rushed in. They formed a wedge, then pushed through the yelling crowd and began leading the shaken protesters toward a safer place across the street. Still, Firsters ran in front of and behind them, jamming the way, being shoved aside by police, falling over each other. Violence simmered just beneath the surface. Anything could happen tonight. Anything was possible. These days, anger rippled across the country like waves, turning American against American. Neighbor against neighbor.

Flashbulbs popped as press photographers captured it all.

A couple of Firsters stepped assertively toward a reporter. Would the press cover the rally fairly this time? they wanted to know. Or would the newspapers be biased and inaccurate as usual? Many rally-goers believed the media couldn't be trusted. Their hero, the face of America First and the man they'd come to hear speak tonight, had told them so. "Contemptible," he'd called the press. "Dishonest parasites." In a recent speech he'd even told supporters that the press was controlled by "dangerous elements," men who placed their own interests above America's. That was why he had to keep holding rallies, he explained. Someone had to tell it like it was. Someone had to speak the impolite truth about the foreigners who threatened the nation. It was time to build walls—"ramparts," he called them—to hold back the infiltration of "alien blood." It was time for America to close its borders, isolate itself from the rest of the world, and focus solely on its own interests. It was the only way, he claimed, "to preserve our American way of life."

At 5:30 p.m., the Garden's doors opened and a crush of people began pushing and shoving, eager to get inside. As the enormous space filled, it grew hot and deafeningly loud. There was anger here, too, brewing, seething, waiting to be channeled toward some common enemy. It seemed to fill every seat, all the way up to the dim balconies.

Down in front, rally-goers discovered a protester in their midst. Pointing, shouting, their faces flushed, they called out a tall, sullen man. Men and women climbed onto their seats for a better look. The boos and roars reverberated to the far-off corners of the building. "Throw him out!" they screamed. People were standing up all over the arena now; the aisles were filling; lines of police gathered. "Throw him out!"

The protester backed up the aisle, his eyes fastened anxiously on the policemen walking toward him. The officers followed him slowly, controlled and rigid. All the while a low, grumbling sound came from the mob, like thunder about to break into a storm. It felt, recalled one rally-goer, like "the rumbles of revolution."

Onstage, the warm-up speakers approached the podium. Rally organizer John T. Flynn was first, followed by well-known orator and Presbyterian minister Norman Thomas. Both men gave brief, heartfelt speeches about building up the nation's defenses. But hardly anyone in the audience listened. They were waiting for one man.

At last, he walked slowly toward the podium.

Pandemonium. It was as if every voice in the place fought to shout the loudest, the noise building and building until it was, as one rally-goer described it, "a deep-throated, unearthly, savage roar, chilling, frightening, sinister and awesome."

"Give it to them!" shouted some in the crowd. "Give them the truth!"

"For six full minutes," a reporter would later recall, "he stood, smiling, as the mob leaped to its feet, waved flags, threw kisses and frenziedly rendered the Nazi salute."

At last, he leaned into the line of microphones to utter words that would be broadcast far beyond the arena to millions of Americans across the nation. "We are assembled here tonight because we believe in an independent destiny for America."

Foot-stomping, whistling, and clapping erupted.

The speaker waited, accepting it. When the crowd settled down a bit, he continued, pressing home his usual message. The country's survival depended on three things: increased defense spending, isolation, and putting America first. As he ticked off each, the audience howled its approval.

The speaker didn't try to tamp it down. He didn't repudiate violence. He just nodded and waited for the howling to end before he continued, his fiery words repeatedly punctuated by shouts.

Sitting behind him onstage, his wife recognized the truth even if he did not. The crowd wasn't really listening to her husband's speech. It wasn't his words that moved them, but the man himself. The celebrity. The personality. The hero, famous for his historic flight; the father whose family was the victim of the "Crime of the Century."

Now the mob chanted his name: "Lindbergh! Lindbergh! Lindbergh!"

THE RISE

PART ONE
GROWING UP

"A sound individual is produced
by a sound life stream."
—*Charles Lindbergh*

CHAPTER ONE

IN THE BEGINNING

THE ORIGIN STORY

On a sticky summer day in 1861, Charles Lindbergh's grandfather, August, accidentally cut off his left arm. It happened at the local sawmill. While guiding a log into the spinning blade, the young man slipped. Blood splattered across the room, and he saw both his arm and a slab of his back lopped off before he was hurtled across the room. His neighbors wrapped him in a quilt, delivered him to his bed, then went for the preacher. They expected him to die.

Lying there, gripping his shoulder socket with his right hand to stanch the blood, he stared out his bedroom window at the farm he'd carved from the Minnesota wilderness. August would not permit himself to die. His wound, he knew, was bad, so deep it exposed his beating heart and part of his lung. But he believed dying was the lazy way out, and August Lindbergh was anything but lazy.

He'd come to America two years earlier to escape prison. Back in Sweden, where he'd been called Ola Månsson, he'd been a wealthy dairy farmer, as well as a member of the Swedish parliament and—through his government position—an officer of the state bank. But in 1858, political opponents accused him of embezzlement. Ola had responded to their claims with his typical irreverence. When prosecutors handed him a sheaf of legal documents in court, he'd ripped them in half, dropped his trousers, and used the pieces to wipe himself. The judges found him guilty.

Ola, however, was not in court to hear their verdict. To everyone's shock—most especially his wife and children's—Ola had run off. With him went a solid gold medal once given to him by his constituents as a token of their esteem, as well as his twenty-one-year-old mistress, Lovisa, and their seventeen-month-old son, Karl.

Ten weeks later, Ola resurfaced in another courtroom, this one in Minnesota's Sixth District. Declaring his desire to become an American citizen (and "forgetting" to mention he was a fleeing felon), he gave officials his new name—August Lindbergh. His wife, he said, was Louisa Lindbergh. And their son was Charles August Lindbergh, called C.A. for short.

Thrilled to be in America rather than a Swedish jail, Ola-now-August settled into pioneer life. He traded his gold medal for a plow, built a log cabin, and began clearing trees. Lovisa-now-Louisa planted a garden, milked the cow, gave birth to a baby girl, and cried a lot. But to August's mind, life was good—until the day of the accident.

For months afterward, August lay in bed, refusing to give in to either pain or death. Because he was poor and isolated, with no medical care beyond an unlicensed and itinerant doctor, nothing could be done for him. When he was finally able to stand, he demanded to see his lost limb. Four-year-old C.A. brought it to him. Entwining the healthy fingers of his right hand with the stiff, dead ones of his left, August said to his arm, "You have been a good friend to me for fifty years. But you can't be with me anymore. So good-by. Good-by, my friend."

After placing his arm in a blanket-lined box, he buried it in the garden.

Then the stubborn farmer rigged up a belt with pockets and rings into which he could fit the handles of his plow, and got on with harvesting his crop. Soon he was doing as much with one arm as he used to do with two.

〜

Charles Lindbergh never knew his paternal grandfather. August died ten years before his grandson was born. But the story of the old man's extraordinary gumption, told to Charles time and again by his father, made a deep impression on the boy. He never heard it without wonder. And as he grew, he came to develop a much clearer, broader understanding of the story's importance. He saw himself as coming from exceptional stock, being shaped by the inherited traits of courage, physical toughness, stoicism in the face of adversity, and stubborn individualism. This "genetic composition," he later said, explained his "individuality and extraordinariness." It left him with an unwarranted belief in his superiority, as well as an exaggerated confidence in his own capabilities that would stay with him for the rest of his life.

IN THE BEGINNING

"I was born a child of man, in the city of Detroit, on February 4, 1902," Charles Lindbergh wrote nearly seventy years after the event. "[H]orses still dominated the streets and Orville Wright had not yet made the first power-sustained airplane flight."

His mother was Evangeline Land Lindbergh. Raised in Detroit by a science-minded family, Evangeline Land had been encouraged by her parents to attend the University of Michigan. It was rare in those days for a woman to go to college, even rarer to graduate with a degree in chemistry, but that was exactly what she'd done. Always unconventional, she'd then accepted a job teaching high school science in faraway Minnesota. Within months of her arrival, she married Charles August Lindbergh—still known as C.A. Yearning for independence and adventure, she'd found love instead.

Seventeen years older than Evangeline, C.A. had grown up to become a successful country lawyer and real estate investor—and one of the wealthiest men in Little Falls, Minnesota (population five thousand). He was also a widower with two daughters, fourteen-year-old Lillian and ten-year-old Eva, whom he rarely saw. Soon after his first wife's death, grief-stricken and craving solitude, C.A. had packed the girls off to a boarding school in Minneapolis. The girls would return to Little Falls only for an occasional visit. (Years later, when Charles reminisced about his boyhood, he never mentioned his half sisters. As far as he was concerned, they hardly existed.)

It wasn't long before Evangeline became pregnant. As soon as she was aware of her condition, she insisted on returning to her parents' home in Detroit. She absolutely would not give birth anywhere else, she declared. And she would have no other doctor but her uncle Edwin Lodge at her bedside.

C.A. had no choice but to agree. Three months of marriage had taught him that there was no arguing. What Evangeline wanted, Evangeline got.

And so, in the ninth month of her pregnancy, in the bitter winter of 1902, the couple traveled by train to Detroit. Once there, Evangeline was tucked comfortably into the front bedroom of the family's house on West Forest. Pampered and petted, the center of everyone's excited attention, she settled in and waited.

Less than a week later, in the early-morning hours of February 4, her nine-and-a-half-pound baby was born.

"Is it a boy?" asked Evangeline, who, along with C.A., had been hoping for a son.

"It is," Uncle Edwin replied.

"Are you sure?" she asked.

"Dead sure!" he exclaimed. "Just look at the size of those feet."

The baby also had startling blue eyes, a fuzz of light hair that soon grew into golden curls, and the same dimpled chin as his father.

His mother named him Charles August, after his father. But Evangeline was determined he would have his own unique identity. And so she added an extra syllable to his middle name, so he would not be a "junior." Then she bundled up her newborn and laid him on a chair beside an open window. After all, it was never too early to make a man out of a boy.

Charles Augustus Lindbergh took his first breaths of fresh winter air.

UP IN FLAMES

Five weeks later, baby Charles—he was *never* called Charlie because Evangeline believed nicknames were demeaning—returned with his mother to the family's big house in Minnesota.

Years earlier, his father had bought some land on the outskirts of Little Falls—120 acres of imposing bluff and thick woodland on the banks of the Mississippi River. In the months after their wedding, C.A. had built a grand three-story house on the very edge of the bluff, complete with a billiard room, servants' quarters, and an impressive front hall with a curved staircase. His Minnesota neighbors gossiped about his sudden spending. Until then, C.A. had always lived simply. He wore the same suit day in and day out, ate the nickel lunch at the Buckman Hotel, and used country expressions like "begorry." What could have caused such an about-face? they wondered. It had to be the fault of his young, college-educated wife. Full of airs, Evangeline Land was sure to lead C.A. into financial ruin.

C.A., however, could easily afford it. Both real estate and the business of law were generally booming, and his country lawyer practice provided a healthy income. Despite what his neighbors thought, the house was as much his dream as Evangeline's.

Young Charles's earliest memories were happy ones. He remembered sitting at the long dining room table set with gleaming silver and stemware while his father fed him raw carrots. He remembered his mother planting irises around the front of the house and playing sprightly songs on the piano in the living room. And he remembered watching from his bedroom on the second floor, the stars "curv[ing] upward in their courses . . . a flock of geese in westward flight—God's arrow shooting through the sky."

He also remembered the day it all came to an end.

On a Sunday morning in August 1905, three-year-old Charles was playing with his tin soldiers on the living room floor. Suddenly, he was jerked away from his toys by his mother and rushed out the back door.

Outside, everything was in chaos. Workmen raced across the grass with shovels and buckets while his father shouted orders and his mother sobbed into her hands. The air around him crackled and popped. When he took a deep breath, it tasted of soot.

His nurse grabbed his arm. "CHARLES!" she cried, and dragged him toward the safety of the barn. "Charles, you *mustn't* watch!"

He wiggled free of her grip.

"CHARLES, COME BACK!"

A huge column of black smoke rose from the house, spreading out and blackening the sky. The boy stared, eyes wide. Now he understood why he'd been yanked from his play. His house was burning down.

Across the lawn, the house seemed to give a huge sigh. Then, in a shower of flames and ash, it collapsed.

The next day, Charles and his mother poked through the smoldering ruins of the only home he'd ever known. Twisted pipes. Melted glass. Everything covered with the gray snow of ash.

His mother tried to comfort him. No one had been injured or killed in the fire. Besides, "Father will build us a new house," she said.

But my toys, thought Charles sadly, *and the big stairs and my room above the river, are gone forever.*

"EXPERIMENTING IN NEW FIELDS"

"It was a dreary winter that came after the burning of our house," Charles later recalled.

The Lindberghs rented an apartment in Minneapolis, but its small rooms were no substitute for the boy's beloved first home. He desperately missed its space and freedom. Now he spent "hours on end in dry, heated rooms." He grew pale, listless, and bored. Painfully shy, he did not play with other children. Instead, he stuck close to his mother, who almost never let him out of her sight.

Around this time, the four-year-old developed what became a lifetime practice of asking himself unusual questions, "experiment[ing]," as he called it, "in strange new fields." "Why can't I hold ten marbles between ten toes?" he asked himself. "How long can a cream-filled chocolate last if I eat it with a pin?"

Summer found the Lindberghs back in Little Falls. Since their new house wasn't built yet, they lived in a hotel. But Crook, their skittish horse, pulled their wagon the two miles to the construction site almost every day. While the carpenters and masons worked, Charles hovered nearby. He didn't ask questions; he was too shy for that. But his wide blue eyes took in everything.

Did he notice that the new house was only half the size of the old one? C.A. let it be known around town that he was scaling back because of financial problems. But the truth was, he and Evangeline weren't getting along. Beyond physical attraction, the two had little in common. Evangeline was brittle and demanding. C.A. was aloof and severe. "I don't tell people when I'm pleased," he once admitted. His annoyance with her demands and her frustration at his cold reserve had driven a wedge between them. Even before the fire, C.A. had moved out of their bedroom. Why build another grand house if he was considering leaving altogether?

The new house, when completed, wasn't much more than a summer cottage, and the family started referring to it as the camp.

Just seven small rooms clustered around a middle hallway, its attic unfinished, it lacked indoor plumbing and central heating. To four-and-a-half-year-old Charles, the best part was the screened-in sleeping porch. He chose it as his bedroom. "I was in close contact with sun, wind, rain, and stars," he recalled. "My bed, a wide, folding-cot affair, was in the northwest corner. On stormy nights rain blown in through the screen would mist it."

Already, Charles understood his deep need for the outdoors. "I am not happy living away from water or where I cannot see the sky on a clear night," he admitted years later. Indeed, he would always be happiest alone, outside with nature.

POLITICS AND GOD

In June 1906, a group of Republican men urged C.A. to run for the United States Congress in Minnesota's Sixth District.

At first, he demurred, saying he had better things to do with his time.

But the men persisted. Because he was the son of a farmer, C.A. understood their problems. And since two-thirds of the district's population was farmers, C.A. was sure to be a shoo-in.

Still, C.A. hesitated. He talked with friends and clients. Some told him it would be good for his law practice. Others told him it would be good for his bank account. But one client inadvertently hit on the most appealing reason of all. Being in Congress, he warned, would mean spending less time at home. Was C.A. prepared to give up family time?

Was he ever! C.A. had been searching for a socially acceptable way of separating from his wife. In those days, divorce was considered scandalous and ruinous to reputations. Instead, many unhappy couples found ways to live apart.

C.A. decided to run.

Evangeline did what she could to support his political ambitions. Since candidates and their families were expected to be regular churchgoers, she dressed up her not-quite-five-year-old son in an itchy flannel suit and dragged him to the Lutheran church in Little Falls.

Charles didn't like it one bit.

Week after week, he found himself trapped in the airless sanctuary, his legs itching in their tight stockings and the starched collar pinching his neck. He knew the preacher was talking about religion. "But you have to be grownup to understand [it]," said Charles. "When you don't . . . it's awfully uninteresting."

On his sleeping porch with his spotted mutt, Dingo, snuggled beside him, Charles stared out at the star-speckled sky and pondered God. As had become his habit, his questioning was expressed as a long internal conversation. "If there were no God," he recalled thinking, "then how could man have been created? But if there was a God, how did He begin? He couldn't very well have made Himself up out of nothing. And how did the universe begin—the stars, and space, and all the planets? . . . And if God existed, why didn't He show Himself to people, so there'd be no argument?" No, the boy finally decided, "God was as remote as the stars, and less real—you could see the stars on a clear night; but you never saw God—"

In November 1906, voters elected C. A. Lindbergh to the United States House of Representatives. It brought "certain changes in life for me," Charles admitted later, "a number of which were disagreeable."

The most disagreeable was the loss of a permanent home. His father's election meant the boy had to divide his time among three places: the "camp" in Minnesota, his grandfather Land's house in Detroit, and Washington, DC.

Rootless, his childhood fractured, Charles Lindbergh would move around so much over the next ten years that he never really became a part of anything.

CHAPTER TWO

ROOTLESS

DETROIT

As the eight-year-old leaped from the train to the platform, steam from the locomotive dampened his cheek. Behind him, his mother struggled with their suitcases, but Charles was too excited to help her. He scanned the crowd behind the gate eagerly. A man with a white mustache and gold-rimmed spectacles raised a black felt hat in the air to catch his attention.

There he was—Grandfather Land!

Twice a year, Charles and his mother came for a long visit, usually on their trips to and from Washington, DC. "I never had a dull moment at Detroit," Charles recalled, adding, "[There was] even more to do than [at the camp]." That was because Grandfather Land introduced him to the marvels of science.

The Lands lived in a gray frame house on West Elizabeth Street with flowers, a flagstone path, and a brass sign on the front door that read C. H. LAND, DENTIST.

Charles raced ahead of the adults and flung open the door. Was everything waiting for him exactly as he'd left it? An obsessive list-maker, Charles kept detailed accounts of his possessions. It was, one biographer would remark, as if he were "taking inventory of himself through his things." As always, he made a checklist:

There are the steps my tricycle once rolled down. There's the stuffed head of the Rocky Mountain sheep that I use as a target for my unloaded rifle. Here's the safe, which holds platinum foil and bright sheets of dental gold. And . . . the cabinet full of polished stones and fossils. On one of its shelves is a piece of a mammoth's tooth. . . . There are my old toy fire engines, high on the back hallway shelf. There's Grandmother, smiling and getting up from the kitchen table, and at her feet my battle-scarred tomcat, Fluff.

The place was a treasure trove, and the boy was given complete freedom to investigate and discover. In his grandfather's downstairs dental lab, Charles examined plaster casts of patients' mouths. He rode up and down on the hydraulic foot-pedaled dental chairs. And he used the dental wheel to polish stones he'd brought from Minnesota. He fiddled with microscopes, Bunsen burners, and ceramic ovens. "There were drills of all sizes and drawers for hand instruments, bottles of acid, amalgam powder, rubber sheets, little wads of cotton to put under the tongue."

When he wasn't with patients, Grandfather Land answered Charles's endless questions and helped him with his projects. He also made a point of teaching the boy how to use all the tools. He showed him how to mix clay and make molds, how to cast metal and handle electrically charged wires.

"Charles," he often reminded his curious, overeager grandson, "you must have patience."

Patience. It was, the boy came to realize, one of the most important requirements of scientific experimentation. He willed himself to slow down, to think logically and to construct systematically. And over the years, at his grandfather's side, he learned more chemistry, anatomy, electricity, biology, and mechanics than most adults ever do.

Equally stimulating was the talk around his grandparents' dinner table. The Lands' conversations ranged from arguments about philosophy to discussions of the latest scientific discoveries and theories. Their talk didn't "hum in my ears like a church sermon or a political speech," acknowledged Charles. Science was something he could grasp. He liked the quick way it could provide a definite answer. At the Lands' house he learned that "science is a key to all mystery." That was what his grandfather always said. "With this key, man can become like a god himself. Science is truth; science is knowledge; science is power."

Charles didn't doubt Grandfather Land's words. After all, Dr. Land was also an innovator and inventor. Using fixtures and hardware he'd developed, he wired his home with electricity—an impressive accomplishment in 1910. He'd designed a self-rocking cradle for baby Charles. He'd refurbished a dental foot engine into a pottery wheel so he could throw his own flowerpots. He grew mushrooms in his basement and wildflower hybrids that he'd cultivated himself in his garden. He even created an air filtration system using cheesecloth and fans to keep Detroit's sooty air out of his house. "My Grandfather is as wise as he is old," Charles bragged as a child, "and he can make *anything* with his hands."

Like his grandson, he also pondered the question: What is death? And he wondered if the human body could be treated like a machine with a collection of replaceable parts. After all, if he could replace teeth with perfectly fine artificial ones, then why not a heart and lungs? Dr. Land was convinced that it would happen one day. And then . . . was it possible that humans could live forever?

The vocal and opinionated Dr. Land expressed these ideas to his family. And Charles, with his curious mind and his own questions about life and death, soaked them up. *Is there something within one's body that doesn't age with years?* the boy wondered. The question "throb[bed] in my mind."

Around the age of ten, Charles began thinking about becoming a doctor when he grew up so he could "explore the mysteries of life and death."

He felt confident he could solve them.

WASHINGTON, DC

Despite her estrangement from C.A., Evangeline went to Washington eight out of the ten winters he was in Congress so that father and son could see each other daily. The couple did not live together. Instead, C.A. slept on the black leather couch in his office while Evangeline rented a series of inexpensive rooms in hotels and boardinghouses.

Charles hated his winters in Washington. "For me," he said, "the city formed a prison." He felt hemmed in by the solid rows of red-brick buildings and bustling streets. He longed for woods and fields, the sigh of wind through the pines and the hoot of an owl echoing across the darkness. Often, the clanging of the streetcar jarred him from his sleep. At those times, he would have liked to get up and play with his tin soldiers, but their rooms were always too small for that. One year, he and his mother shared a large front room with just one bed. Another time, a curtained alcove with a small mattress served as his bedroom. Only once did they rent rooms with a kitchenette, enabling Evangeline to cook. Most years, they took their morning and evening meals in the dining room with the other boarders. "Surrounded by strange adults, there was never room for Charles to misbehave, or just be a boy," noted one historian. "The boardinghouses constricted his already strained personality; at an early age he became an overly polite silent sufferer."

Concerned about her son's lonely existence, Evangeline took him on trips around the city. He climbed the Washington Monument, watched money being printed at the Treasury Department, and visited the National Zoo.

One morning when he was ten, Charles and his mother traveled by streetcar to Fort Myer, Virginia, to see a demonstration of military aircraft. There, on a crescent-shaped field just west of Arlington National Cemetery, a half dozen pilots from the newly formed US Army Air Service (the forerunner of our modern-day air force) readied their planes for takeoff. Propellers whirred. Engines rumbled. Mechanics puttered around wings and wheels.

Charles watched, wide-eyed. Like most of the other spectators standing at the far edge of the field, he'd never seen an airplane. He could hardly believe such a thing existed. They were astonishing and marvelous. And they'd been invented during his short life.

On December 17, 1903—two months before Charles's second birthday—Orville and Wilbur Wright had made the first airplane flight. Though it had lasted just twelve seconds and traveled just 120 feet—a mere skip across the sand at Kitty Hawk, North Carolina—it was the start of a new future in transportation.

Over the next years, the Wright brothers continually improved their invention. And by 1909, they had what they considered a "practical flyer." A variation on their Model A airplane, it was designed to carry two people sitting upright and shoulder to shoulder in two seats on the leading edge of the wing. Controlled by two simple levers (or "sticks"), the plane was equipped with a more powerful, four-cylinder internal combustion motor. The original plane had used a two-cylinder engine.

That year, Wilbur Wright wowed the world by circling the Statue of Liberty in the Model A. His demonstration convinced US Army officials to invest in aircraft. Within the year, they hired the Wrights to build the first military planes. Smaller than the Model A, these planes were designed for speed and—to the army's amazement—could reach a top speed of 42 miles per hour. (Modern commercial jets fly at a speed of between 460 and 575 miles per hour.) With the purchase of these machines, the army also enlisted its first pilots.

A few civilians took to the skies, too, once the Wrights began selling planes to those who could afford the asking price of $5,000 (about $137,000 today). These buyers, like those first military pilots, were trained to fly by the brothers themselves. And still the Wrights kept improving their product. With each passing year their planes flew higher, faster, and farther. By 1912, they'd designed an eight-cylinder motor that could reach 80 miles per hour and fly for one hour and twelve seconds. They improved directional control. And they added wheels for takeoffs and landings, dispensing with the launch system (similar to a catapult) they'd been using.

These were the type of plane Charles saw that morning in Fort Myer—called pushers because their propellers were behind the pilot, thus pushing the machine through the air. (It would be another two years before "tractors"—propeller-first aircraft—would be introduced.) All were biplanes—that is, they had two pairs of wings stacked one above the other for added strength and lift. And all looked fragile. Made of wood and fabric, with open cockpits and no fuselage (main body), they seemed to be held together with nothing but struts and wire.

After wrapping themselves in leather and wool for protection against the cold, the pilots perched at the front of what looked to Charles like box kites—oblong wooden crates without sides. Incredibly, they flew. "One of the planes took off," recalled Charles. "You could see its pilot clearly, out in front—pants' legs flapping, and cap visor pointed backward to streamline the wind."

A second plane bombed a chalked outline of a battleship, with oranges thrown by hand.

A third was forced to make an emergency landing in nearby woods.

And Charles's imagination soared with visions of flight.

〰️

When alone, Charles roller-skated on the Mall or played in the self-service elevator at the Library of Congress. One afternoon he amused himself by locking all the doors to the Cannon House Office

Building's bathroom stalls from the inside. Another day he dropped lightbulbs off the building's roof. He didn't get in trouble for either of these pranks. A congressman's son, he quickly learned, could get away with all sorts of mischief.

Charles took it for granted that he had little in common with other children. Perhaps if his parents had sent him to school more often, he would have developed a rapport with those his own age. Despite their college educations, neither parent felt school was especially important. Evangeline disapproved of rote learning and believed she could do a better job of teaching Charles at home. ("I like my mother. My mother likes me" were the first sentences she taught her son to write.) Though C.A. did occasionally prod his wife to send the boy to school, he had little respect for formal education and thought it cruel to keep youngsters cooped up inside all day.

And so their son attended school sporadically. By his own count, Charles went to eleven different schools between the ages of eight and sixteen. His first was the Force School in Washington, DC. Admitted as a second grader, he hated having to "sit still in a strange room, amid strange children, and surrounded by strange conventions . . . countless hours . . . waiting, waiting, waiting for school to close."

Later, he went to the Sidwell Friends School, a name Charles scoffed at. "I did not find much friendship among the children there. I did not understand them, nor they me." They made him the butt of their jokes, nicknaming him "Limburger or simply Cheese."

Despite this, he remained at Sidwell for two years, in the seventh and eighth grades—the longest of any school. Even then, he didn't attend the entire academic year. His mother's habit of stopping in Detroit for several weeks on her way to and from Washington meant he always started the school year weeks late and left weeks early. Is it any wonder he was inattentive and bored in class? And while he never flunked any subjects, his grades were poor.

Duller still were the hours he spent in the House of Representatives' gallery. "It was always too hot, and rather stuffy, and [the] speeches went on and on like sermons from a pulpit. . . . Sometimes you got a headache as you listened—" But his father liked having him there whenever he spoke . . . and C.A. spoke often.

C.A.'s favorite topic to rail about on the House floor was banking reform. A congressional maverick, he relished the idea of battling America's financial institutions. Declaring war on banks and investment firms, he demanded to know why they "who are no smarter than the rest of us" continually got richer. This "Money Trust," he claimed, had seized sinister control of America. Something had to be done before they "undermined free speech, free press and the freedom of thought."

His opinions were unpopular with his fellow congressmen. But C.A. didn't care. "It is better to speak the truth than be liked," he told his son.

They were words Charles would come to live by.

LITTLE FALLS

The wheels clattered on the track, changing tempo as the train curved and crossed a white-watered river. Charles looked out the window. He could see the tops of the tall Norway pines that marked his "camp."

"L-l-l-ittle-e-e Fa-a-a-l-l-l-s!" sang out the conductor.

The train slowed, jerked, came to a stop.

"Winter's school is over," ten-year-old Charles rejoiced. "Summer has come; and with it, our Minnesota home."

As they did every June when they returned, mother and son stopped at Ferguson's Grocery to order food and arrange for their trunks to be delivered from the station. Then they set out on foot to the camp.

When they reached the neighbor's house where Dingo had spent the winter, Charles whistled and the dog bounded out to greet him.

Frantic with joy, Dingo barked, wiggled, wagged. And Charles—always more affectionate with animals than people—thumped Dingo's side and scratched him all over. Then they started together down the shady country path that curved through meadow, woods, and tangled thickets.

At last, Charles pushed open the camp's gate and, with Dingo at his heels, raced toward the cottage. Short-tall, his pet chipmunk, scampered out onto the rock pile beside the back porch steps. The boy was relieved to see him, and the house. Ever since fire had destroyed his first home, Charles worried about losing the second.

After turning the key in the lock, he pushed into the kitchen. The place smelled musty. They didn't have a caretaker, so no one had been inside all winter. As Evangeline flung open windows to let in the fresh summer air, Charles ran through the rooms, making sure all was in order.

Once his indoor inventory was complete, he dashed back outside. Was his rope swing still hanging? Had the cave he'd dug out around an old stump fallen in? Could he still keep his balance on the stilts he'd made? "There's the maidenhair patch to visit and the bluff on the creek to slide down," he told himself. "I have my guns to clean and hawks to hunt. Dingo has gophers to catch."

⁂

One day, as Charles played outside, he stumbled across a dead horse, black flies buzzing above its bloated belly. Its four rigid legs looked like exclamation marks.

Charles stopped. Where had the horse come from? And why had it died here in his woods?

Beside him, Dingo barked and lunged. Charles gripped the dog's collar to hold him back. The boy certainly hadn't expected to find *this* when he'd set out in search of adventure.

Practically every morning since his return, he'd tramped through the pinewood. He liked to pretend he was a pioneer, blazing new trails through the wilderness, or a soldier, protecting the frontier. Except for Dingo, he was always alone. He wasn't sorry about that. Charles found the children in Little Falls, like the ones in Washington, DC, a bit disappointing. He knew the neighboring kids thought he was odd, but he didn't care. Why bother spending time with other people when you were your own best company?

Dingo barked again. The air no longer smelled of fresh forest pine. The boy inched closer to the horse. The sight left him both sickened and spellbound. He had seen dead things before, but never anything this big.

Charles crouched down. He couldn't find any obvious wounds. So why had the horse died? Why did anything have to die? He grew still, thinking hard. "The difference between life and death was so apparent in that rotting hulk," he later wrote, "and yet it was not understandable! What stopped life from living?"

"Why does [God] make you die?" he asked his mother when he got home.

Replied Evangeline, "When you die, you go to God and he takes care of you."

Charles shook his head. That wasn't what he'd asked. He tried again. *If God was so good, why did he make you die? Why didn't He let people live forever?*

Evangeline still didn't have an answer.

So Charles came to his own conclusion. *"There was nothing good about death,"* he said. *"It was terrible."*

When he wasn't tramping through the woods, Charles could often be found lying on his back in the meadow, hemmed in by the tall grass and hidden from passersby, watching the clouds drift overhead and thinking. "Those clouds, how far away were they? Nearer than the neighbor's house, untouchable as the moon—unless you had an airplane," he figured. He wished he had one. "Wings with which I could fly up to the clouds and explore their caves and canyons—wings like that hawk circling above me. Then, I would ride on the wind and be part of the sky."

Charles thought a lot about airplanes. He remembered the excitement of the airplane demonstration his mother had taken him to in Virginia. And then there was the day when he'd heard the sound of a distant engine while reorganizing his rock collection in the cottage's attic.

At first, he'd assumed it was a car. More and more people in Little Falls were buying automobiles, and the sound of them on the road had become common. But as the engine sound grew louder, Charles leaped to his feet, sending stones skittering across the wood floor. No automobile engine made *that* noise. And it was approaching too fast.

The boy hurried to the window and climbed out and onto the roof.

There, above the treetops, passed a "pusher" like the ones he'd seen in Virginia. But what was it doing here?

He watched until it flew out of sight. Then he raced downstairs and shared the exciting news with his mother.

Evangeline knew all about it. She'd read in the local newspaper about a pilot coming to town. He was taking people up for a dollar a minute. But it was terribly dangerous. "Suppose the engine stopped, or a wing fell off, or something else went wrong?" she explained to Charles.

Disappointed, Charles pushed down his longing to fly. But for months afterward, he imagined himself with wings, "swoop[ing] down off our roof into the valley, soaring through air from one riverbank to the other . . . above the tops of trees."

There were risks in everything that was worthwhile or interesting. "Danger was a part of life not always to be shunned," Charles said later. "It was dangerous to climb a tree, to swim down rapids in the river, to go hunting with a gun." Or, as he soon learned, to drive a car.

One July afternoon in 1912, C.A. arrived at the camp in a brand-new Ford Model T. Charles quickly took inventory of the marvelous machine with its "foot-pedal gearshift, four-cylinder engine . . . carbide headlights, hand crank, squeeze rubber-bulb horn . . . and quick fasten-on side curtains for rainy days." C.A. announced that he'd bought the car for his campaign trips and intended to leave it with them the rest of the year. Evangeline, he added generously, was welcome to drive it anytime.

But it was soon clear that Evangeline was a nervous driver. She'd drive the two miles into town white-knuckled, her foot clamping down on the brake, causing the car to stall out. When she wasn't braking and stalling, she was weaving and swerving. Once, she drove into a ditch.

Ten-year-old Charles knew he could drive better than *that*. And even though he was so short that he had to stand up to reach the pedals, he climbed behind the wheel and, without any supervision, headed down the road. Soon, he taught himself how to handle the car. Neither parent tried to stop him. They did not impose their ideas of what he should do or how he should behave. And they seemed not to notice that he was still a child. "Age seemed to make no difference to [them]," Charles later wrote. "My freedom was complete. All [they] asked for was responsibility in return. . . ."

The Model T needed lots of maintenance. Even on short trips, Charles often had to stop and tinker with the engine, change the tires, and make adjustments to the gas headlights.

This didn't bother him. He knew he possessed exceptional mechanical abilities. Even as a small boy, he'd shown a remarkable aptitude. He'd taken apart and reassembled a shotgun before he could read. When he was seven, he'd fixed the camp's motor-driven water pump. And recently he'd designed a way to move heavy blocks of ice from the icehouse to the kitchen using pulleys, levers, an inclined plane, and a toy wagon.

"[The] kid . . . loved machinery and knew how to handle it," recalled Martin Engstrom, owner of Little Falls's hardware store. Engstrom was so impressed he gave the boy free use of the store's workshop, and Charles spent long hours tinkering back there—so many that Engstrom started to worry. It seemed to him that machines had become more real to Charles than most people were. "Nobody recalls [him] ever having attended a social function, or having looked at a girl. His favorite pastime was to hang around [the] hardware store, where he could gaze at the latest mechanical gadget. . . ."

Charles was, one Little Falls girl recalled, "a grubby youth . . . [with] engine grease under his fingernails."

CHAPTER THREE

CHANGES

"BUNCOED!"

C.A. Lindbergh was furious. War had erupted in Europe in 1914, and the congressman from Minnesota—in typically loud fashion—was fighting to keep America out of it. Wall Street, he railed from the floor of the House, had "buncoed the citizens." This war wasn't about national security. It was about money. Financiers wanted to get rich from a war fought with the blood of American fathers, husbands, and sons. Congress could not let this happen.

But no one seemed to be listening to Congressman Lindbergh. So C.A. decided to run for the United States Senate. Senators, he believed, had a bigger platform than congressmen. He announced his candidacy in the spring of 1916, then returned to Minnesota and began campaigning across the state.

Fourteen-year-old Charles drove him everywhere. For weeks they traveled over rough roads and through bad weather. Wherever his father spoke—churches, town halls, courthouse squares—Charles handed out an antiwar pamphlet C.A. had written, titled *Why Is Your Country at War?*

Charles claimed not to care about politics. "While I wanted very much to have my father win," he admitted, "my primary interests in his campaign trips lay in the opportunity they gave me to . . . drive." Still, when C.A. said, "The trouble with war is that it kills the best and youngest men," it obviously made an impression. Little did the boy know that twenty years in the future, he would emulate both his father's sentiments and his fervor.

C.A.'s antiwar stand made him unpopular with voters. He was trounced by his opponent and retreated to Washington and his congressional seat, where he continued his fiery crusade against getting involved in Europe's war.

But even as C.A. was shouting on the House floor, Germany was sinking American ships. In April 1917, President Woodrow Wilson asked Congress for a declaration of war.

Congress gave it to him.

And suddenly, C.A. supported it. "The thing has been done," he wrote, "and however foolish it has been, we must all be foolish and unwise together, and fight for our country." For the first time since entering the House, Congressman Lindbergh fell quiet. Patriotism held his tongue.

WIRE AND STRUTS GO TO WAR

Airplanes remained, at the beginning of the war, boxy and slow. But governments on both sides of the conflict pushed for improvements. They recognized aircraft's usefulness during battle. Planes could scout over enemy territory, shoot down other planes, and drop bombs. Across Europe and the United States, aeronautical manufacturers sprang up, cramming decades of technological progress into just a few years. Their goal was to enhance aircraft speed, distance, and maneuverability. Soon, planes became more enclosed, although cockpits were still open. Some aircraft even used metal in their construction, although most were still framed with wood, trussed with wires, and covered with linen. At the start of the conflict in 1914, the average speed for a plane was seventy miles an hour; by war's end in 1918, it was twice that fast. With their more streamlined shape, long, graceful wings, and more powerful motors, airplanes could go farther, too, with cruising ranges of five hundred miles. They could also bank (turn) more sharply and climb more quickly.

However, they could not fly at great altitudes. Anything above 8,000 feet caused pilots to grow light-headed from lack of oxygen. (Air gets thinner with every foot climbed.) Unlike modern commercial jets, whose typical flight altitude is 35,000 feet (made possible by pressurized cabins), pilots in World War I flew below the clouds. This left them subject to rain, snow, flocks of birds, and every gust of wind. Not until World War II would high-altitude flying become possible.

Still, the technological strides made during the First World War were impressive. So was the number of planes produced. At war's beginning, there were approximately twenty thousand planes worldwide. By its end, that number was two hundred thousand. Once considered foolish and fatal, flight had proven itself. And some people began to see commercial possibilities: If planes could serve in war, why not in peace?

"RESCUED BY WORLD WAR I"

Evangeline and Charles didn't follow C.A. to Washington for the winter of 1917–1918. Instead, they remained at the camp, and at C.A.'s urging began stocking it for the first time with cattle and sheep. "Food Will Win the War" had become the national slogan, and anyone who could grow crops or raise livestock for America's soldiers and its French and British allies was urged by the government to do so. And so the camp was transformed into a farm.

C.A. believed his fifteen-year-old son could manage it all.

Charles knew he could, too. "We'll make our hundred and twenty acres of field and woodland produce all the food they can," he declared—even though he'd never farmed. Hadn't he taught himself how to repair an internal combustion engine? If he could do that, he could certainly raise crops and animals.

He was less confident about the task Evangeline had given him: to graduate from high school. Having enrolled at Little Falls High School in September 1917, he bicycled to classes each morning. But it was, he admitted, "a gesture." While his teachers droned on about history or civics, he doodled in the margins of his notebooks— airplanes, motorcycles, automobiles. His grades soon fell so low he doubted he could pass the exams required to graduate. And then . . .

"I was rescued by World War I," recalled Charles.

On a snowy morning in January 1918, Principal Michie gathered all the students in the gymnasium to share some astounding news. The army needed food, but because so many men had been drafted for military service, there was a shortage of farmworkers. Therefore, any student willing to do farmwork could leave school and still grad- uate.

Charles had his hand in the air before the principal finished speaking. He'd trade in his textbooks for a tractor any day! A week later, he bade farewell to high school. He would return only once— in June 1918, to pick up his diploma.

A SCIENTIFIC FARMER

"Farm work enabled me to combine my love of earth and animals with my interest in machinery," said Charles. Deciding to use mod- ern methods, he confidently ordered up a tractor, a gangplow, a disc harrow, and a seeder. His neighbors thought him impractical. How could he possibly farm without a team of horses? But the teenager sniffed at their shortsightedness. Mechanization would increase productivity. To this end, he installed a milking machine—the first in the county—cutting his milking time in half. He bought incubators, successfully hatching a thousand chicks in just one season. And after reading a government pamphlet on breeding stock, he bought a pure-blooded Guernsey to improve his herd's gene pool.

Even with the help of modern methods, however, farming was hard work. All by himself, Charles tended three dozen dairy cows, sixty sheep, countless chickens and geese, and two ponies named Queen and Prince. He raised fifty acres of corn. And he chopped down trees to build fences and log houses for the hogs, built a silo and a swinging bridge across the creek, pitched hay, hauled ice, and repaired the tractor . . . and the milking machine . . . and the incubators.

The sixteen-year-old became hard-muscled and physically fit, and he reached his full height of six feet three inches. Lithe and slender, he had high cheekbones, a dimpled chin, and a full mouth that rarely smiled. In his startling blue eyes glimmered a faint arrogance.

At the end of each workday—after shaking his mother's hand by way of good night—Charles went out to the screened-in porch. Even in the winter, he slept there. He'd wrap himself in an old fur-lined coat of his father's, then burrow under the bed's mountain of quilts. His fox terrier, Wahgoosh (Dingo had died years earlier), pushed in beside him.

Some nights when the stars were extraordinarily bright, Charles would look out at the constellations and imagine a life beyond farming. He had only a vague notion of what he wanted from life. Freedom, yes, and to work with mechanical things. But also a little danger, and physical achievement.

Meanwhile, he plodded through his days, shearing sheep and milking cows.

When the war ended in November 1918, his father, who had just been voted out of the House of Representatives, did not return to Little Falls. Instead, he moved to Minneapolis and opened a law practice there.

Charles turned seventeen.

What should he do next?

College occurred to him, but he hesitated. He hadn't cracked open a book in two years. What if he was "too rusty to keep up?"

He put off his decision and kept working the farm. He bought himself a twin-cycle Excelsior motorcycle and in his spare time roared all over the county. He longed to travel farther—all the way to California, or maybe Alaska. "I loved . . . our Minnesota home," he later explained, "but two years on the farm was enough."

He thought about studying engineering. It made sense because of his interest in science and mechanics, and yet he chose to attend the University of Wisconsin in Madison, "probably more because of its nearby lakes than because of its high engineering standards," he admitted.

Charles left for college at the beginning of September 1920. As he straddled his Excelsior, he looked back at the cottage and felt a moment's bittersweet nostalgia. "I knew that day that childhood was gone. My farm on the Mississippi would become a memory, of which, sometime, I'd tell my children."

Revving the motor, he roared off into his future.

PART TWO
AIRBORNE

"I tasted a wine of the gods."
—*Charles Lindbergh*

CHAPTER FOUR

SCHOOLED

FISH OUT OF WATER

By the fall of 1920, an entire generation infected with the spirit of "eat, drink, and be merry, for tomorrow we die" had returned from the battlefields of Europe. Used to speed, excitement, and living on the edge, they found it impossible to settle down into the humdrum routine of American life as if nothing had changed. *Everything* had changed. They were sick and tired of heroic efforts, disillusioned by war and cynical about peace. They wanted fun and freedom and release from those stodgy prewar morals and ideals. Awash in rebellion, they pursued both pleasure and profit recklessly. They were uninhibited and "emancipated." The whole country, declared novelist F. Scott Fitzgerald, was "going hedonistic."

Thus the Roaring Twenties was born—age of jazz babies and flappers, bootleg whiskey and true crime magazines. And at the University of Wisconsin, students were flinging themselves into the new decade with abandon. Female students shortened both their hair and their hemlines, and cigarettes became their new diet fad. Male students donned raccoon coats and carried around ukuleles in hopes of wooing these newly emancipated girls. To the shock of their elders, they sipped gin (now illegal with the passage of the Eighteenth Amendment to the US Constitution in January 1920) from hip flasks, sat in parked automobiles for "petting parties," stayed up into the wee hours, and gleefully pushed each other into Lake Mendota.

Into this world rode Charles Lindbergh.

He did not fit in.

Shy and clean-shaven, he was remarkably wholesome. He didn't drink or smoke. He didn't touch caffeine, not even Coca-Cola, and he cared nothing for fashionable clothes. He'd never learned to dance or been on a date.

He also lived with his mother.

Incredibly, Evangeline had followed her son to college. Renting a two-bedroom apartment close to campus, she went about keeping house for the eighteen-year-old freshman. Charles didn't mind; being with his mother was better than living with strangers in a dorm.

Charles steered clear of most people. He found the other students childish and their activities pointless. It wasn't long before his classmates left him as alone as he seemed to want to be. They judged him different and odd, a boy who "went home every night to have dinner with his mother."

Things were no better in the classroom. Unable to concentrate, he daydreamed and doodled and took long hikes beside the lake instead of completing assignments. Despite his mother's help (she wrote his papers), his grades were poor. "Why should one spend hours of life on formulae, semi-colons, and our crazy English spelling?" he asked himself. "I don't believe God made man to fiddle with pencil marks on a paper. He gave him earth and air to feel. And now even wings to fly . . ."

Charles had followed newspaper accounts of aerial combat during the war, and he'd briefly considered joining the army in hopes of training to be a pilot. Now his interest in flying and his frustration over college coalesced. In late fall 1921, he wrote to a handful of flight schools. No matter that he'd never even gotten close to a plane, much less flown in one. He was certain he could be a pilot. Soon he was poring over the flight school's pamphlets. *This* was the kind of learning he knew he would like—hands-on instruction in the air and practical lessons on all aspects of airplane mechanics.

The nineteen-year-old was most impressed by a program offered by the Nebraska Aircraft Corporation in Lincoln. Courses began the first week of April, and the literature urged potential students to apply early, since enrollment was limited.

Should he apply? His parents, he knew, would be dead set against his quitting school.

The university made the decision for him. Midway through his sophomore year—after failing mathematics, physics, and mechanical design—he was expelled.

No reasonable parent in 1922 would have wanted his or her child to become a pilot. Civilian aviation in those days was perilous, and completely unregulated by the government. Anyone could buy a plane, in any condition, and take up paying customers. These planes were almost all former warplanes that had been sold off by the government. Small and unstable, the wood-and-fabric crates held just one or two passengers—*if* the passengers didn't weigh too much. Since anyone with a plane—skilled or unskilled—could take to the sky, accidents were common. It was claimed that the average pilot could expect to fly just nine hundred hours before suffering a fatal crash. No wonder the majority of Americans thought airplanes were wildly unsafe.

Flying was also considered slightly seedy. At that time, there were no commercial airlines in the United States; not a single company had yet to move people and cargo by air. Only the United States Postal Service used airplanes, but in a very limited capacity. Without airlines to employ them, pilots took whatever work they could find—giving rides at county fairs, dragging advertising banners across the sky, and performing spectator-thrilling aerial stunts. In good-weather months, these men—and women, too—crisscrossed the country, "vagabond[ing] in the air," as one pilot put it, in constant search of a job. Most just barely managed to eke out an existence.

Her son's decision disappointed Evangeline, but she hid her emotions. "All right," she finally said. "If you really want to fly, that's what you should do." She paused before adding, "You must lead your own life. I mustn't hold you back. Only I can't see the time when we'll be together much again."

Evangeline would eventually take a teaching job in Detroit.

And Charles would soar into history.

But first he had to learn to fly.

ABOVE

Charles stood in the big, half-open door and blinked. What a sight! Airplanes, a half dozen, lined the Nebraska Aircraft Corporation's factory floor. The surplus army training planes, now converted for civilian use, that Charles gazed at were Lincoln-Standard Turnabouts. Biplanes with forward-mounted propellers, they were powered by a 150-horsepower engine that could reach a speed of ninety miles per hour.

Charles didn't know any of this yet. This was the first time he'd been close enough to an airplane to touch it. His fingers stroked wooden struts and trailed down slender wires. His nostrils filled with the acrid odor of acetate.

Ray Page, the company president, gave the gangly twenty-year-old the once-over. What did the kid want?

Charles explained that he'd come to enroll in the flying school.

Page didn't know about any flying school. He'd bought the company just a month earlier, and the previous owners hadn't said a word about it—probably because there'd never been one. Genuine flying schools were rare in 1922. Why train people for a career in which there were no jobs? The literature sent to Charles had been nothing more than a come-on to lure potential airplane buyers. Still, there were plenty of pilots and mechanics around who could show the kid the ropes. Was Charles willing to pay?

Charles handed over a check for $500, money he'd saved from his farming days.

It was a princely sum for a scraping-by aviator. "Welcome . . . to school," announced Page.

Right away, he put his one and only student to work. That first week, Charles took apart an engine and learned how to waterproof wings with a special varnish aviators called dope. He became proficient at straining fuel into a plane's tank and hooking up rudders. He was learning airplanes inside and out. And he marveled at all of it.

Only a week later, on April 9, 1922, Charles climbed into the front cockpit of a newly converted Liberty biplane for his first airplane ride. With his goggles strapped on and a leather helmet on his head, he turned to look at the pilot in the rear cockpit.

"CONTACT!" hollered the pilot.

The engine coughed, then caught with a roar. The wings trembled. The propeller blade became a blur. Then the plane moved forward, bumping over rough ground, going faster and faster and—

"Now!" exclaimed Charles. "The ground recedes—we are resting on the air—Up, past riggers and mechanics—over tree tops—across a ravine—like a hawk . . ."

He felt weightless . . . transformed . . . *above.*

"I lose all conscious connection with the past," said Charles. "I live only in the moment in this strange, unmortal space, crowded with beauty, pierced with danger."

Too soon, the plane descended. The engine sputtered, and with a shudder, everything came to a stop. Charles felt overwhelmed with sadness. He didn't want to be on the ground. He wanted to be part of the clouds and sky, soaring through blue, forever and forever.

BIFF AND SLIM

While Charles made up the school's entire student body, Ira Biffle had been appointed by Ray Page to be its entire faculty. With a weatherworn face and a propensity for colorful cursing, Biff, as he was called, had trained pilots in the war. But after seeing a friend die in a plane crash, he'd lost his desire to fly.

Time and again, on clear blue mornings, Charles rode his motorcycle out to the airfield. He expected to be taken up, but most times, Biff didn't show.

When he did, he was full of excuses for not going up. "The air's too turbulent at midday, Slim," he'd say, using Charles's new nickname. "Meet me at the flying field when it smooths out this afternoon." Or, "Slim, it was just too rough. Let's try at sunrise tomorrow—that's the smoothest time of day."

Charles did get into the air occasionally, sometimes even managing to make a half dozen takeoffs and landings before Biff called it a day. Charles's quick reflexes and exceptional mechanical aptitude made him a natural pilot.

In May, after just eight hours of flying time, Biff decided Charles was ready to solo. "You can get up and down all right," the instructor said. He paused. "As long as the air's not too rough."

It was a lukewarm endorsement. Still, soloing was all that stood between Charles and his flying certificate. And he wanted that certificate, no matter how meaningless it was to the rest of the aviation world.

There was just one problem. He couldn't take a plane up by himself without Ray Page's permission. And Page wasn't giving it. What if the kid cracked up (damaged) or crashed (wrecked) the plane? Page wasn't about to risk his expensive machine on a beginner.

Charles considered his options. Sure, he hated not soloing. But even if he did solo, there wouldn't be a pilot job waiting for him. He was still a novice. People weren't going to trust their lives or machines to him. If he wanted a career in flying, he was going to have to get in lots more hours in the air . . . any way he could.

CHAPTER FIVE

DAREDEVIL LINDBERGH

"WINE OF THE GODS"

Days later, Charles teamed up with several pilots, including H. J. "Cupid" Lynch, and spent the next four months barnstorming above the golden fields of Kansas, the badlands of Nebraska, and the Bighorn Mountains of Wyoming. Barnstorming meant crisscrossing small-town America, dropping into county fairs and homecoming events, or using farmers' fields in hopes of selling fifteen-minute plane rides to country folks for five dollars each. It meant luring customers by performing death-defying stunts. And for Charles, it meant experiencing those brief but thrilling moments of anticipation mixed with dread as he walked on a plane's wing.

With Lynch at the controls, the two barnstormers would swoop low over a town to attract attention. Then Charles crawled out of the open passenger cockpit. Inching his way along the wing, he felt courage *and* fear course through him. From the ground, folks couldn't see the finger-width wire strung between the biplanes' stacked wings, and as Charles gripped it to gain his balance, he looked like he was floating. Once he'd steadied himself, Lynch gained altitude. Higher and higher climbed the biplane before it finally turned back toward the crowd. Then, pulling back the throttle, Lynch stopped the propeller blades with their eighty-mile-an-hour blast of wind that could blow Charles off the wing.

With the plane gliding on the air, Charles let go of the wire.

Weaving between the struts near one of the bottom wings' end, he balanced on the narrow wooden spar that made up its spine—the only part of the structure strong enough to hold his weight. The wind screamed in his ears and buffeted his body. He wobbled. Tottered. Flailed. Hundreds of feet above the ground and without a parachute, he was truly defying death. If the plane hadn't remained level, or if a bird had flown into him, there was nothing Charles could have done.

A feeling of exhilarated calm shot through him.

He was at the wing's end now. He waved to the tense crowd below, then stretched out his arms and raised first his left foot, then his right foot. He bent at the waist as if tying his shoes. From afar, it looked as if he were doing intricate balances. In reality, he was stepping into a pair of steel cups connected to the wing and attaching four cables too thin to be seen from the ground. He signaled to Lynch.

The plane, which had been losing altitude all this time, started up with a roar. Once again it rose higher into the sky. With the crowd gasping below, it looped the loop once . . . twice . . . three times before finally leveling out. Then, just as theatrically, as Charles stood firm on the wing, he undid the cables and stepped out of the steel cups. After waving once more, he started back toward the cockpit, careful step by careful step. Once he'd climbed in, Lynch circled down for a landing.

This stunt never failed to attract plenty of customers now eager to pay for a plane ride.

And even though he didn't gain any piloting experience, Charles never tired of the thrill. His every sense was sharpened, placing him on a higher level of existence. No longer was he one of the ordinary people below. His life was richer because of the danger, freer because he was not bound by earth. "I tasted a wine of the gods . . . I decided that if I could fly for ten years before I was killed in a crash, it would be a worthwhile trade for an ordinary life."

A PLANE OF HIS OWN

Souther Field in Georgia looked like a ghost city, with its empty wooden barracks and neglected streets. Once, it had been a bustling army base, but by the time Charles arrived in April 1923 it had been abandoned for years. Now just a handful of civilian mechanics worked in one of the dozen hangars, reconditioning surplus planes. Word was, they sold them cheap.

Charles sure hoped so. He was desperate to buy his own plane. He knew it was the only way he'd ever gain any flying experience. But all he had was a few hundred dollars in cash and checks. Some of it was savings from stunting. The rest he'd borrowed from his father.

The mechanics gave him a good deal. For $500—every penny Charles had—he bought an army surplus Curtiss JN 4D, called a Jenny. Widely used during World War I to train beginning pilots, the Jenny was a twin-seat (two cockpits), dual-control (it could be flown from either cockpit), "student-in-front-of-instructor" biplane. Light and maneuverable, it could do seventy miles an hour if the wind was favorable. Charles also chose a "brand-new Curtiss OX-5 engine . . . a fresh coat of olive gray dope . . . and an extra twenty-gallon fuel tank installed in the fuselage."

Unable to afford a hotel, Charles lived on the field for the two weeks it took for his Jenny to be assembled and painted. At night, he slept by its side in the hangar.

At last, the chief mechanic said, "Well, she's ready. When are you going to test her out?"

That was when Charles realized it'd been six months since he'd last been behind the controls of a plane. He'd had just eight hours of "stick time." And he'd never soloed. He was sweating all over as he climbed into the cockpit. He cautiously taxied across the field, bouncing, skidding, and fishtailing from side to side. To his embarrassment, a group of pilots and mechanics gathered outside the hangar to gape and point.

The plane rose into the air a few feet before thudding back to earth . . . rose and fell . . . rose and slammed back to the ground on one wheel.

"What an exhibition I'd made!" recalled Charles. Sweaty and humiliated, he wished he could switch off his engine and stay right there in the middle of the field. But the mechanics would just drive out and ask what the trouble was. Red-faced, he turned and taxied slowly back toward the hangar.

One of the pilots sauntered over to him. "Why don't you let me jump in the front cockpit before you try that again?" he asked.

Charles's cheeks burned. He stammered out an excuse about rough air.

Waving him off, the pilot climbed in. "Why don't we make a few rounds right now?"

With the pilot's help, Charles taxied out onto the field again and rose into the air. It was easier to fly, he admitted, when someone was there to correct his mistakes.

They made a half dozen takeoffs and landings together.

By late afternoon, Charles was ready to solo.

It was, he admitted, "far different from all other flights. You are completely independent, and terribly alone in space. . . . There's no hand to motion the nose down before a stall, no other head to check your fuel or watch your r.p.m. You can choose your point of compass and fly on as long as you like. . . . I kept climbing that day, higher and higher. . . . I might not have stopped climbing then, but the sun was almost touching earth, and dusk makes landing difficult for amateur's eyes."

Charles felt ready to make some money.

For the next five months, and mostly alone, he barnstormed across the Midwest. And he gained valuable flying skills. He learned to read the weather and pick out safe landing places. He learned to steer a course using just a compass and landmarks below, and to do barrel rolls, spins, and dives. He slept in a canvas hammock hung from an upper wing, cooked canned beans over an open fire, and accumulated 250 hours of seat-of-the-pants flying. On some days he barely earned back his expenses, while on others he carried passengers all day long for five dollars each. "This is sure a great life," he wrote his mother.

He also made mistakes.

There was the time he landed upside down in a swamp and two kids out fishing had to cut him from his seat belt.

And the time he decided to give the crowd a thrill by doing loop-the-loops . . . without knowing how. The Jenny stalled and dropped from the sky like a stone. He regained control just seconds before he would have crashed.

And then there was the afternoon he tried to impress the locals by taking off from their town's Main Street, a challenging plan considering the street's telephone poles were forty-eight feet apart and his plane's wingspan was forty-four feet. All went well until one of his wheels hit a rut in the road, causing the plane to swing around and clip one of the poles with its wing tip. Out of control, the Jenny crashed through the front window of the hardware store. Miraculously, no one was hurt.

Still, by September, Charles felt so confident in his skills that he invited Evangeline to join him. She quickly accepted. "I'd go with you no matter if my heart jumped out of my mouth," she declared.

CHAPTER SIX

SILVER WINGS

SECOND-RATE PILOT

The chilly fall weather brought an end to the 1923 barnstorming season. Land-loving folks just didn't want to go up in a freezing-cold open cockpit. With time on his hands, Charles steered a course toward the St. Louis Air Meet. Held at Lambert Field, it was meant to showcase advances in aircraft's speed and reliability. Not only would there be landing contests, speed races, and flying demonstrations, but also the latest military aircraft would be on display—from little sport racers that could zoom at 125 miles an hour to big army bombers. Charles was wild to see it all. It would be fun "to view the show as an insider—as a pilot in my own right."

The place was crowded with military planes, and the star performers were the army fliers, with their up-to-date equipment. After landing in a weedy area at the far end of a long row of civilian planes, Charles walked around the field, studying aircraft and growing more and more self-conscious. With his unpolished boots and oil-stained clothes, he looked like a country bumpkin beside the crisply uniformed army pilots. He tried to absorb himself in watching their flying maneuvers—many of which he'd never even heard of. But by day's end he was itching to escape into the air himself.

That was when he learned the field was being thrown open to visiting pilots. "I couldn't stay on the ground any longer and watch all those planes overhead," he said. He had to show them—and maybe himself—that he was just as good a pilot.

"I felt highly professional as I climbed into my cockpit and started the warm-up," he recalled. Meticulously, he idled the engine for three minutes to check temperature and pressure. Then he pushed the throttle wide open. "Everything was perfect."

Until he heard the yelling.

Charles turned. Behind him billowed a thick cloud of yellow dust thrown up by his plane. Through it he could vaguely see several angry, rudely gesturing men. Charles gulped. "I'd been used to flying from sod-covered pastures, not a crowded and newly graded airport, baked dry by Missouri's sun."

Coughing and dust-covered, an air official emerged from the cloud. "God Almighty!" he sputtered. "Where did you learn to fly? Don't you know enough to taxi out to the field before you warm up your engine? Get out and lift that tail around. Hold that throttle down. All right, damn it, go ahead!"

Charles felt "like a forty-acre farmer stumbling through his first visit to the state fair." Carefully, he taxied out and took off. But any joy he'd hoped to find in the flight had evaporated. He realized that while he had loads of practical experience, his six hours of flight instruction with Ira Biffle had provided little technical training.

As a pilot, he was second-rate.

And second-rate would never do.

Within weeks, he sold his Jenny and enrolled in a one-year course in the army reserve—the most advanced and challenging flying program then available. Just months later, in March 1924, he reported for duty at Brooks Field in San Antonio, Texas. The twenty-two-year-old was one of 104 cadets. Half of them, warned his commanding officer, would be kicked out before they graduated.

Charles did not intend to be one of them.

IN THE ARMY

On the first morning of flight training—March 19, 1924—Master Sergeant Bill Winston gathered seven new recruits, including Cadet Charles Lindbergh, around him on the dew-wet flying field. "Now you fellows are going to think you're pretty good," he said, looking pointedly at Charles, who wore an expression of cocky assuredness. "I just want you to remember this: in aviation, it may be all right to fool the other fellow about how good you are—if you can. *But don't try to fool yourself.*"

Then he waved the young pilots toward the army's training planes—Jennies, just like the one Charles had been flying for the past year. Supremely confident, he climbed into the back cockpit behind Winston. He couldn't wait to show off his skills. That was when he realized the controls were mounted on the left side of the fuselage. He'd only flown planes with right-hand throttles.

Changing hands on the stick threw Charles off. His first landing was far from perfect. It took three times around the field before he got the hang of the controls and Winston finally let him go up on his own.

It was a wobbly start.

Charles was also wobbly when it came to his classwork. "Photography, motors, map-making, field service regulations, radio theory, military law—twenty-five courses we took in our first half-year of training," he recalled. On his first exam, he scored 72 percent—just two points above failing. Sliding by wouldn't have worried him in high school, but it did now. Any cadet who failed two exams was automatically "washed out" of the program. And Charles did *not* want to be washed out.

"I studied after classes, through the weekends, far into the night," he recalled. "At times I slipped into my bunk with swimming head, but I had the satisfaction of watching my grade average slowly climb through the 80's and into the 90's." For the first time, "school and life became both rationally and emotionally connected."

Even though he lived in a crowded barracks, Charles remained aloof and alone. As one historian put it, he was "able to blend into any environment—to be a part of any group, but always apart." He joshed with the other cadets, even played practical jokes on a few, but nobody became a close friend—nobody, that is, except a stray white mutt he adopted and named Booster.

At the end of April, Charles received bad news. C.A., diagnosed with an inoperable brain tumor, was dying. "I may be 'washed out' . . . for going up home," Charles told a fellow cadet, "but that can't be helped." He hurried to the Mayo Clinic in Rochester, Minnesota, to find his father paralyzed and barely able to speak. Still, C.A.'s eyes brightened at the sight of his son. Charles sat holding his hand for most of that first day. A week later, C.A. lapsed into a coma.

Charles was willing to stay until the end, but Evangeline argued against it. C.A. wouldn't have wanted him to sacrifice all that hard work, she said. Reluctantly, Charles returned to Brooks Field, where he crammed to catch up on all the work he'd missed. On May 24, a telegram arrived. C.A. had died, but no one expected Charles to attend the funeral. "Later," wrote Evangeline, "when you come, you [can] comply with your Father's wish about throwing his ashes 'to the wind' . . . near the old farmstead he cared so much for." And so, on the day C.A.'s life was being eulogized, his son studied for a navigation exam.

By September, only 33 of the 104 cadets remained in the program. One of them was Charles Lindbergh, who graduated second in his class.

After he'd packed his footlocker, he and the other "veteran" cadets headed ten miles west to Kelly Field for advanced training. Gunnery and bombing, dogfighting and flying in formation were just a few of the difficult skills the men learned. The course was so tough that by the time graduation rolled around on March 14, 1925, only nineteen remained. Charles, who earned a commission as second lieutenant in the Air Service Reserve Corps, graduated first in his class.

The next day, the graduates made a promise to stay in touch. But Charles never tried to see any of them again, and except for chance encounters, he didn't. Already, the loner was living a "compartmentalized existence," explained one biographer, "always packing light, carrying few people from one episode of his life to the next."

Charles boarded a train for St. Louis. During his time in the army, his mind had kept turning back to Lambert Field and the air meet and the camaraderie he'd felt there. Now that he was a civilian again, what better place to start looking for a job? There would certainly be student pilots to teach at Lambert Field, and planes to take out barnstorming. "St. Louis is a city of winds," said Charles. He believed they'd blow favorably for him.

"IF ONLY I HAD A BELLANCA"

Carved from a cornfield, Lambert Field was 170 acres of hard clay sod. There were no runways, just a triangular landing space in its middle. This was fine in the summer, but in the winter, gusty winds and deep, frozen ruts made taking off and landing difficult for even the best pilot. Like other airfields in those days, its facilities were rudimentary. It didn't have navigational aids—no revolving beacons or boundary markers or floodlights. It didn't have a control tower or even a weather service bureau. For weather reports, pilots simply telephoned railroad stations along their route and asked the ticket agent to stick his head out the door and tell them what he saw.

Most of Lambert Field's commercial activity centered on Frank and Bill Robertson, who had set up the Robertson Aircraft

Corporation. The corporation mostly reconditioned and sold army training planes and engines, but the brothers were looking to expand. They set their sights on the airmail business.

The United States had been flying mail between California and New York since 1920. Now the government wanted to add feeder lines to other areas of the country from that single cross-country route. Members of Congress did not want to pay for this expansion with federal funds. So they auctioned off the new lines to private businesses. The Robertson brothers proposed to run the St.-Louis-to-Chicago mail route.

And Charles proposed to be their chief pilot. Flying the mail was exactly the kind of job he wanted—a permanent, responsible position in aviation. But the first time he walked into the Robertsons' office, they could hardly believe the baby-faced, gangling twenty-three-year-old was a veteran flier. Then Charles took up one of their planes and put it through its paces. He was the real thing. "There was never another like him," recalled Bill.

Soon afterward, the Robertsons won their bid.

And Charles got his job.

He spent the winter of 1925–1926 surveying the 285-mile route, arranging for emergency landing spots along the way. He chose nine in all—one for every thirty miles. These were simply cow pastures and farmers' fields fitted out with a little gasoline, a telephone, and somebody nearby to help the pilot. Of course, none of these fields were lit. If a pilot needed to land at night, he had to drop an emergency flare first and hope the sputtering orange flame shed enough light to avoid fences and ditches. Each plane was outfitted with one—just one—flare. For additional illumination, the pilot carried a pocket flashlight. Like everything else connected with civilian flying in 1926, the Robertsons' mail route operated on a shoestring.

On April 15, 1926, Charles flew the first airmail from St. Louis to Chicago, the canvas sacks of letters piled in the front cockpit of his plane—a rebuilt army salvage De Havilland. The Robertsons' contract with the government called for five round trips a week, and during the spring and summer Charles and the other two pilots completed 99 percent of their scheduled flights. "Ploughing through storms, wedging our way beneath low clouds, paying almost no attention to weather forecasts, we've more than once landed our rebuilt army warplanes on Chicago's Maywood field when other lines cancelled out [and] older and perhaps wiser pilots ordered their cargo put on a train," said Charles with pride. Because of their efforts, a letter arriving at the St. Louis post office before 3:30 in the afternoon could reach the New York post office by the next morning's delivery—a whole day faster than mail sent by train.

Nonetheless, week after week, the mailbags remained nearly empty. To potential customers, the savings of a few hours was seldom worth the extra cost per letter (ten cents in postage as opposed to three cents for regular letter mail). Still, Charles and the others flew doggedly on. Their efficiency, they believed, would eventually prove to the public that commercial aviation was transportation's future. "Whether the mail compartment contains ten letters or ten thousand is beside the point," he explained. "We pilots have a tradition to establish. The commerce of air depends on it [and] we have faith in the future. Some day we know the sacks will fill."

It didn't take long, however, for Charles to realize that his permanent, responsible job in aviation bored him. He could no longer just "fly . . . where the wind blows," he confessed in a letter to Evangeline. Instead, delivering the mail meant following the same route day after day. "The monotony of [it] is terrible," he wrote. More and more he daydreamed of barnstorming in Alaska, or competing in long-distance airplane races. In search of a new challenge, he wrote to the National Geographic Society, asking if they needed an experienced pilot for future expeditions. And he joined the Missouri National Guard simply so he could do maneuvers with army planes that were too dangerous for civilian aircraft.

Adventure. That was what he longed for. The birth of the airplane had spurred the most exciting time in exploration since Columbus. Recently, Italian pilot Francesco de Pinedo had traveled from Italy to Australia via Japan in a series of short flights, covering thirty-four thousand miles in seven months. British pilot Alan J. Cobham had just started out on what would be a four-month trip by air from London to Cape Town, South Africa. And US Navy Commander Richard Evelyn Byrd was preparing to fly over the North Pole.

And what was Charles doing?

Flying back and forth between St. Louis and Chicago.

"Unless something new turns up, I expect to leave [St. Louis] soon," he told Evangeline.

⁂

It was September 1926, and the last pink rays of sun had disappeared from the sky. Charles sat in the plane's cockpit on his way to Chicago. The evening's weather was perfect. Too perfect. There would be no flying challenge tonight. With his hand resting gently on the stick, he let his mind drift.

As he'd done since childhood, he posed questions and rolled around possible answers. He felt so detached from earth. Why couldn't he just "fly on forever through space . . . beyond mountains, over oceans?" Tonight, though, he had to land in Chicago. It seemed a "roundabout method," he thought, flying the mail north to Chicago just to transfer it to another plane (and another mail carrier) headed east. Why didn't he have a plane that could fly all the way to New York? Such a plane *did* exist—the Wright-Bellanca—a monoplane, so called because it had just one pair of wings. One pair of wings meant less drag, allowing the Bellanca to fly faster and burn half the fuel.

If only I had a Bellanca, he thought. *I'd show St. Louis businessmen what modern aircraft could do.* He'd start by flying passengers from St. Louis to New York in just eight or nine hours.

No, wait!

If he had a Bellanca, he'd fill it with fuel tanks instead of passengers, and with the engine at low speed, the plane might be able to stay aloft for days. He could break the world's endurance record and "set a dozen marks for range and speed and weight. Possibly—"

His mind took another leap, and a sudden notion startled him.

I could fly nonstop between New York and Paris.

PART THREE
NEW YORK TO PARIS

"The greatest feat of a solitary man in
the records of the human race."
—*New York Evening World*

CHAPTER SEVEN

PLANS AND FRUSTRATIONS

THE PRIZE

New York to Paris. That night in his Chicago hotel room, Charles repeated the phrase to himself, whispering it in wonder. *New York to Paris.* It sounded like a dream, like some fairy-tale vision born of night and altitude and moonlight. And yet he believed he could do it. *I'm almost twenty-five,* he told himself. *I have more than four years of aviation behind me, and close to two thousand hours in the air. I've barnstormed over half of the forty-eight states. I know the wind currents over the Rocky Mountains and the storms of the Mississippi River . . . [A]s a flying cadet, I learned the basic elements of navigation. I'm a Captain in the 110th Observation Squadron of Missouri's National Guard.* All he had to do was *lay a plan, and then follow it step by step no matter how small or large each one by itself may seem.*

Charles wondered about other aviators' plans. After all, he wasn't the first flier to come up with the New-York-to-Paris idea. Pilots considered the Atlantic Ocean aviation's biggest obstacle. And plenty of them had tried to cross it—seventy since World War I—leapfrogging from one strip of land to the next. But no one had crossed nonstop in an airplane until 1919. That year, British fliers John Alcock and Arthur Brown decided to give it a go. In June they climbed into a slow and boxy biplane made of wood and canvas and took off from Newfoundland, the closest point on the North American continent to Europe. Sixteen hours and almost two thousand miles later they landed in Clifden, Ireland. Their perilous adventure earned them front-page headlines, a cash prize of £10,000 (about $1.1 million in today's money) awarded by the British newspaper the *Daily Mail,* and a banquet at Buckingham Palace, where King George V knighted them. Sadly, Alcock died six months later after his plane crashed during a forced landing in heavy fog. As for Brown, he gave up flying and retired to a private life. It wasn't long before the world forgot all about both men.

Coincidentally, around the time Alcock and Brown were making their milestone flight, a New York City hotel owner named Raymond Orteig decided to create a prize—$25,000 to anyone who could fly nonstop between Paris and New York. The distance between those cities was more than twice what Alcock and Brown had flown, 3,315 miles, a trip that would take thirty to forty hours. But no one even tried for the prize; planes simply weren't capable of making such a long flight. Then suddenly, in 1926, a window in aviation history opened. The Bellanca was built, and other aircraft designers began working on long-range planes, too.

In the same month that Charles seized on the idea to fly from New York to Paris, newspapers had been following the exploits of French pilot René Fonck and his ill-fated attempt to make the flight and win the Orteig Prize. Fonck's plane—a big biplane equipped with three powerful engines—had been luxuriously finished in red leather and contained sofas, chairs, and a bed. For the four-man crew's additional comfort, it was stocked with wine and champagne, as well as a lavish dinner of turkey, terrapin, and duck to be eaten in celebration when they landed in Paris. At the last minute—just before takeoff—a bag of croissants was put on board.

As Fonck's plane bounced down the rutted dirt runway at Roosevelt Field on Long Island, a section of its landing gear fell off. Instead of cutting his switches, Fonck kept going, opening the throttle wide in hopes of getting up enough speed to get his overladen plane off the ground.

It didn't lift, not even an inch. While horrified spectators watched, it rolled past the end of the runway and tumbled over a steep slope. Several seconds of shocked silence followed. Then an enormous fireball shot into the air as the plane's 2,380 gallons of fuel exploded. Fonck and his navigator managed to crawl free of the wreck, but two other crewmen burned to death. The biplane was a complete loss.

Though the incident shocked the aviation community, it didn't stop other fliers from trying for the prize. With his successful North Pole flight behind him, Commander Richard Evelyn Byrd began planning an attempt. He announced his intention to take off the following May, as soon as winter weather over the Atlantic cleared.

Wanting to beat Byrd, other hopefuls began making noises about getting planes for their own crossings. Renowned aviation pioneer Clarence Chamberlin declared his plan to make the flight, as did popular naval officers Noel Davis and Stanton H. Wooster.

Reporters sensed a story, hoping for a sensational headline-grabber. That was what the American public demanded in those days—stories about social scandal and murder trials. They were riveted by fashions and fads, transfixed by boxing matches and beauty contests. And while Americans loved the radio, it wasn't yet an effective news medium. They listened to short bulletins but still relied on newspapers to "read all about it."

Responding to these sensation-seeking readers, publishers had introduced a revolutionary type of newspaper—the tabloid. Tabloids focused on sports, crime, and celebrity gossip, giving these trivial topics a false importance. By distilling the news to its most sensational or salacious essence and reporting on it in a minutely detailed and hyperbolic style, writers could grab readers' attention and hold it over the course of days, or even weeks. It was a manipulative kind of journalism, one that created news as much as it reported it. And with headlines like **RED HOT CUTIES OF ATLANTIC CITY** and **I KNOW WHO KILLED MY BROTHER**, tabloids had a huge readership. By 1924, one of the most popular, the *New York Daily News,* was selling 1.32 million copies every day.

In order to compete with these numbers, conventional newspapers also adopted a more gossipy tone. Even the highly respected *New York Times* occasionally devoted its pages to scandal—**WIFE BETRAYS PARAMOUR**—or cheap heroics—**[MAN] SHAVES HIMSELF WHILE SITTING ATOP FLAGPOLE**. News that mattered was buried on the inside pages, while popular attention was focused on one trivial person or event after another.

And so reporters began making news out of the flurry of activity surrounding the Orteig Prize. Framing it as a rivalry among celebrated fliers and a race with life and death in the balance, they sought to create "Atlantic Fever." "Somebody *will* fly from New York to Paris this spring," the *New York Times* teased its readers. "The question is, Who?"

SCRAMBLING

Charles believed the success of his flight depended on simplicity— one set of wings, one engine, one man. If he could get a Bellanca, he would strip out everything unnecessary, including a crew, to save room and weight for extra fuel. But he was getting ahead of himself. First, he needed a plane.

He had a few thousand dollars in the bank—not nearly enough to buy a Bellanca, with its $15,000 price tag. How could he get the rest of the money? He mulled over the question as he flew above the farmlands of central Illinois. He couldn't ask his fellow pilots. Most of them were broke. What he needed were investors, rich and prominent St. Louis businessmen, to fund his project. But what could *he* offer *them*? Businessmen would want some kind of return on their investment. Certainly, if he won the Orteig Prize, the money would cover that. They'd own the plane, too. That was something, but it wasn't enough. He needed more.

By the time his plane's wheels touched down in St. Louis, Charles knew what that "more" would be: community spirit. That was what he'd sell them. His flight would spotlight St. Louis as an aviation city with one of the finest commercial airports in the nation. "It would show people what airplanes can do [and] it would advance aviation." Most importantly, his flight "would advertise St. Louis."

Over the next few months, Charles spoke with insurance executives, bank officers, newspaper publishers, and the president of the city's chamber of commerce. Some said no, but enough said yes. By January 1927 he'd put together a group of nine backers. "From now on . . . leave the financial end to us," they told him.

In return, they had just one request. "What would you think of naming [the plane] the *Spirit of St. Louis*?" asked Harold Bixby of the State National Bank of St Louis.

The Spirit of St. Louis, Charles thought, *it's a good name.* He nodded. "All right, let's call it [that]."

Bixby grinned and handed him a check for $15,000.

But raising the money was almost easier than spending it. Since the market for long-range planes was minuscule, only a handful of manufacturers produced them. It was next to impossible to find an aircraft like a Bellanca that was already built and ready to fly. Instead, most long-range planes were constructed only after an order was placed. And not every order was accepted. Manufacturers often refused to build planes for inexperienced—or in Charles's case, unknown—pilots. A crack-up or crash could ruin a brand's reputation, so companies like Boeing, Douglas, and Curtiss were extremely particular about accepting orders. And when it came to pilots vying for the Orteig Prize, well, manufacturers were even more selective.

The event was sure to bring world attention to their airplanes. They couldn't risk having an amateur at the controls.

Travel Air, maker of a long-range aircraft, had already refused Charles's order. The speed and definiteness with which the company had turned him down had depressed him. "I expected at least some interest on their part," he confessed. So he couldn't believe his luck when Charles Levine, president of the Columbia Aircraft Corporation and owner of the one and only existing Bellanca, agreed to sell it.

Charles placed his cashier's check on the businessman's polished desktop. How soon could he get the plane and start preparing it for flight? He had ideas about modifications to the design, and if he wanted to be ready when weather over the Atlantic broke, he needed to get started right away.

Levine leaned across his desk. "We will sell our plane, but of course, *we* reserve the right to choose the crew that flies it."

Charles shook his head. "I'm afraid there's been a misunderstanding," he said. "If [the St. Louis organization] buys a plane, we're going to control it, and we'll pick our own crew."

"The Columbia Aircraft Corporation cannot afford to take such a chance with our airplane," explained Levine. He smiled before adding, "It would be wise for you to let us manage the flight to Paris. You should think it over. What I tell you is best."

"There's no use thinking it over," Charles retorted. "We either buy the plane outright, or we don't buy it. Will you accept this payment, or must I find another plane?"

"You are making a mistake," Levine argued.

Too angry and insulted to reply, Charles snatched up his check and stormed out the door.

Next he tried the Fokker Company, famous for its trimotored long-range planes. But he didn't want three engines. One set of wings, one engine, one man, that was the plan. When he asked how much it would cost for a single-engine Fokker, the salesman cut him off. "Our Company would not be interested in selling a single-engine plane for a flight across the ocean," he said firmly.

Charles grew frustrated. He knew Byrd and the other pilots were already preparing their planes with an eye toward taking off in late spring. Every day, he fell farther and farther behind.

Who would take his order? He considered wiring Boeing and Curtiss. Then he thought of a small outfit, Ryan Aeronautical Company in San Diego. Weren't airmail pilots on the West Coast route flying Ryan's high-wing monoplanes?

On February 3, he wired Ryan: CAN YOU CONSTRUCT A WHIRLWIND EN-GINE PLANE CAPABLE OF FLYING NONSTOP BETWEEN NEW YORK AND PARIS STOP IF SO PLEASE STATE COST AND DELIVERY DATE.

The next day—Charles's twenty-fifth birthday—the president of Ryan Aeronautical, B. F. Mahoney, wired a reply. His company could do it. It would take two months and cost $6,000.

Two months, thought Charles; *that would let me start test [flights] sometime in April. I could still be ready to take off when the weather breaks in spring.*

It was the best birthday present Charles had ever gotten.

THE *SPIRIT OF ST. LOUIS*

The odor of dead fish from the waterfront cannery next door mingled with the smells of the airplane factory. Ryan Aeronautical Company—dusty, paper-strewn, and located in a falling-down warehouse—was obviously neither rich nor successful. But Charles trusted the chief engineer, Donald Hall, within minutes of walking into the plant that February morning. They spoke the same language. Their minds worked the same way.

Right off, the two began talking about the plane's design. Charles had definite ideas about what he required for an ocean flight. As he described his vision, Hall went to his drafting board. Soon, pencil lines curved and angled over the paper. He sketched what he heard without questioning—increased wingspan, changed placement of the engine. But one request startled him: just a single cockpit for a single passenger.

"You don't plan on making that flight alone, do you?" asked Hall.

Charles explained his belief that he'd be better off with extra gas rather than an extra man.

Hall listened, nodding, instantly grasping the advantages of a solo flight. The engineer's mind whirred with ideas. The fuselage, the main body of the plane, should be shorter and lighter, he suggested. They'd have to rebuild Ryan's existing model, but—yes!—the plane could carry another 350 pounds of gasoline. Still, was Charles sure he wanted to fly alone?

Charles was. He could make his own decisions and carry them out as he saw fit, packing light both physically and emotionally.

So where did he want to put that single cockpit? wondered Hall.

Behind the gas tanks, Charles told him. Pilots who sat behind had a better chance of surviving—they didn't get trapped between the engine and the rear fuel tanks in a crash. Yes, he understood the tanks would block his forward view during flight, but that didn't matter. What was there to crash into over the Atlantic Ocean? If he needed to see in front of him, he could always poke his head out the side window.

What about night-flying equipment? asked Hall. Flares, illuminated instruments, landing lights, and such?

Charles couldn't afford the weight. Every six pounds of jettisoned equipment meant another gallon of fuel he could carry. He also decided against a parachute. "That would cost almost twenty pounds," he told Hall.

So concerned was he with weight that he even decided to go without gauges on the gasoline tanks. Not only were they heavy, but they often didn't work. If he had to, he would figure his fuel use manually, using rpms (revolutions per minute) and the nickel-plated pocket watch he'd inherited from Grandfather Land. But really, it was a useless activity. Either he'd have enough gasoline or he wouldn't.

Within days, Hall had finished drawing up the designs. The unusually heavy load of fuel required for a trans-Atlantic crossing meant he had to redesign not only the fuselage, but the landing gear and wings as well. And he had to do it fast. Time, Hall knew, was of the essence. He worked around the clock, staying at his desk for thirty-six hours straight.

All thirty-five of Ryan's employees were working full bore, too, day and night, seven days a week. They knew Charles desperately wanted to be in New York by the end of April. And even though he tried their patience by constantly hovering and questioning their every move, they felt inspired by the lanky youth.

News stories spurred them to work even faster. The press continued to whip up "Atlantic Fever," with daily bulletins about what they exaggeratedly called "the most spectacular race ever held." One story reported that Commander Byrd—who would be flying in the big three-motored Fokker—had his sights set on a takeoff in May, the earliest time when weather over the Atlantic would permit using "the most advanced . . . navigational devices known to science."

Charles wouldn't be flying with *any* navigational devices. In his obsessive search to strip away pounds and ounces, he'd traded a sextant for twenty-five pounds of gasoline, a radio for ninety more.

Hall worried about that last choice. Without a radio, Charles would not be able to communicate with people on the ground. And they would not be able to contact him. He'd be completely cut off—no messages, no news bulletins, nothing. Charles must be sure he wanted to do that.

Fuel, Charles reminded the chief engineer, was all that mattered.

To save another few ounces, Charles designed special lightweight flight boots with soft soles. He ripped spare pages from his logbook and even trimmed the white edges off his charts to eliminate a little weight. He decided to restrict himself to a single quart of water in flight. Water was heavy, and really all he needed was enough to wash down the five sandwiches he'd be taking along. "If I get to Paris, I won't need any more, and if I don't get to Paris I won't need any more either," he told Hall.

Meanwhile, a flurry of newspaper articles touted the latest exciting air news: famous plane designer Igor Sikorsky was building a bigger, better plane for René Fonck's next attempt across the ocean; flying in Charles Levine's Bellanca, Clarence Chamberlin and another top pilot, Bert Acosta, broke the world's endurance record for staying in the air fifty-one hours; and from the other side of the Atlantic, French fliers Charles Nungesser and François Coli had decided to try for the prize. They planned to fly from Paris to New York.

A black mood fell over Charles. His competitors were so far ahead of him. He'd started his preparations too late. *There's no use blinding myself to reality,* he thought. *Almost everyone else would have to fail before I could succeed.*

Convinced another flier would get across the Atlantic first, he began making plans for a trans-Pacific flight.

Then came startling news. Byrd's plane had crashed on landing after a test flight over Long Island with designer Anthony Fokker piloting it. Byrd had broken his arm in two places, two other crew members had been badly injured, and the plane had suffered serious damage. Only Fokker had walked away unscratched. Reporters speculated that the commander would have to abandon his plans for a May takeoff.

Eight days later, word came that Chamberlin had cracked up the Bellanca when part of its landing gear tore loose during a test flight takeoff. He managed to land on one wheel, and no one was hurt, but the plane required repair. His intended start across the Atlantic would have to be pushed back, too.

And then, horribly, impossibly, just two days later the *American Legion,* a triple-motored biplane manned by Noel Davis and Stanton

Wooster, crashed at Langley Field in Virginia during its final test flight. Both men were killed.

"My God!" exclaimed Charles when he learned of the accident. "Every one of the big multi-engine planes built for the New York to Paris flight has crashed. . . . What happened?"

He believed he knew. The planes had weighed too much.

On April 28—two months to the day after Charles placed his order—the *Spirit of St. Louis* stood in front of the hangar, sleek, silver, and . . . *finished*!

He couldn't wait to take the plane up. After climbing into the cockpit, he settled into his seat, a wicker porch chair that he'd chosen because it weighed less than a pilot's chair. It took up so much space, however, that Charles could not stretch out his legs. He would have to fly with the control stick between his knees.

In front of him two large fuel tanks filled the nose of the aircraft, blocking his forward view. Worried about this, one of the workers, a former submariner, had installed a simple periscope that extended through the left side of the fuselage. A simple instrument panel had also been installed. Among its ten basic instruments were a speedometer, an altimeter, oil temperature and pressure gauges, and the magneto, or ignition switch.

Charles took a moment to gather his focus before calling out the side window for the mechanic to spin the propeller.

It was a metal prop—a vast improvement over the wooden ones used until just recently. People often mistook the rest of the plane for metal, too. That was because she'd been painted with an aluminum-pigmented dope. But the *Spirit of St. Louis* was nothing but thin cotton stretched tight over a wood and tubular steel frame. Only a thin layer of fabric lay between Charles and the sky. It was like "flying in a box with fabric walls," he admitted.

The motor caught, the roar deafening. Charles pulled out a couple of cotton balls from his jacket pocket and plugged them into his ears. Then he signaled for the blocks to be pulled away from the plane's wheels.

Turned loose, the *Spirit of St. Louis* accelerated faster than any plane he'd ever flown. It leaped into the air, and Charles spiraled it up to two thousand feet. Within minutes, he was flying over the Ryan factory. At the sound of the plane's motor, the employees came running out. As they looked skyward, Charles circled over them and rocked his wings—the pilot's salute—before heading out over the bay.

He noticed some minor glitches. The fin needed adjustment, and a section of the wing rode too high. He wrote these points on his data board. They'd be easy fixes once he was back on the ground.

The biggest issue, though, was stability. Because of all the design compromises, it was a challenge to keep the plane flying straight, much less make it do what Charles wanted. "The Spirit is high-strung and balanced on a pinpoint," he noted. "If I relax pressure on the stick or the rudder for an instant the nose veers off course." Still, he figured the constant attention required just to maintain an even keel would keep him alert during the flight.

Twelve days and thirty-seven test flights later, Charles stopped in at the Ryan factory to say goodbye to the people who'd put their all into his dream. He knew they felt as thrilled by the *Spirit*'s performance as he did. He also knew he'd be flying with a piece of them. Weeks earlier, every man and woman working at the plant had signed the plane's nose cone before the propeller had been set in place.

With a final wave, he walked out the big double doors. A worker called after him, "Send us a wire when you get to Paris."

CHAPTER EIGHT

THE FLYING KID

THE NATION BENEATH HIS WINGS

As Charles winged his way eastward, he flew across a country whose citizens should have felt optimistic and happy. The national debt was lower than it had been since the war, the unemployment rate was less than 4 percent, taxes were at an all-time low, and the stock market was at an all-time high.

"The chief business of the American people is business," President Calvin Coolidge had said in a speech two years earlier, "producing, buying, selling, investing and prospering." And the public agreed. By 1927, everyone seemed to own everything—pop-up toasters, ready-to-wear clothing, vacuum cleaners, refrigerators, wristwatches, hair dryers. Spurred on by scores of new inventions, cheap mass production, and easy credit, the nation had gone on a spending spree. No longer did Americans identify themselves by their jobs, religions, or political parties. They *were* what they bought. Things, they believed, could make them happy.

That year, too, the public saw a mind-boggling leap in technology. Americans could make an overseas phone call from New York to London, although at the cost of $75 for the first three minutes (about $1,000 nowadays), few ever did. A far more popular invention was the radio. Introduced at the beginning of the decade, the radio by 1927 was a fixture in practically every home. Americans marveled at being able to hear what was happening as it happened. Another marvel, the Hudson River Vehicular Tunnel (later renamed the Holland Tunnel), would soon allow cars to drive *beneath* the Hudson River. And in October, the first "talkie," a motion picture with sound, would be released, astonishing moviegoers used to silent films. Even America's drinking habits changed that year, after a powdered, flavored beverage mix called Kool-Aid hit the grocery store shelves.

So why was the nation glum? Most people could not have pinpointed a reason. But the decade's earlier euphoria and rebellion had been eclipsed by "a widespread neurosis, like a nervous beating of the feet," wrote novelist F. Scott Fitzgerald. More leisure, and more prosperity, more dancing, more parties, more movies, and more distractions had not brought happiness. Instead, they had wrought a world that felt shallow and corrupt. In 1927 alone—seven years after Prohibition was enacted—more people died from alcohol-related deaths than at any other time in history. Crime rates were soaring. So were suicides. And a sudden, sharp rise in divorce had made the United States second only to the Soviet Union in failed marriages. Obviously, cars and Kool-Aid, tabloids and "talkies," dancing until dawn and bootleg gin had not filled the country's spiritual void. Something else was needed.

And then, wrote Fitzgerald, "In the spring of '27, something bright and alien flashed across the sky. . . ."

THE LONG WAIT

Up to now, the name Charles Lindbergh had been mentioned only briefly in the nation's newspapers, and despite "Atlantic Fever," no one had bothered to run a photograph of him or his plane. His arrival on Long Island on May 12, 1927, changed all that.

As the *Spirit of St. Louis* rolled to a stop on the muddy runway at Curtiss Field, newspaper photographers rushed toward the plane, shouting and pushing, while a line of heavy motion-picture cameras mounted on tripods swiveled to follow its every move.

Blinking, Charles stepped from the cockpit.

One of the reporters tossed out a question. "When are you going to take off for Paris?"

"My engine needs servicing, and I'm having new compasses installed," he replied. "After that's done, I'll take off as soon as the weather clears up."

It had been raining for weeks in New York, turning the airfield slick with mud. Puddles spread across the paths between the hangars. But it was the weather over the Atlantic that concerned Charles. The entire route was blocked with fog, snow, and sleet.

"How's about letting the camera boys get a picture of you in front of the plane?" came a request.

With difficulty, the reporters cleared enough room for Charles to take his place next to his plane. As they'd asked, he placed his hand on its propeller.

The press saw it immediately. Standing there, modest and wholesome and smiling shyly, the "flying kid" was special. There was something old-fashioned and heroic about his attempt to make the perilous journey alone. And he was so handsome. Even better, he was an "everyman," a young, seemingly ordinary middle-class Midwesterner, the kind of person their readers thought they knew. *This* kid was a headline-grabber. Dubbing him "Lucky Lindy" (a nickname that he would always detest, but that reporters thought pithy and memorable), they turned the spotlight of publicity on him.

And so it was that overnight the previously unknown airmail pilot from Missouri became the country's favorite flier.

His competition, however, believed Lindbergh was outclassed and didn't stand a chance—especially against the likes of *them*. For weeks the airfield had swarmed with fliers and mechanics testing and perfecting the two other planes that would attempt the flight—Commander Byrd's rebuilt Fokker, and Chamberlin in Levine's repaired Bellanca. Like Charles, these pilots kept a close eye on the weather. Each intended to be the first to take off.

The morning after Charles's arrival, Commander Byrd dropped by the *Spirit*'s hangar. Still with a cast on his arm, the famous pilot clapped the younger man on the back and promised to help any way he could. He began by offering to share his private weather reports. Even more generously, he gave Charles use of his runway at Roosevelt Field (right next door to Curtiss Field). Byrd had leased the airstrip for his exclusive use, including its longer, smoother—and therefore safer—runway. To his credit, the admiral insisted all his competitors use it.

Over the next few days, Chamberlin also showed up at the *Spirit*'s hangar, along with other big names in aviation. One of them was Harry Guggenheim, a fabulously rich ex–navy pilot who administered a fund that promoted aviation. Like Byrd, he worried about the young pilot. Without a radio, *"this fellow will never make it,"* Guggenheim said to himself. *"He's doomed."* Still, he masked his fears and tried to sound positive. "When you get back, look me up at the Fund's office," he told Charles.

Days passed, and the atmosphere at the airfield grew more and more tense. Pinned down by the weather, Charles went to Coney Island one day along with two publicists from the Wright Corporation, Dick Blythe and Harry Bruno. The seaside Brooklyn amusement park relaxed the twenty-five-year-old. He munched on popcorn and hot dogs, played some carnival games, and splashed down the Chutes, the park's famous water ride. "He was happy as a kid," recalled Blythe.

Suddenly, a woman recognized him. She started shrieking his name.

"Get me out of here," said Charles.

The three men hightailed it back to Long Island.

Not that he had any more privacy there. Every day, crowds

arrived at the airfield in hopes of catching a glimpse of the pilot who was on the front page of every newspaper. The Sunday after he arrived, thirty thousand people descended on Curtiss Field—as many as would attend a Yankees game. And reporters never stopped badgering him for interviews. When he agreed, they wasted his time with questions like "What's your favorite pie?" "How do you feel about girls?" "Do you carry a rabbit's foot?" He found it embarrassing and intrusive. What did any of *that* have to do with flying?

In the middle of this frenzy, on May 14, Evangeline arrived to wish him a safe journey. It should have been a private moment between mother and son. Instead, reporters surrounded them. Standing stiffly side by side, the Lindberghs endured a barrage of thoughtless and insensitive questions. Did Evangeline know what a dangerous trip her son was undertaking? Wasn't she afraid he'd be killed in the attempt?

It wasn't until they demanded that Evangeline kiss her son farewell that she balked. Mother and son *never* kissed. Instead, she patted Charles on the shoulder and said, "Well, son, good-bye and good luck."

The next morning, newspapers featured a photograph of the Lindberghs' faces spliced onto the bodies of two people hugging. Charles wasn't surprised. Accuracy, he'd learned, was secondary to a newspaper's circulation. "But accuracy means something to me. . . . Every aviator knows that if mechanics are inaccurate, aircraft crash. If pilots are inaccurate, they get lost—sometimes killed. In my profession life itself depends on accuracy."

Thursday, May 19, dawned gray and rainy . . . again. Charles paced the hangar floor. Every minute he remained on the ground seemed to suck his attention away from flying. "My problems are already shifting from aviation to reporters, photographers . . . and requests for autographs," he grumbled.

That night, Charles drove into New York with Blythe and Bruno to see a Broadway show. On the way, he decided to check the weather reports again. It didn't seem likely the forecast had changed. A misty rain was falling and the tops of skyscrapers were buried in fog. Still, he pulled over to the curb and Blythe ran into an office building to call the meteorologist. Minutes later he was back. And Charles could tell by his expression he had good news.

"Weather over the Atlantic is clearing!" he cried. "It's a sudden change."

Charles turned the car around. He wouldn't be able to take off tonight—the plane had to be fueled first, a tedious process that involved filtering all 450 gallons of gas through cheesecloth to clean out impurities. Besides, the skies over New York were still too thick with haze. But he could be in his cockpit ready to take off at dawn— if one of the other planes didn't beat him to the runway.

Back at the airfield, he was surprised to find no lights burning in either Byrd's or Chamberlin's hangar. He soon discovered why: the other pilots were waiting for confirmation of the weather report. After all, there were only *indications* of a clearing sky.

It was the opportunity he'd been hoping for. With his mechanics, he began readying the *Spirit* for the flight, filling gas tanks and making last-minute checks of instruments. After working until almost midnight, Charles—who'd already had a long day—left for his hotel. He needed some sleep.

After posting an acquaintance, George Stumpf, outside his door so no one would disturb him, Charles let his head sink into the pillow. But sleep evaded him. His mind was spinning. What if there were still patches of fog tomorrow? Should he cancel the takeoff? No, a pilot should never turn down a break in the weather. But what if he was too tired to fly? Earlier he'd calculated that it would take him about thirty-six hours to fly to Paris. Did he have the reserves to fly that long without sleep? He believed so. He'd done it on the mail run. Nonetheless, he thought, *a pilot should be fresh for the start of a record-breaking transoceanic flight. Your mind doesn't work as well when it's short of sleep—*

Stumpf burst into the room, interrupting his thoughts. "Slim," he wailed, "what am I going to do when you're gone?"

Charles must have thought this a strange question, considering the two had known each other only a week. "Good Lord!" he exclaimed in exasperation. "I don't know. There are plenty of other problems to solve before we think about that one."

With any luck, tomorrow he'd be well on his way to Paris.

And tonight? Obviously he wasn't going to get any sleep. He might as well return to the airfield.

It was 3 a.m. when he arrived at the hangar. Somehow, reporters had heard about his planned departure. They were already there, shouting questions, but Charles ignored them. He looked up. The weather was still bad but getting better. He felt the wind. A gentle headwind. He tested the ground. It was muddy and soft. These were definitely *not* the conditions he would have chosen.

His mechanics, still fueling the plane, turned to watch him. What would he do?

If the weather was too bad, he could always turn back, he told himself. There was no shame in that. But did the *Spirit* have enough power to get off the ground? He was asking her to lift thousands of pounds in mist, off a mud-thick runway. *Wind, weather, power, load.* The words went around and around in his mind.

Then his thoughts quieted. Conviction surged through him.

He nodded to the men.

"I'll start at daybreak."

TAKEOFF

At 7:40 a.m. on Friday, May 20, 1927, Charles Lindbergh climbed into the *Spirit of St. Louis*'s snug-fitting cockpit. After buckling his safety belt, he pulled on his leather flying helmet and adjusted his goggles over his eyes. Then he signaled to a mechanic to spin the propeller.

The plane's engine coughed and gave three sharp explosions from its exhaust stacks before finally catching.

"It's the weather!" the mechanic hollered to Charles through the cockpit's side window. "[Planes] never rev up on a day like this."

Charles leaned against the window and looked through the propeller's whirling blades. The long runway, shimmering with puddles, stretched out before him. At its end he noted a parked tractor and, higher up, the twist of telephone wires. Beyond them, a thick curtain of mist shut off all traces of the horizon.

Along with the usual mob of reporters and newsreel crews, the other airmen and their teams had come out to watch his takeoff. One of them, a representative of the Fokker Company, had driven his sedan loaded with fire extinguishers to the other end of the runway. This was where René Fonck had crashed nine months earlier. Scorch marks still marred the spot.

Charles signaled to the men to remove the blocks in front of the plane's wheels. The *Spirit* was free. He eased the throttle wide open.

A soft runway. An overload of weight. And a wind that had changed from head to tail—"five miles an hour *tail*!" exclaimed Charles.

Would the plane lift?

The plane crept heavily forward. It wasn't vibrant with power like before. He could feel its great weight pressing its tires into the spongy ground. He could sense the fragility of its wings and the fullness of its oversized tanks of fuel. *Nothing about my plane has the magic quality of flight,* he thought.

Gradually, the *Spirit* picked up speed. But half the runway had already passed beneath them before he finally felt "the load shifting from wheels to wings." He had to make a decision. Should he close the throttle and abort the takeoff, or could he really get airborne? *Is there still time, still space?* he wondered. The wrong decision would mean a fiery crash.

Charles eased the stick forward. They were almost at flying speed. The plane was so close to lifting . . .

The *Spirit* rose.

And dropped back to the ground.

Charles tried again. In his hand the controls felt "taut, alive, straining."

The plane rose clumsily. Five feet—twenty—forty—

The telephone wires loomed straight ahead.

Clarence Chamberlin clamped his hand to his mouth, then shouted with relief when—

Swoosh!

The *Spirit* cleared the wires with just twenty feet to spare.

"My heart was in my throat," said Chamberlin. "It seemed impossible. It took guts."

Later, people who witnessed the takeoff would claim Charles Lindbergh "*willed* his plane into the air."

Commander Byrd raised his hand in farewell. "God be with him," he said.

The official recorded takeoff time was 7:52 a.m.

The spectators watched in silence until the *Spirit of St. Louis* disappeared into the mist.

⌇⌇⌇

In Detroit, Evangeline Lindbergh received a telegram from Dick Blythe: her son had taken off an hour earlier and was now on his way to Paris. Evangeline, who was teaching school that day, stuck to her normal routine—until reporters showed up. Surrounding her during her lunch break, they clamored for a statement. Instead, she simply went home to the tall brick house she shared with her brother. Not until she reached her front porch did she turn and face the crowd in the yard. "My heart and soul is with my boy on his perilous journey," she said simply. Then she went inside and closed the door. She would not come out again until she'd heard from Paris.

CHAPTER NINE

33 HOURS, 30 MINUTES, 29.8 SECONDS

FRIDAY IN THE SKY

Takeoff behind him, Charles lined up his compass and set his course. Heading across Long Island Sound, he flew toward Connecticut. A newspaper plane soared up beside him. Cameras stuck out cockpit and cabin windows. He stiffened in his seat. It had never occurred to him that newspaper companies would hire a plane to follow him. He willed it to go away.

As he crossed into Connecticut, he got his wish. After dipping its wing in farewell, the plane turned and soared off.

The sky belonged to the *Spirit of St. Louis.*

Charles flew on, and by late afternoon, he'd passed over Rhode Island and Massachusetts and was winging his way toward Nova Scotia.

The sun came out, warming up the cockpit. It made Charles— awake for more than twenty-four hours—groggy. He unzipped his blanket-lined flying suit and took a sip of water from his canteen. It would be pleasant to doze off for a few seconds. "But I mustn't feel sleepy at this [point]," he scolded himself. "Why, I'm less than a tenth of the way to Paris. . . . There's still the rest of today, and all of tonight, and tomorrow, and part—maybe *all*—of tomorrow night."

At noon, Nova Scotia appeared. As the forest-thick landscape passed beneath his wings, he reached for one of the five sandwiches he'd brought along.

No, he thought, drawing his hand back. Why eat when he wasn't hungry? He'd save it, just in case he was forced down at sea.

His legs began to cramp. He tried to ignore it, knowing his muscles' complaints would grow worse over the next few hours. Eventually, though, his legs would get accustomed to their bent position. The pain would subside.

He kept himself busy. Every hour, he would need to adjust the lever regulating the flow of gasoline from one tank to another. He kept a mark on his instrument panel for each changeover. He also entered hourly notations on his log sheet, marking speed, altitude, and other data. And then there was the *Spirit*'s instability. It required his constant attention to stay on course.

⌇

Four hours later, Nova Scotia was behind him. But now his eyes felt dry and hard. Keeping them open seemed impossible. Sleep was winning. He let them close for a moment before forcing them open again.

The sun was starting to set. Hours of darkness lay head . . . and thousands of miles of ocean. How would he get through the night without falling asleep? He forced himself to focus on stick and sky and the rumbling of his engine.

⌇

He was over Newfoundland now, "the last point on the last island of [North] America—the end of land; the end of day," he realized. Sacrificing some of his precious fuel, he veered slightly off course and circled low over the little town of St. John's. Men on the wharves looked up, pointed, waved. He wanted them to see him. If he got lost over the Atlantic, at least people would know he'd made it this far.

Then he turned his plane toward the open sea and the blackness of night.

Ireland lay two thousand miles ahead.

FRIDAY ON THE GROUND

Something like a miracle was taking place across America. No sooner had word flashed across the wires that Charles had taken off than a hundred million people were suddenly seized with hope and yearning. Young and old, rich and poor, farmer and stockbroker, churchgoer and skeptic—everyone fastened their attention on the young man in the *Spirit of St. Louis.* Would Charles Lindbergh make it? Could he? In the minds of the public, his flight had taken on epic proportions. Not only would his success be a source of national pride, but it would also be an achievement for all mankind. Imagine it! Because of Lindbergh, the world would be changed. People, countries, continents once separated from each other would be brought together by flight. Everyone would be within reach. And this man— this *boy,* really—was doing it alone. The sheer audacity of it took people's breath away.

All along Charles's early route, people climbed into trees and onto roofs or gathered on the street to catch a glimpse of his plane. They huddled before radios and in front of newspaper offices to hear or read the latest "flash bulletin."

In New York City, a crowd mobbed Times Square, expecting reports of Lindbergh's progress to be posted on the side of the Times Square Building. When information didn't come fast enough, people telephoned the newspaper—ten thousand calls in total. And as the hours passed, reports trickled in. Lindbergh had been sighted over Connecticut . . . Massachusetts . . . Novia Scotia. Across the nation, in factories, stores, restaurants, and homes, atlases were opened and maps tacked up on walls so the earthbound could envision his route.

Night fell, and the public turned sober.

"No attempt at jokes today," wrote America's famous cowboy humorist, Will Rogers, in his syndicated newspaper column. "A . . . slim, bashful, smiling American boy is somewhere over the middle of the Atlantic Ocean, where no lone human being has ever ventured before. . . . If he is lost it will be the most universally regretted loss we've ever had."

Several radio stations broadcast a new song written and sung by the trio the Bonnie Laddies. So moved were listening audiences that the lyrics were printed in newspapers coast to coast the next morning.

> *Captain Lindbergh, we're with you.*
> *Won't you please come smiling through?*
> *Keep her going, give her the steam.*
> *You'll soon reach the land of your dreams.*

And in Yankee Stadium, two heavyweight boxers, Jim Maloney and Jack Sharkey, fought before a crowd of forty thousand. Suddenly, a bow-tied announcer stopped the action and stepped into the pool of light in the center of the darkness. "Rise to your feet and think about a boy up there tonight who is carrying the hopes of all true-blooded Americans," he said. As one, the entire crowd stood and bowed their heads. For a full minute they kept quiet, before Sharkey knocked out Maloney.

In little towns and big cities, wherever people gathered, they prayed for their hero. It was all they could do. But by sending a few words heavenward, many felt they'd become part of his journey.

NIGHT FLIGHT

It was pitch dark, the sky thick with mountains of clouds. Feeling lonely, Charles once again sacrificed some fuel to climb above them. Up, up, up he ascended, until at last, at five thousand feet, stars pierced the haze. A feeling of security washed over him. *The stars have always been there,* he thought. *As long as I can hold on to them I'll be safe.*

With his eyes on them, his mind wandered back to his boyhood days. It was as if he were traveling with their twinkling vision, back and forth through time. His head nodded. His eyelids felt heavy.

Suddenly, he noticed how cold it had gotten inside the cockpit. He snapped back to attention. At this altitude, cold meant ice—ice that could deform the shape of a wing, weigh down a plane and force it into the sea.

He pulled his flashlight from his pocket and shined it out the side window. A pillow of clouds had closed over the stars. At their edges he spied shiny, threadlike streaks. He shined the light on one of the *Spirit*'s struts. Ice already coated it.

Charles was fully awake now. His first instinct was to dive steeply toward warmer air. But the *Spirit* was too sensitive for that. It required careful flying every minute. As the plane bounced—buffeted by sudden strong winds—he maneuvered out of the ice clouds and into clear air. He flew, shining the light on wings and struts again and again. At last, the ice melted and fell away.

Charles relaxed, and once again, sleep threatened. He had to stay awake. He had to keep his eyes open. But after sixteen hours in the air and almost thirty-nine hours without sleep, all he wanted was to close them. Fighting the urge, he stuck his hand out the side window, diverting a strong gust of air into his face. He took deep, gulping breaths and let his eyelids fall shut for a few seconds, then tried to raise them. But they weighed too much. He didn't have the strength. After forcing one open with a thumb, he lifted the muscles on his forehead to hold it in place. One hand on the stick, the other on his face, he flew on.

⌇⌇

Five more hours in the air. Five more hours without sleep. He no longer felt attached to his body. It was as if he were "an automaton, flying mechanically." Both hands were now on the stick, his feet on the rudder, and his eyes on the compass. But his consciousness, like a winged messenger, soared from the cockpit, skimmed the white-caps of the ocean below, played in the clouds. At one point he jerked back into his body to discover he'd fallen asleep with his eyes open. Terrified of what might have happened, he descended until he was just above the ocean, close enough for cold spray from the waves to moisten his face. He shook his head until it hurt.

⌇⌇

Twenty-two hours into his flight, the ghosts came. "Vaguely outlined forms, transparent, moving, riding weightless with me in the plane," he later said. They filled the fuselage behind him. Charles felt no surprise at seeing them. He felt no fear. These phantoms weren't strangers. They were more like "a gathering of family and friends after years of separation." He felt he'd known them all in "some past incarnation."

The ghosts spoke with human voices. First one and then another pressed forward and leaned into his ear so as to be heard above the engine.

What did they say? Charles never told. But their words, he believed, were gifts—special knowledge not shared with ordinary mortals. He felt his body disintegrate and re-form. He felt his mind expand beyond its "solid walls of bone" to the "immortal existence that lies outside." He felt reconstructed . . . reincarnated. "Death no longer seems the final end it used to be, but rather the entrance to a new and free existence which includes all space, all time. . . . I live in the past, the present, the future, here and in different places, all at once. . . . Vistas open up before me as changing as those between the clouds I pass. I'm flying in a plane over the Atlantic Ocean; but I'm also living in years now far away."

The spirits stayed until the night's darkness lifted and the early-morning mist faded. And like the mythical phoenix, reborn and renewed, the *Spirit of St. Louis* burst into dazzling sunlight.

SATURDAY MORNING IN AMERICA

Below on earth, Americans awoke clamoring for news of their hero. Of course, there wasn't any. Charles had been out of touch for hours and would continue to be until he reached Ireland. What papers lacked in real news they made up for with editorial cartoons, tributes, and special photo sections. But it was a cartoon by *St. Louis Dispatch* artist Daniel R. Fitzpatrick, depicting a "wide, empty sea [and] an immense, gloomy sky," that best summed up the nation's emotions. In the middle of this desolate picture, looking both "defiant and pathetic," a solitary plane flew.

THE SECOND DAY

Charles was more than two hours ahead of schedule. Miraculously, a tailwind had whipped up just after his ghostly visitors departed. Even more astonishing, he felt alert and strong again. It was as if he'd recovered from a serious illness. Hands on the stick, eyes on the horizon, he pondered his otherworldly experience. He believed he would unravel its deeper meaning in time. But discovery would have to wait. Now in his twenty-seventh hour of flight, Charles could see the coast of Ireland.

Haze-covered hills, clumps of trees, rocky cliffs—Ireland was a glorious sight. As the *Spirit of St. Louis* soared above villages, people streamed into the streets, waving and waving. Thought Charles, *For twenty-five years I've lived on [earth], and yet not seen it till this moment.*

On he flew. Daylight was fading when he saw the coast of France. One more hour to Paris, he told himself. In celebration, he ate one of his sandwiches—his first food in more than thirty-five hours. It didn't taste all that good, but he chewed, swallowed it down, then gulped some water. He didn't have to conserve *that* anymore. He crumpled up the sandwich wrapper and started to throw it out the window. At the last second he thought better of it and stuffed it back in the bag. "I [didn't] want the litter from a sandwich to symbolize my first contact with France."

Soon he picked up the patterned lights of Paris's streets and the Eiffel Tower. He circled it, of course. Then he headed northeast toward Le Bourget airport. He thought he saw it, but what was happening with its lights? They made no sense. There was a black square framed by regularly spaced lights, but on one side the airfield was a jam of erratic light.

He circled over the black square. And circled again. More of the airfield revealed itself. Those erratic lights, he realized, were the headlights of automobiles stuck in traffic. Why would they put the airport so close to the city?

He circled the square a third time, choosing a spot for his landing. He pulled back on the stick, closed the throttle. His wheels touched ground, and the *Spirit* bounced and rolled, at last coming to a stop in the middle of the dark field. It was 10:24 p.m. in Paris—thirty-three and a half hours since he'd left New York, and two and a half hours ahead of his schedule.

Suddenly, out of the blackness surged a wall of people, arms waving, shouting, crying, frenzied. The first to reach him were airport workmen. *"Cette fois ça va!"* they shouted. "This time, it's done!"

Charles shouted back, "Are there any mechanics here?"

His words were lost in the pandemonium. Wave after wave of people kept coming—more than 150,000 in all—breaking down the barricades set up by the government, surging onto the field.

Charles opened the cockpit door and tried to put his foot on the ground, but dozens of hands grabbed him. They lifted him into the air, then passed him around over the heads of the cheering mob. "It was like drowning in a human sea," he recalled.

In the chaos, two French pilots found themselves close to him.

"Come!" said one to the other. "They will smother him!"

Snatching the flying helmet off Charles's head, they slapped it onto a tall American reporter, pointed at him, and shouted in French, *"There is Lindbergh!"*

The crowd dropped the real Lindbergh and surged after the startled imposter.

Meanwhile, Charles's rescuers linked their arms around him and began moving him unnoticed through the crowd. Charles protested. He needed to go back and make sure the *Spirit* was safe. But the pilots promised the plane would be taken care of. They bundled him into a nearby car and drove him to a quiet hangar on the other side of the field.

Two hours passed before the American ambassador to France, Myron T. Herrick, found him. "Young man," he said, "I'm going to take you home with me [to the embassy] and look after you." Charles was grateful, but he couldn't leave until he'd seen his plane.

It took another hour for the crowds to disperse. Then Charles's French rescuers drove him to the hangar where the *Spirit* had been stored. Shocked, Charles ran his hand over the plane's frame. Souvenir hunters had torn it apart. Gaping holes pockmarked its fuselage, and fittings from its engine had vanished along with the flight log. Still, a careful inspection showed no serious damage. A little repair would make it airworthy again. After leaving the *Spirit* protected by policemen in the hangar, Charles got back into the car with his rescuers.

And then?

After battling both traffic jams and people dancing in Paris's streets; after visiting the Arc de Triomphe and the tomb of the Unknown Soldier (the French pilots' idea, not his own); after eating a light supper of bouillon and an egg; after bathing and putting on a pair of the ambassador's too-short pajamas; after giving a brief interview to the reporters who clogged the street in front of the American embassy (the ambassador's idea, not his own); Charles finally, *finally* climbed into the narrow twin bed in the embassy's guest room and closed his eyes. It was 4:15 in the morning. He had been awake sixty-three hours.

CHAPTER TEN

THE MOST FAMOUS MAN IN THE WORLD

AMERICA

The nation went berserk. Word of Lindbergh's successful flight reached New York City at 5:15 in the afternoon—forty-five minutes after he landed in Paris. Minutes after that, thanks to radio, it was known across the country. Horns honked. Church bells rang. Kids ran up and down the sidewalks, banging pots and pans.

Fire companies sounded their sirens and rolled out into the streets to spread the news. People hugged and sobbed and danced and shouted.

They tore up their phone books to make confetti and flung it out windows. They waved flags and burst into rousing renditions of "The Star-Spangled Banner." They turned up their radios full blast to hear the details—although there was little more to say than that Lindbergh had landed—being broadcast on every station across the country. "We just went dippy with joy," recalled one Ohio college student.

In Detroit, a tearful but smiling Evangeline Lindbergh came out of her house to greet the crush of reporters in her front yard. "I am proud to be the mother of such a boy," she said simply.

At Long Island's Glen Cove Community Hospital, newborn Charles Lindbergh Hurley became the first baby to be named after the hero.

And at Harlem's Savoy Ballroom, reveling patrons shouted, "Lindy's done it!", then created a new dance on the spot. Called the Lindy Hop, it quickly became a national craze.

The gripping, drawn-out drama of Lindbergh's Atlantic crossing would become, remarked historian Richard Bak, "one of those shared national experiences that binds a generation until its last member dies."

Newspapers struggled to articulate Lindbergh's momentous achievement. The *New York Evening World* called it "the greatest feat of solitary man in the records of the human race." And the *North American Review* proclaimed "the long-awaited joy of humanity at the coming of the first citizen of the world, the first human being truly entitled to give his address as 'The Earth,' the first Ambassador-at-Large to Creation."

They gave him another nickname, too—the Lone Eagle. A nod to Charles's solitary bravery, it also linked his success to the bald eagle, a national emblem symbolizing the proud independence, strength, and freedom of the United States. Charles's feat had become a matter of civic pride. His was an American victory, and citizens reveled in the knowledge that it had been accomplished through Yankee grit and know-how, not to mention technology. Noted President Calvin Coolidge weeks later, "We are proud that in every particular [the *Spirit of St. Louis*] represented American genius and industry . . . [in its] construction."

Still, most people viewed Lindbergh's triumph as something far more. It was, wrote one reporter, "a victory for the entire human race. By this act of pulling himself from one continent to the other Lindbergh transcended nationality and rose to the level of citizen of the world." And indeed, congratulatory cables arrived from all corners of the globe—Italy, India, Argentina, Japan. "The victory of Lindbergh is, above all, a moral victory," editorialized the Paris newspaper *Le Petit Journal.* "He succeeded as much with his soul as with his muscles."

America's theologians agreed. That Sunday in churches all across the country, millions of Americans bowed their heads in thanksgiving. Sermonized one church leader, "While everyone else jockeyed for money and publicity . . . this young man simply flew." Declared another, "[Like Lindbergh,] it is necessary for us all to discipline the flesh with its appetites and lusts [if] the heroic adventure of Christian life is to succeed."

Practically overnight, Charles had became a true hero for a generation who'd sworn off true heroes. This wholesome and modest young man who'd flown alone had demonstrated that even in an increasingly shallow age, the individual spirit could still triumph. And his achievement did more than amaze Americans. F. Scott Fitzgerald wrote that it made them "set down their glasses in country clubs and speak-easies and [think] of their old best dreams."

It had taken just thirty-three and a half hours for Charles Lindbergh to go from "the flying kid" to the Second Coming.

ADULATION

"I wonder if I really deserve all this?" Charles said as he stood on the deck of the USS *Memphis*. It was June 11—Charles Lindbergh Day—and four navy destroyers, two army dirigibles, and eighty-eight army air corps planes escorted the *Memphis* through Chesapeake Bay en route to Washington, DC, where President Calvin Coolidge, along with members of Congress, top military brass, important business leaders, and 250,000 euphoric Americans waited on the National Mall to honor him. Millions more would be listening on their radios. (In the days before Charles's return home, twelve thousand miles of telephone wire had been converted to radio use, giving the country its first coast-to-coast broadcast, and practically every American tuned in.)

It all bewildered Charles. He understood the meaning of his flight for the future of commercial aviation—his was the forerunner of regular air service between the two continents. But the laurels heaped on him in Europe had stunned him. The president of France had awarded him the Legion of Honor, the first time that nation's highest honor had been given to an American. He'd ridden in a parade attended by millions, been given the key to Paris, then traveled to London to meet both the prime minister and the royal family. He'd been embarrassed when King George V had pulled him aside and whispered, "Now tell me, Captain Lindbergh. There is one thing I long to know. How did you pee?" Blushing, he'd managed to explain his use of a "funnel and an aluminum can." He'd been decorated with the British Air Force Cross, pinned with the Badge of a Knight of the Order of Leopold (a Belgian award), awarded the London *Daily Mail*'s gold cup, and honored with a gold medal from the city of Brussels. He'd received plaques from both the Belgian and the British Royal Aero Clubs, laid wreaths at the Tomb of the Unknown Soldier in Paris, Brussels, and London, and for sixteen hours a day attended dinners, receptions, and other ceremonies. "From the moment I woke in the morning to . . . when I fell asleep at night, every day was scheduled," he complained. "There was no time for the things I wanted most to do: walk through the streets of Paris . . . talk to French pilots, maybe fly some French planes. I did not even have time to be with my *Spirit of St. Louis*. . . . I was a prisoner of the ceremonial life that had been arranged for me."

Charles would face far more adulation at home. Americans were clamoring for his return. Already, proposals had been put forward in Congress exempting him from paying income taxes for the rest of his life; creating a new department of aviation, with him as its long-term head; and establishing May 21—the day he landed in Paris—as a permanent national holiday. While none of these proposals passed, Congress did vote to award him the Congressional Medal of Honor, previously reserved for heroism in combat. At the same time, the United States Postal Service rushed out special airmail stamps

depicting the *Spirit of St. Louis*—the first time a stamp had been issued in honor of a living person. And the US Army promoted him to
the rank of colonel.

Across the country, schools, parks, bridges, streets, and even
a mountain peak in Colorado were named after him. A newborn female elk at the Brooklyn Zoo was christened Lindy Lou. A Times
Square restaurant featured a Lindbergh Sandwich. Novelty companies churned out Lindbergh buttons, flags, plates, ashtrays, statio-
nery, spoons, and other souvenirs by the millions. Music companies
cranked out scores of popular songs, with titles such as "The Eagle of
the USA" and "Like an Angel You Flew into Everyone's Hearts," while
ordinary Americans churned out odes and poems in his honor. Five
thousand gushing verses, such as Willis A. Boughton's "American
Rhapsody to Lindbergh," were published in magazines and newspapers just in the first three weeks after his landing. They expressed
not only the dizzying heights of the public's adoration, but the ex-
tent to which Americans identified with him:

> *Once more I stand, America abreast the world*
> *Carrying as banner your bright deeds*
> *Your glory and your simple pride.*
> *The wonder of your virtues.*
> *As if they were my own,*
> *For they are my own!*

If the public wasn't writing about him, they were writing *to* him.
Awaiting his return were a hundred thousand telegrams and cables,
three and a half million letters (mostly from females), and fourteen
thousand packages containing an astonishing array of gifts and me-
mentoes. Among the presents were a replica of the *Spirit of St. Louis*
carved from soap, an embroidered handbag (for his mother), a lifetime pass to all National League baseball games, a dress sword, dozens of Bibles, rings, watches, religious medals, a diamond stickpin,

a German shepherd, a silver chest, automobiles from the Franklin, Ford, and Cadillac-LaSalle companies, and a five-seater monoplane from his friends at Ryan Aircraft.

Was it any wonder Washington, DC, erupted in a cacophony of church bells, sirens, factory whistles, and car horns when the USS *Memphis* came alongside the navy yard dock? "Here comes the boy!" exclaimed the radio broadcaster when Charles stepped onto the gangplank. "He stands quiet and unassuming. . . . He looks very serious and *awfully* nice. A darn nice boy!"

Listeners around the country tensed with excitement. Their hero was home.

Meanwhile, crowds waiting at the dock could not contain themselves. When Charles appeared, they surged forward, rushing the marines who stood with fixed bayonets. Charles was hustled into a waiting car to head under military guard to the Washington Monument. Many people wept. Charles occasionally waved, but mostly he just stared—looking a bit shell-shocked—at the cheering mob.

When at last he reached the speaking platform, he nodded to the sea of people stretching from the Capitol to the Lincoln Memorial. The crowd roared. Then President Calvin Coolidge, after making a brief speech, pinned the Distinguished Flying Cross on the lapel of Charles's plain blue suit. He gestured for the flier to say a few words.

Charles leaned into the microphone (it was set too low for him) and the Mall fell silent. Most had never heard the sound of his voice.

"On the evening of May twenty-first," he began in his clipped, reedy voice, "I arrived at Le Bourget, France. I was in Paris for a week, in Belgium for a day, and was in London and England for several days. Everywhere I went . . . I was requested to bring a message home to you. . . . Always the message was the same. 'You have seen . . . the affection of the people of France for the people of America demonstrated to you.'" Charles paused before adding, "I thank you." He stepped back from the podium.

The listeners stood stunned for a moment. That was all he had to say? Charles Lindbergh was obviously as economical with words as he was with plane fuel. But then, recalled one eyewitness, "came long applause. . . . Men and women clapped until their palms were numb. Again, many wept."

Two days later in New York City, Charles rode bareheaded in an open car up Broadway in the biggest ticker-tape parade the world had ever seen. Eighteen hundred tons of paper rained down from skyscraper windows—a blizzard of ticker tape, shredded phone books, and confetti so thick that at times some of the more than four million people lining the street could not see their hero as he passed. The next morning, city workers cleaned debris from the street that in places stood five feet high.

And still the parades and dinners and speeches continued. By the end of June—just two weeks after his return to the United States—Charles was so heartily sick of people that he was unable to pretend otherwise. He no longer smiled for photographers, and when they begged him to look happier, he refused. He *wasn't* happy. How could he be? He couldn't take a walk without being mobbed. Crowds formed around any building he was in, and waiters fought over a corncob left on his plate. His laundry disappeared every time he sent it out, and he couldn't write checks because people kept them instead of cashing them. Girls on the streets flung themselves at him, and once, when he was lunching in a restaurant, a middle-aged woman came over and peered into his mouth to see what he was eating.

Charles had to admit that since touching down in Paris, he'd felt a strange sense of loss. He couldn't shake the feeling that his success had swallowed up everything he treasured—work, respect, privacy. The life he'd known had vanished.

He tried transferring the public's interest in him to his cause—aviation—by only talking about America's need for an airport in every city, or the safety of flight and a future in which people could fly to Europe in mere hours.

No one appeared to be listening. "Is it true, Colonel, that girls don't interest you at all?" asked one reporter just moments after Charles had spoken about his vision of linking countries through commercial aviation.

"If you can show me what that has to do with aviation, I'll be glad to answer," the pilot snapped back.

Now the most famous man in the world, Charles was deluged with business proposals to endorse products, speak on stages, star in movies, write newspaper columns, and lend his name to various ventures. A French theatrical agent guaranteed him $250,000 for five appearances in South America. And one Hollywood producer offered $1 million for him to appear in a movie in which he actually got married.

Charles said no to most of them. Certainly he hoped to profit from his flight, but he didn't want to do anything that felt cheap or profiteering. So he chose the cleanest, most respectable of the offers. He accepted assignments from the *New York Times* and the *Saturday Evening Post* on the strict condition that he wrote about aviation and not himself. He accepted the Orteig Prize of $25,000. And he took on technical consultant positions (and stock options) in both Pan American Airways and Transcontinental Air Transport (TAT). Commercial airlines were still in their infancy, but Charles firmly believed they were the future, and he wanted to be a part of that. And he took $50,000 from Harry Guggenheim's Fund for the Promotion of Aeronautics. At the end of July, he would fly to all forty-eight states as a way of stirring popular interest in aviation while showing how safe it was.

Charles also signed a $50,000 book contract with George Putnam of G. P. Putnam's Sons that allowed for a ghostwriter to pen a quickie account of his flight. When Charles read the completed manuscript, however, he refused to approve it. The ghostwriter's version, he claimed, made him seem like a "dumb, Midwestern hayseed."

Putnam didn't care. He'd paid for a book and was already

publicizing it. So for three weeks, Charles locked himself into a suite of rooms in Harry Guggenheim's Long Island estate and worked fourteen hours a day to produce the forty thousand words that was specified in his contract. He didn't try for any literary flourishes. Instead, he wrote a terse, listlike account of his flight to Paris that included little about his personal life but plenty about the remarkable performance of his American-made earth-inductor compass and his Wright Whirlwind engine. Writing the book, he later confessed, was one of the worst tasks he'd ever undertaken, done not for pleasure, but because of obligation. He hoped never to have to write another.

But it hardly mattered. The book was published on July 27 under the title *We* (because of Charles's tendency to refer to himself and his plane in the first person plural) and was bought by 190,000 people in less than six weeks. Just four days after handing the completed manuscript over to Putnam, on July 20, he set off on his forty-eight-state tour. Over the next three months he flew 23,350 miles, spent 263 hours in the air, visited 82 cities, gave 147 speeches (all on the topic of aviation), was the guest of honor at 69 dinners, drove 1,285 miles in parades, and was seen by an estimated 30 million people (an astonishing *one-fourth* of the nation). When the tour ended, the public idolized him more than ever.

And Charles was more miserable. "I wish the public would just remember my flight to Paris as something that happened in the [past], and then forget about me," he said to Donald Keyhoe, an aide assigned to his tour by the Department of Commerce. The two men were hunkered down in a hangar at an airstrip in New Jersey. Through the closed double doors, reporters shouted questions.

Impossible, Keyhoe replied. "You are a public figure, and everyone insists on keeping you in the foreground."

"I can either be in public life, or go back to private life," replied Charles. "It might help aviation if I [keep] . . . talking about flying, but I think there are more important things to be done."

Keyhoe asked him what those things were.

"I'd like to be free to work on some scientific problems," answered Charles vaguely.

He didn't tell Keyhoe about his ghostly experience over the Atlantic, or how it had gotten him thinking more and more about that nagging question from childhood: What was death? Somehow—although it was still unclear in his mind—his next journey would involve his long fascination with biology and the mysteries of life and death. *If [man] could learn to fly,* he remembered thinking at the time, *why could he not learn how to live forever?*

PART FOUR
COPILOT

"[He] has swept out of sight all the other men I have ever known . . . my world—my little embroidery beribboned world is smashed."
—*Anne Morrow*

CHAPTER ELEVEN

CHARLES AND ANNE

LOVE AT FIRST SIGHT

December 1927. Anne Morrow felt annoyed. She'd been counting the days until Christmas break, eager to be alone with her family. But now a stranger was horning in on the family's holiday . . . Charles Lindbergh, no less!

She supposed it *was* the polite thing to invite him. The only reason the aviator was even in Mexico was because her father, Ambassador Dwight Morrow, had asked him to make a goodwill flight to that country. After landing in Mexico City just ten days before Christmas, Charles had been asked to stay on at the American embassy and spend the holidays with Morrow and his wife, Betty. It would, Betty assured him, be a wonderful family get-together. All the Morrows would be there—twenty-three-year-old Elisabeth, fourteen-year-old Constance, and nineteen-year-old Dwight Jr. Even their middle daughter, twenty-one-year-old Anne, was traveling all the way from Smith College in Massachusetts.

Charles had hesitated. The thought of an old-fashioned Christmas surrounded by a large, loving family made him very uncomfortable. But the alternative—reporters trying to ferret out his holiday traditions (of which he had none)—was far worse. Morrow's home, with its gates and guards, was a haven of privacy. For a few days, at least, he'd be free from prying eyes. He'd accepted the Morrows' invitation.

Now, on the ride from Mexico City's train station to the American embassy, Anne guessed what he'd be like—"a regular newspaper hero, the baseball-player type." Of course, that sort of man didn't interest her. She wanted someone with whom she could share her stories and poems, a man as passionate about words as she. From the newspaper photographs, she knew Lindbergh was good-looking. But who wanted a lady killer? She certainly had no intention of "worship[ping] Lindy" like everyone else.

The car came to a stop in front of the embassy, and Anne climbed out of the backseat. She hurried up the wide marble stairs and found Charles leaning against a stone pillar, "a tall slim boy . . . so much slimmer, so much taller, so much more poised than I expected. A very refined face, not at all like the grinning 'Lindy' pictures—a firm mouth, clear, straight blue eyes, fair hair and nice color."

Feeling suddenly "very confused and overwhelmed," Anne held out her hand.

An expressionless Charles shook it.

Anne spent the rest of her visit in a state of distraction and bewilderment. She stammered and could not meet their guest's eyes. "Why is it that attractive men . . . always terrify me and put me at my worst?" She felt like a lump, the dark-haired middle daughter who wasn't nearly as pretty as her sparkling older sister. Meanwhile, she was experiencing an utterly surprising emotion. The flier had "swept out of sight all the other men I have ever known, all the pseudo-intellectuals, the sophisticates, the posers—the 'arty' people. All my life, in fact, my world—my little embroidery beribboned world is smashed."

Although she kept her feelings secret, Anne had already fallen in love with Charles Lindbergh.

〰

On the last day of his visit, Charles borrowed a five-passenger silver trimotor plane and took Anne, along with her sisters, Elisabeth and

Constance, and her mother, Betty, for a ride. As she climbed into the seat directly behind him, Anne said to herself over and over, "God, let me be *conscious* of it . . . *while* it's happening. Let me realize it and feel it vividly. . . . Let me be *conscious* of it."

The propeller whirled. The engine sputtered. The plane rumbled across the field, picking up speed. Anne could feel every bump and rut. The ground came toward her faster and faster . . . the ride became bumpier and bumpier . . . until suddenly it was smooth. She felt suspended in time, suspended in air, her heart rising in her throat as they went up, up, up. A *"real* and intense *consciousness* of flying" flooded over her.

On they soared, above fields where cows and sheep were mere specks and the embassy looked like a dollhouse. "Oh, to go on and on . . . I could understand why people never can give [flying] up," she later wrote in her diary.

Soon, though, she found herself more mesmerized with the pilot than the flight. "He was so perfectly at home. . . . Every movement quiet, ordered, easy—and *completely* harmonious. I don't know how I can say that, really, for he moved so *very* little and yet you felt the harmony of it," she noted. And his hands! "One hand on the [stick]— one hand! He has the most tremendous hands . . . the grasp, the strong wrist, the grip of the thumb."

When the flight ended, she stumbled from the plane, dazed. "I will not be happy till it happens again," she confessed in her diary.

A week later, Anne returned to Smith College to finish her senior year. Even with the frenzy of that last semester—classes, papers, final projects—she couldn't get Charles Lindbergh out of her mind or heart.

And Charles? He got back to the business of flying. It would be months before he gave Anne another thought.

THE IMPORTANCE OF GOOD GENES

In the spring of 1928—not long after his twenty-sixth birthday—Charles sat in an Indiana hotel room with pen and paper. He'd made a decision. "[I]t was time to meet girls." And so, in the same way he outlined specifications for a plane, he listed the best qualifications for a wife:

"[G]ood health, good form, good sight and hearing," he wrote. More importantly, "a girl who like[s] flying," because he "would take her with me on the expeditions I expect . . . to make in my plane. That ought to be great fun." Intelligence? Absolutely, but he didn't care about formal education. It was an "attitude of mind" he wanted, "not a mass of knowledge." He also sought a "mental attractiveness," although he didn't exactly define that.

Above all, she had to come from superior stock, genetically. "My experience in breeding animals on the farm had taught me the importance of good heredity," he said. Environment, Charles believed, had little to do with physical and mental superiority. "When you saw the mothers and fathers, you could tell a lot about their offspring."

Charles believed "mating [was] the most important choice of life. . . . One mates not only with an individual, but also with that individual's . . . ancestry." And he had no intention of diluting his extraordinary Lindbergh-Land genes by marrying a woman whose own were not "conducive to evolutionary progress."

He was hardly alone in this thinking. After World War I, groups with names like the Race Betterment Foundation and the American Breeders Association had sprung up around the country. Their goal was to spread the word about eugenics, a pseudoscience that advocated improvement of the human race through controlled breeding. Eugenicists believed heredity determined not only a person's physical features, but also their mental and moral character. Desirable traits like honesty, intelligence, and industriousness were passed on from generation to generation. So, too, were undesirable traits such as shiftlessness, criminality, drunkenness, and "feeblemindedness," a catchall term that included everything from severe mental illness to learning disabilities. Even poverty, they claimed, could be blamed on inferior genes.

During the 1920s, it was common for eugenicists to host "better baby" and "fittest family" competitions at state fairs and local exhibitions. Contestants completed a questionnaire about their physical and mental health, their churchgoing, their hobbies, interests, and other matters. Their answers were then scored on a scale created by the American Eugenics Society, a national organization dedicated to promoting eugenics education to the public. Families earning a B+ or higher received a medal engraved with the words "YEA I HAVE A GOODLY HERITAGE." It was an award for "best" human stock—not unlike the blue ribbons given for the prize hog or biggest pumpkin.

Certainly, Charles had encountered these genetic competitions during his barnstorming days when he dropped in on local events to sell airplane rides. He may also have come across the theory while at the University of Wisconsin. By 1921 the eugenics movement had become so mainstream that most college-level biology textbooks devoted a chapter to it. And doctors, politicians, philanthropists, and the general public readily adopted it.

Most eugenicists were middle- to upper-middle-class, white, Protestant, and educated. They celebrated the qualities of the Nordic and Anglo-Saxon "races" and disparaged others who threatened the nation's "racial strength." This was largely due to World War I, which had given many Americans a greater fear of foreigners at a time when immigration to the United States was increasing. Since the turn of the twentieth century, the country had experienced a surge of immigrants, mostly from Russia and Southern Europe—close to half a million people a year. To many white Americans it seemed as if the nation was being invaded by the poor and uneducated, people who didn't speak English and did not look American. Afraid of being overrun, these white Americans embraced eugenics. They believed the genetically fit—themselves—should be encouraged to have large families. But how to keep the unfit from reproducing?

In 1924, Harry Laughlin, president of the American Eugenics Society and a man who believed that "the central mission of all politics is race hygiene," lobbied Congress, urging its members to change the nation's immigration policy. Speaking before the House of Representatives Immigration Committee, Laughlin told members what they already wanted to hear: immigrants were polluting America's bloodline with "feeblemindedness, insanity, criminality, and dependency." The resulting legislation, the Immigration Act of 1924, did everything Laughlin had hoped for. It set strict quotas on various "undesirable races"—Jews, Asians, and people from Southern and Eastern Europe—while still welcoming large numbers from Britain, Ireland, and Northern Europe. Said President Calvin Coolidge as he signed the act, "America must remain American."

Just three years later, in 1927—the same year Charles flew across the Atlantic—the federal government legalized sterilization for the "socially unfit." In an eight-to-one ruling by the Supreme Court, the State of Virginia won the right to forcibly tie the fallopian tubes of seventeen-year-old Carrie Buck, whom the state had declared "feeble-minded." In his majority opinion, Justice Oliver Wendell Holmes wrote, "It is better for the world, if instead of waiting to execute degenerate offspring for crime, or let them starve for imbecility, society can prevent those manifestly unfit. . . . Three generations of imbeciles are enough."

By 1931, thirty-two states had passed eugenic sterilization laws, and over the next forty years, between sixty and seventy thousand Americans of both sexes were sterilized. (Most of these laws would not be repealed until the 1960s and 1970s.)

So it wasn't surprising that Charles insisted on a wife from genetically good stock. Since he considered himself a superior specimen, he felt duty bound to choose carefully.

Having completed his checklist, he began his search.

"Girls were everywhere," Charles said, "but it was hard to get to know them." Because of his fame, they didn't act natural. Instead, they treated him with awe or curiosity. They were too shy, or worse . . . too forward! If he actually talked to a young woman for more than five minutes, the newspapers had him instantly engaged. And if he ever did manage to ask one out, he couldn't take her to dinner or a movie without its becoming front-page news.

By September 1928 he changed his strategy. He would, he decided, confine his search to the families of the political and business leaders he'd gotten to know in the past year. Not only did some of them have daughters his age, but their large, well-protected homes provided him privacy from the press.

It was this pragmatic thinking that led him back to the Morrow daughters. Not the sparkling, vivacious Elisabeth, but the one "resting in [her] shadow"—Anne. Charles admitted surprise that she'd resurfaced in his memory. In Mexico he had "noticed her [only] casually."

Could it have been that Anne came to mind after he became aware of Elisabeth's heart condition? Having contracted rheumatic fever as a child, the Morrows' oldest daughter suffered from a damaged heart valve—hardly the superior physical specimen he was seeking.

Whatever the reason, Charles began making more plans, this time for "achieving my objective with the girl." Not only had he never been on a date with Anne (or *any* female, for that matter), he hadn't even been in contact with her since Mexico. Still, he was already determined to marry her.

A DATE IN THE AIR AND ONE ON THE GROUND

After some thought, Charles decided "to approach Anne with an invitation to fly, and then extend it into a date on the ground." But not until he had a detailed, practicable, and solid plan in place did he telephone the Morrows' home in Englewood, New Jersey.

It was a crisp, clear afternoon in October, and Anne (who had graduated from Smith the previous spring) was home for the month with just servants for company. She'd been writing poetry, filling her diary with rich words, when her mother's social secretary interrupted. Charles Lindbergh, she told Anne, was on the telephone.

Still infatuated, feeling faint and frantic, Anne picked up the phone and whispered weakly, "Hello—hello."

"Hello. This is Lindbergh speaking," came the response. He got right to the point. Would Anne care to go flying?

Surely, he didn't really want to go with her, she thought. He must have called for Elisabeth and, learning she wasn't there, had asked Anne out of politeness. She tried to put him off.

But Charles refused to be diverted. "About what time could I come?" he asked.

"T-tomorrow?" she stammered.

"Tomorrow—what time?"

"Tomorrow afternoon . . ."

"Well, *what time* tomorrow afternoon? Any time you say."

"Any time after three?"

"Well, tomorrow at four, shall we say? . . . I'll see you tomorrow, then."

Anne later admitted to feeling somewhat cornered. He was like "a small boy," she wrote in a letter to her sister Constance. "Action, *decided* action, follows thought at an amazing speed. There are no complications: 'Good day for fishing!' Off! Presto! Like that."

〜

She had forgotten how handsome he was, so "tall and thin," his face "sunburned . . . and his hair so *fair*."

Anne, on the other hand, looked a mess. She'd thrown together an outfit she hoped would be appropriate for flying—Constance's riding pants, a woolen shirt of Betty's, and her father's thick gray golf stockings, which she'd stuffed into a pair of high-heeled shoes. Over it all she wore a red leather coat.

Charles roared with laughter when he saw the high heels.

As he led her to his car, he told her about the day he'd planned. First they'd have lunch at a friend's house, and afterward he'd take her flying in a biplane he'd borrowed for the afternoon.

"Now, *really*, please don't let me be any more bother than is necessary," fussed Anne. She still did not grasp that this was a date.

Replied Charles, blue eyes twinkling, "It's no bother at all."

They drove to Falaise, the Long Island mansion of Harry Guggenheim. Months earlier, the millionaire had invited Charles to make the 350-acre estate his home, and had given him a bedroom suite overlooking Long Island Sound. When he wasn't flying, this was where the aviator could usually be found, swimming, fishing, or taking off from Guggenheim's private airstrip.

Charles seemed entirely at home in the palatial surroundings, "push[ing] open the great carved door without knocking, picking up his mail casually," noted Anne. Here was a completely different side of him. Gone was the cold and reserved hero. "He's just *terribly* kind and absolutely natural and . . . rather a dear," Anne later wrote.

It was all part of his plan. He knew the wealthy, educated Morrows considered him a bit unpolished. By bringing Anne here, he allowed her to see how easily he fit in with society's first families, how at home he felt living among "gatehouses and towers and lawns and peacocks."

After lunch, he took Anne out to the airstrip. He strapped her into her parachute, helped her into the plane, and gave her a few simple flying instructions. Then they climbed into the air.

The wind whistled past Anne's face. The groan of the plane's engine filled her ears. Soon they were so far up, they could see both shorelines of Long Island. "I can't describe the flying," Anne recalled, "it was too glorious."

❊

Three days later, Charles took Anne for an evening ride in his car. The two drove for hours along back roads and through dense fog, talking honestly about what mattered most to them. Charles explained his passion for flight in a way that made Anne see that it was a means to greater ends. Successful flights across the oceans, he believed, would bring nations closer together. They would be "link[ed] up through aviation" in both distance and understanding. Airplanes would become instruments of peace instead of war.

In the nestlike warmth of his car, with the engine purring, Anne felt contented and comfortable. Even the silences in their conversation felt natural. Lowering her guard, she shared her dream of becoming a published writer.

"You like to *write* books?" he said in astonishment, obviously recalling his miserable experience producing *We.* He added, "I like to *live* them."

On the ride home, he asked her to marry him.

"You must be kidding!" she exclaimed. "You don't know me."

"Oh, I do know," he answered.

He knew that, like him, she was basically shy. She was also healthy, intelligent, and attractive.

And she obviously delighted in flying. She could easily be shaped into a dutiful wife and crewmate.

If love entered into Charles's decision, he never mentioned it.

Anne seemed to instinctively understand her expected role. He was, she wrote, "a knight in shining armor, with myself as his devoted page . . . an apprentice to someone more experienced in a world of which I knew little but which I was eager to explore."

What was said after the proposal, neither Anne nor Charles recorded.

But Anne's answer was definitely yes.

CHAPTER TWELVE

I DO

NEW FRIENDS

Because of Charles's status as a public figure, as well as the future son-in-law of the well-connected Dwight Morrow, some of the richest men in America welcomed him into their homes. Often, after a sumptuous dinner, he would join his new friends in their leather-lined smoking rooms or book-lined libraries. There would be scientists, executives, ambassadors, bankers, politicians, high-ranking officers, publishers, and industrialists—almost exclusively men of capital. And almost exclusively Republicans. If Charles didn't agree with all their conservative opinions, he found he shared many of them. Like these men, he worried about the behavior of the nation's youth (odd considering he was still in his twenties). He was concerned about crime and corruption, as well as the decline of American morals. And he heartily agreed with the measures they proposed to preserve the financial status quo.

After all, Charles was a man of capital, too. First, there were the lucrative contracts he'd negotiated after the trans-Atlantic flight with both Transcontinental Air Transport and Pan American Airways. Then there were the six-figure royalty checks he received from *We,* which had earned him $190,000 in just its first two months (about $2.6 million today). A year later, it remained on the bestseller list. And then, of course, there was the money from his stocks. As a favored client of the banking empire J. P. Morgan & Company (of which Dwight Morrow had once been a partner), Charles had the opportunity to purchase blue-chip stocks at discount rates. After buying them at a third of the price quoted on the New York Stock Exchange, he turned around and resold them at the market price. In this way, Charles made a small fortune. By the age of twenty-six, he had enough of a nest egg never to have to worry about money again.

He reveled in the company of his new and powerful friends. He found them a far better class of people than the grease-monkey mechanics and foulmouthed barnstormers he knew. And so, as he'd done after graduating from army flight school, he broke off his old social life cleanly and began fresh. People from his early days of piloting were mostly forgotten. Even Donald Hall, who'd played such a pivotal role in the creation of the *Spirit of St. Louis,* was jettisoned.

Charles was now a full-fledged member of what his father had called the Money Trust.

HUSH-HUSH WEDDING

On February 12, 1929, Dwight Morrow called reporters into his office at the embassy and handed out slips of paper. On each was typed a single sentence: "Ambassador and Mrs. Morrow announce the engagement of their daughter, Anne Spencer Morrow, to Colonel Charles A. Lindbergh." That was it—no wedding date, no details. But it was enough for radio broadcasters to break into their regularly scheduled programs with news bulletins; enough to make headlines across the country; enough for thousands of letters and presents to flood the embassy. Some came from family and friends. Most, however, came from folks who simply wanted to rejoice with their hero. "Unlike most brides-to-be," recalled Anne, "it was *I* who was congratulated, not he."

Reporters swooped down on the couple. Huddled around the embassy gates, they waited, cameras ready. They climbed up trees and onto nearby roofs to photograph the couple in the garden. They bribed servants to share details about the lovebirds, stole letters, talked to unsuspecting friends, and printed distorted anecdotes of the couple's private life. If they ran short of material, they invented stories.

"Never say anything you wouldn't want shouted from the house-tops," Charles instructed Anne.

This directive made Anne feel smothered. "The lid of caution was clapped down on all [my] spontaneous expression," she recalled. She wouldn't be able to speak freely to Charles unless they were "in the privacy of a plane, a wilderness, or a bedroom. And even in a hotel room, I must be sure that the windows and the transom to the hall were closed to eavesdroppers." It was, she admitted, like putting "a string on a wild bird and expect[ing] it to fly."

Meanwhile, Betty Morrow had her heart set on a big, traditional Presbyterian wedding and had already begun a lengthy guest list. This included family members as well as business associates, diplomats, and politicians.

Charles put his foot down. He wanted a small ceremony with just a select group of family and friends in attendance. And he wanted it held at the Morrows' recently completed New Jersey mansion, called Next Day Hill.

Betty was shocked. No church?

Charles explained he wasn't a churchgoer. Therefore, getting married in one would be hypocritical.

But what about Anne? asked Betty. She turned to her daughter. Certainly, she wanted to observe Morrow family tradition.

Anne remained silent, letting Charles speak for her.

Betty had been having problems reconciling herself to this engagement. It wasn't that she didn't like and admire the flier, but she'd never anticipated having him as her son-in-law. Didn't Anne see how different they were? Hers was the cloistered world of books, writing, and introspection. His was action and adventure. Betty believed solid marriages were based on having things in common. How could Anne know what interests and opinions she shared with Charles? They'd met only four times before getting engaged.

Charles suggested a compromise. He would allow a Presbyterian minister to perform the ceremony *if* Charles was allowed to approve all the prayers, verses, and rituals beforehand. Anything he felt compromised his integrity would have to be removed.

Betty agreed.

They set the wedding date for May 27, 1929.

〰

Another list. Another plan. Meticulously, Charles worked out an elaborate charade to fool the press and keep the wedding a secret. Knowing reporters expected a honeymoon by airplane, he decided to take Anne on a boating trip instead. Under a fake name, he ordered a thirty-eight-foot cruiser named the *Mouette* to be anchored at an isolated spot off Long Island Sound. While the boat was being readied, Charles had his plane flown to the Rochester, New York, airstrip. There he left it, fully serviced and ready to go at a moment's notice. As he'd expected, many of the reporters who'd been swarming the gates of the Morrows' estate in New Jersey hurried to the airstrip, convinced they were about to catch a glimpse of the Lone Eagle and his bride. The reporters who remained outside Next Day Hill kept watch for signs of a wedding—florists, caterers, musicians. They felt sure the event would be an elaborate affair.

So they paid scant attention when a handful of people arrived at the Morrow house in the middle of the afternoon. They'd been invited to tea, the guests replied to the reporters' shouted questions. Betty had just telephoned them.

They were shown into the large living room, hidden from the street and overlooking the garden. It wasn't until Reverend Dr. William Brown of the Union Theological Seminary arrived that they realized the truth. This wasn't a tea party. This was a wedding ceremony. So insistent on secrecy was Charles that even the guests had been kept in the dark.

The double doors leading into the dining room opened. There stood a beaming Dwight Morrow. Beside him, her hand on his arm, was Anne in a simple cream chiffon gown the family seamstress had secretly run up. Without music, father and daughter moved through the hushed group toward the fireplace, where Charles waited in his blue suit.

It didn't take long for Reverend Brown to get through the abbreviated wedding service. The groom slipped a gold band onto his bride's finger and awkwardly pecked her cheek. If Anne was disappointed in his lack of ardor, she didn't have time to dwell on it. In an instant, the guests pushed forward to congratulate them. Since Charles didn't have any close friends or family, no one was there from the groom's side except Evangeline. But though there were only a few in attendance, it was a "lovely, warm group," wrote Anne.

She would have liked to stay and bask in her happiness with them. But just minutes after cutting the cake (made weeks earlier and smuggled into the Morrow house during one of Betty's bridge parties), Charles insisted to Anne that they leave. For his plan to work, they needed to get a jump on the press before word of the ceremony leaked out. Disappointed, Anne changed out of her gown, then slipped out the back door with her husband. She crouched down beside him in the backseat of a waiting car with one of the guests at the wheel. After passing the clutch of reporters, they headed to a little-used alley, where Charles's car waited. There they donned disguises of hunting caps and glasses, got into the second car, and headed for Long Island.

Night had fallen by the time they arrived at an out-of-the-way spot. According to plan, they found the dinghy Charles had arranged to have tied to a tree. In the beam from his flashlight, the newlyweds dragged the boat into the choppy water of Long Island Sound and started rowing. Ahead of them, its lights glowing a warm welcome, bobbed the *Mouette*.

CAMP LINDBERGH

If Anne expected a honeymoon filled with candlelit dinners and long, lazy breakfasts in bed, she was disappointed. Charles didn't seem particularly interested in romance. Instead, he spent their first days together learning the ways of his boat. In fact, when he looked back on the trip, that was what he remembered most fondly. "I had never before navigated a vessel larger . . . than a rowboat," he wrote forty years later. "But basic principles of navigation for sea and air were similar."

It didn't seem to occur to Charles that this time might have been better spent getting to know his wife. He treated the trip more like a stay at Camp Lindbergh than a honeymoon.

At Charles's insistence, Anne busied herself arranging all the cans of food on board. "It took a whole day and most of the deck to sort them out," she wrote to her mother. "It took another day to [stow] them all."

When she finished, Charles inspected her work. With his hands on his hips, he said gravely, "The soap powder, the sugar and the brass polish don't belong together."

His comment left Anne feeling impractical and clumsy. Her new husband, she realized, had exacting expectations, strict rules, and specific checklists. And Anne was meant to learn and follow them all. Eager to please, she docilely went along with his demands. "But it takes most of the day," she admitted to her mother, "what with meals and dishes and pans and sink and icebox and stove and floors and decks and the bed to make and the bathroom to clean, etc."

The press found them a week later. The couple awoke to the

harsh, smirking voice of a reporter calling to them from a nearby vessel. "Is this Colonel Lindbergh's boat?"

Now hundreds of reporters surged up the New England coast. A motorboat full of photographers pulled up alongside the *Mouette*. They would leave the honeymooners alone, one called out, if the Lindberghs would come out and pose for a series of pictures. Charles stubbornly and furiously refused. For the rest of the morning and afternoon, the *Mouette* rocked in the wake of the reporters' motorboat as it circled around and around them. Finally, Charles gunned his engine and fled out to sea, dragging the anchor. The couple spent the night in open water tethered to a fishing bank. Fighting to stay in her bunk as the waves roiled and dishes crashed, Anne felt hunted.

CHAPTER THIRTEEN

SETTLING DOWN

VAGABONDS OF THE AIR

In the summer of 1929, despite warnings from some critics that the economy was overheated and the stock market dangerously overpriced, Transcontinental Air Transport (TAT) decided to expand its business by offering the first-ever coast-to-coast travel service. Recent developments in aircraft technology had made this possible. In 1925, the Ford Motor Company had begun building planes as well as cars. Soon it was producing the "Tin Goose," the first all-metal, multiengine (three in total) commercial airplane. Sumptuously equipped with velvet-cushioned wicker chairs, individual reading lamps, and electric cigar lighters with ashtrays, the plane could carry a crew of three (pilot, copilot, and cabin steward), as well as nine passengers. Despite the necessity of landing every 250 miles to refuel, the plane could cross the country in just forty-eight hours—forty hours faster than a train. This time savings, however, came with a big price tag. At $351.94 (about $5,000 today), a one-way flight on TAT cost twice as much as the most expensive railroad accommodation. Understanding the need to appeal to the wealthiest travelers, TAT officials upped the company's snob appeal by giving every passenger on the transcontinental run a solid gold fountain pen from Tiffany & Co.

TAT also sought to enhance its name recognition and reputation by dubbing itself "the Lindbergh Line," since the famous pilot had agreed to lend both his name and his services to the company in exchange for that lucrative stock-sharing deal.

And so, fresh from their honeymoon, Charles and Anne took to the air, crisscrossing the country to christen the new airports along TAT's cross-country route. Everywhere they went, they were followed by whirring newsreel cameras and popping flashbulbs. It was the kind of attention of which Charles approved—publicity for aviation, proof that plane travel was fast, efficient, and, above all, safe. And Anne became TAT's unofficial hostess, smiling alongside her husband. Still, the couple remained always on guard. "We avoid[ed] all personal questions," said Anne, "speaking in discreet banalities."

Vagabonds of the air, they called no place home, living in hotels and embassies and other people's houses. Charles made it clear that his wife was not going to sit at home waiting for him. Where he went, she went—and he was the one who decided where they were going.

Anne resented this at first. "And there he is—darn it all—the great Western strong-man-open-spaces type and a life of relentless action!" she wrote early in their relationship. "But after all, what am I going to do about it?"

To have Anne merely as a passenger in his plane would have been a waste of weight and space. No, she would be a working partner, a member of his crew. Charles expected her to learn to work a radio, become expert in Morse code, and plot a course with charts and compass.

Above all, she needed to learn to fly. Charles, of course, would be her teacher. Concerned for her safety, he bought a special training plane said to be so easy to handle, one could land it in a tree.

But he was a perfectionist. On her first day of instruction, sitting behind her in the dual-control plane, he told her bluntly that he'd rather have a "nonpilot than a poor pilot." Anne got his point.

Sometimes, he had her flying out of the Long Island Aviation Club two or three hours a day, landing and taking off, landing and taking off. Time and again she'd bring the plane down with a bump, a bounce, and a sigh of relief, only to have him say, "Not good. Take her up again."

On August 24, Anne soloed. From the clubhouse porch, Charles watched her take off and circle for several minutes before gracefully bringing the plane back down to earth.

Charles grinned.

And Anne felt glorious! "For the first time, I had a sense of value in the 'real world' of life and action," she said. "Like the bird pushed out of the nest, I was astonished that—flapping hard—I could fly."

Now Charles's mind filled with new possibilities for flights. Truth was, he hadn't realized how lonely he'd been until he'd married Anne. Her being in the back cockpit relieved the long, empty hours of flying. The touch of her hand on his neck, the silly note passed forward because it was impossible to talk over the engines' roar. It had changed him. He still wanted to fly, but now he wanted to fly with his wife.

⌇

That fall, Charles also began his work for Pan American Airways (Pan Am). The airline had originally been an airmail carrier, but its officials had recognized the potential for passenger airlines around the same time as TAT. And they, too, had offered Charles a handsome contract back in 1927. But Pan Am's sights were set on a different territory—Central and South America. They wanted Charles to work out routes spanning the countries in these regions. With Anne behind him, he took off for Cuba, Haiti, Puerto Rico, Trinidad, Panama, Colombia, and Nicaragua.

Everywhere they went, Charles impressed the crowds. But it was Anne, with her physical stamina and fortitude, who surprised people. So small she could stand upright under her husband's outstretched arm, she hiked alongside him at his quick pace across deserts and through dense jungles. She shinnied up and down ropes to investigate canyons and ruins, camped out in heat and cold and thunderstorms.

In March 1930 she allowed Charles to strap her into a glider and propel her over the side of a mountain. She became the first woman to earn a glider's pilot license, although it was not a thrill she longed to repeat.

A month later, in a small sports plane Charles had specially designed, he and Anne broke the transcontinental speed record, flying from Los Angeles to New York in a mere fourteen hours, forty-five minutes—three hours faster than the previous record.

And then "the first couple of the sky," as newspapers called them, did something really surprising. They hung up their flying suits and secluded themselves at Next Day Hill.

Anne was seven months pregnant.

EAGLET

On June 22, 1930—Anne's twenty-fourth birthday—a tired but joyful Charles sent a telegram to his mother in Detroit:

ADVISE PURCHASING PROPERTY.

It was a code Charles had shared with Evangeline weeks earlier, meant to confuse reporters. If the baby was a girl, he would send a telegram reading ADVISE ACCEPT TERMS OF CONTRACT. For a boy it would read ADVISE PURCHASING PROPERTY.

Evangeline had a grandson.

Charles Augustus Lindbergh, Jr.

Gazing down at her six-pound, seven-ounce newborn for the first time, Anne thought, *Oh, dear, it's going to look like me—dark hair and a nose all over its face.* Then she saw the "unmistakable cleft in the chin" and she went to sleep "quite happy."

Charles did not record how he felt about his newborn son.

The day after the baby's birth, churches everywhere said special prayers and blessings for him. A choir director in Florence composed a lullaby in his honor. The congregants of the Magyar Evangelical Reformed Christian Church in Gary, Indiana, named their new church the Charles A. Lindbergh Jr. Cathedral Chapel. And some members of Congress even suggested his birthday be declared a national holiday.

At Next Day Hill the doorbell kept ringing. Poems. Letters. Flowers. Presents. Songs. All this and more poured in. They came from around the world, and mostly from strangers—a candy maker forwarded a specially created box of "Lindy Jr. Pure Honey Kisses"; *Parents* magazine offered the Lindberghs a free subscription; a Hollywood director sent along a small movie camera; a California rancher sent a pony. So many people wanted to forward their good wishes that a Boston printing company created a special greeting card for the occasion that read, "Congratulations to the Happy Lindberghs." Bushels of them arrived at the Morrow estate.

But as months passed, the tone of this correspondence began to shift. Good wishes turned to appeals for money. People began begging for help instead of autographs. And more than two hundred new parents wrote and asked for the baby's outgrown clothing. "Surely a hero like Charles Lindbergh can spare something . . . anything," insisted one letter writer.

Neither Charles nor Anne responded to these requests. But they understood their meaning: Americans were feeling the strains of the Great Depression.

CRASH

"There is something about too much prosperity that ruins the fiber of the people," Charles said one evening in October 1930. He looked down the china- and crystal-laden dining table toward Dwight Morrow. Did his father-in-law agree?

The men were discussing the economic downturn. A year earlier, on October 24, 1929, the stock market had crashed, plunging the entire nation into an economic tailspin. Although only a small percentage of Americans had invested in the market, the impact of plummeting stock prices was quickly felt across the country. Many banks—hard hit when stock investors were unable to pay back their loans—closed their doors. The life savings of millions of Americans were wiped out. And businesses began failing at an alarming rate, leaving more and more people without jobs. In the past year, one in four Americans had found themselves out of work. Stores were closed; factories and mines stood idle; and millions of workers roamed the cities, looking for employment.

Hungry Americans stood in long lines at charity soup kitchens or foraged in garbage cans. Homeless Americans built makeshift shelters out of scrap iron, packing boxes, and other thrown-away items. And some piled their remaining belongings into their cars and headed west, searching for a better life. They didn't find it. It seemed suffering and despair were everywhere—except at Next Day Hill.

Within the manicured borders of the Morrow estate, maids still polished silver; the cook still whipped up delicious meals served by the white-gloved butler; the chauffeur still waited beside the gleaming Rolls-Royce, ready to drive the family wherever it wished. As if living in their own fairy tale, the Lindberghs and Morrows went untouched by the Depression. With the help of their friends at J. P. Morgan & Company, both men's fortunes had survived the stock market crash almost intact.

As servants moved around the table, Charles went on with his thoughts about the economic crisis. "It will furnish a fine test of American capability and character," he declared. That he wasn't being tested himself did not seem to occur to him.

It had occurred to Dwight Morrow, however. The previous January he'd left his ambassadorial position in Mexico and returned to New Jersey to run for, and win, election to a vacated seat in the United

States Senate. Now he often lay awake at night worrying about the growing numbers of hungry and homeless.

Still, Morrow chose not to contradict his son-in-law. He'd learned it was easier to hold his tongue than to argue with Charles. Eventually, as Morrow had hoped, the conversation drifted to other subjects.

Despite living under the same roof, the two men had not bonded. Instead, they treated each other with utmost politeness—so much so that Charles always felt like a weekend guest. He detested not being in charge.

⌇

Not long after the baby's birth, Charles decided it was time to build his own home. He'd already purchased the land—425 acres of fields and woodlands in New Jersey's Sourland Mountains. It even had its own little brook. Best of all, it was private. No one except a few poor farmers lived nearby, and the closest town, Hopewell, was three miles away. An architect was currently drawing up plans for a house, and some of the acreage had been cleared and leveled for an airstrip. Charles spent much of his time there, chopping down trees and supervising construction. Still, it would be another year before their new home was ready.

Anne, meanwhile, settled into motherhood. She'd fallen in love with little Charles. Not immediately, but over time and through a series of "terribly dear" moments. She called him her "fat lamb" and confessed that it broke her heart every time she left him to go shopping or out to tea with her mother.

She worried that Charles would want to return to flying long distances soon. She knew he couldn't remain earthbound for long. So she was overwhelmed with relief when he suddenly directed his passion and energy toward an earthbound question that had nagged at him since childhood: Why couldn't people live forever?

CHAPTER FOURTEEN

IMMORTAL

NOVEMBER 28, 1930

The scientist who stood to meet Charles Lindbergh in the dining room of the Rockefeller Institute of Medical Research in Manhattan was a foot shorter than the pilot. He was stocky and pink-cheeked, and his eyes—one blue, the other brown—peered up through his pince-nez. As he scanned Charles's face, he didn't say a word. Besides being a Nobel laureate and experimental surgeon, Dr. Alexis Carrel was a practitioner of physiognomy—that is, he believed the quality of a man's soul could be read on his face, imprinted there, he claimed, by "brain waves controlling the facial muscles." If Dr. Carrel's scrutiny of someone left him with a good impression, the doctor would talk freely. If not, he would shrug and turn away.

He took to Charles instantly. And the pilot, who rarely warmed up to people quickly, had a similar response to Dr. Carrel. When they shook hands, claimed Charles, an electrical current passed between them. Carrel described it as being "linked by strong psychic bonds."

Over tea and sandwiches, Charles explained to Carrel why he'd come.

Months earlier, Charles's sister-in-law Elisabeth had suffered a mild heart attack. The doctor's prognosis was grim: the twenty-six-year-old had lesions on her heart valves that would only worsen with time. He doubted she'd live long.

Charles was puzzled. Why couldn't the doctor just operate and remove the lesions?

Elisabeth's doctor had explained that the heart could not be stopped long enough for the surgery to be performed. Blood, he explained, "had to be kept circulating through the body."

Charles persisted. Wasn't the heart simply a pump? It seemed as though it should be "quite simple to design a mechanical pump capable of circulating blood through a body during the short period required for an operation." Why hadn't one been invented?

The doctor didn't know.

Charles had been taken aback. *Could it be that no one had seriously thought of designing a mechanical heart for use in surgery?* he wondered.

He hadn't forgotten what he'd said to Donald Keyhoe years earlier. He still wanted to work on scientific problems. He still wanted to explore the possibility of immortality. And the idea of a mechanical heart seemed a good place to start. His mind tumbled with exciting possibilities. *Why could not a part of the body be kept alive indefinitely if a mechanical heart was attached to it—an arm, or even a head? Why could not the* entire body *be kept alive after the heart it was born with became too old and worn out to function?*

Charles had posed these questions to the anesthesiologist who attended Anne during the baby's birth. The anesthesiologist didn't have an answer, either. But he could send the pilot to someone who *did* know—Dr. Alexis Carrel.

This was the reason Charles sat across from Carrel now.

Patiently, Dr. Carrel answered all Charles's questions. No, he said, a mechanical heart made of glass or metal could not be used to circulate blood through the body while surgeons operated on Elisabeth Morrow because "blood soon coagulates [solidifies] in contact with surfaces of glass or metal." However, he added, he *was* working on something the pilot might find interesting. "If you like, I will show you what we are doing here," he said.

THE LABORATORY OF DR. CARREL

Charles and Dr. Carrel climbed a spiral staircase to the fifth floor, to a lab few scientists at the institute knew about. Tucked beneath the attic eaves, it was hidden away from general view. And despite the hefty sums spent by administrators to fund the experiments going on there, it had remained largely a secret. But now, taken with Charles Lindbergh, Dr. Carrel was eager to reveal its mysteries.

Upstairs, the scientist asked his guest to change into a black surgical robe and cap. The color surprised Charles. Patiently, Carrel explained his belief that black was more antiseptic than white. For this reason, every surface in his four operating rooms was also black. He knew some people found this eccentric, but he didn't care. He was used to criticism from the scientific community, especially in recent years as his experiments strayed from the objective, rational science of medicine to what he called "metaphysical researches." Clairvoyance. Miracle healings. Hypnotism. His experiments, remarked one of Dr. Carrel's colleagues, were a cross between "medieval alchemy and the weird experiments of [Dr.] Frankenstein."

He led Charles into the animal rooms.

Here, said Dr. Carrel, were his "patients"—dogs and cats inside cages—some with open sores on their backs. Carrel explained his search for substances that healed wounds quickly and without infection. A discovery like that, he noted, would save millions of human lives. As for the animals' whimpering and moaning, it didn't bother him. The advancement of science, he believed, required their sacrifice. "To learn how man and animals live, we cannot avoid seeing . . . them die," Dr. Carrel liked to say.

Next, he led his guest down the hall to a large glass-walled structure filled with hundreds of boxes and soil-filled pens. This was Dr. Carrel's mousery. Charles stared, transfixed, despite its nose-wrinkling stench. Fourteen thousand mice—a city of rodents—scratched through dirt, gnawed on cage bars, hissed, rested, fought, ate, groomed, and gave birth. Some looked sleek and fat, their fur silky and their eyes bright. Others, covered with scars and wounds, cowered nervously in tunnels or hid beneath sawdust bedding. With their sharp yellow teeth, bigger mice slashed at smaller ones. There were squeals of fear and pain. There was blood.

The mousery's purpose was to "re-create real life and the struggle for existence," Dr. Carrel would later explain. Seeing the strongest dominate and kill the weakest was merely to observe what was right and natural. Here was "the pure mechanism of natural selection at work." The fit eliminated the unfit. Or, put another way, the strong and intelligent procreated and the weak died without coddling. This was how superior civilizations developed, he claimed.

The men at last turned away. With the odor of blood and fear still thick in his nostrils, Charles followed Carrel into a microscope-lined laboratory. The scientist opened a refrigerator door to reveal bits and pieces of tissue. He held up a glass container. A cat thyroid, he said, identifying the thumb-sized organ within. He went on to explain his interest in attaching the parts of one animal to another of the same species. He'd first tried this twenty-five years ago when he'd attached a puppy's kidney to the carotid artery of an adult dog. To Carrel's amazement, the kidney had functioned normally for several hours. Sadly, other such attempts had not been so successful. Still, he held out hope, especially for skin grafting.

The next room was the incubator room. Warm and moist, thanks to steam jets in the walls, this room was where Dr. Carrel kept microscopic pieces of tissue alive—some from laboratory animals, some from humans. Dozens of culture flasks lined the counter. But his most famous experiment sat on a table all by itself.

On January 17, 1921, Carrel had taken a minute sample of heart muscle from a chicken embryo and placed it in a flask containing nutrient fluid. Within two days, the tissue sample had doubled in size. Within four days, it had grown to four times its original size.

Now, eighteen years later, the embryo tissue was still alive and still growing. Every January 17, Dr. Carrel's staff gathered around to sing "Happy Birthday" to it.

As Charles peered through a microscope at the chicken embryo tissue, his mind took a leap. If this tissue could survive for years, why not entire organs? he asked Carrel. Could they be kept alive outside the body, too?

Charles's perceptivity startled Dr. Carrel. He'd been wrestling with the same question for the past ten years. He opened a cabinet and showed his guest a collection of variously designed devices called perfusion pumps. Built to the doctor's specifications, each was meant to keep organs living outside the body, but each had failed.

Keeping an organ alive after its removal from the body was far more difficult than sustaining embryo tissue, Carrel explained. Organs remained alive only if they were "perfused"—that is, supplied with a steady stream of nutrients and oxygenated blood. The doctor had already perfected a synthetic substitute for the body's natural fluids. What he needed was a way to properly circulate his fluid around the organ.

How could he experiment on living organs if he could not find a way to keep them alive for a prolonged period? There was no telling what medical advances might be possible if he could. Dying organs might be "removed from the body and placed in the . . . pump," he said, "to be revived, and repaired, and returned to function once more."

Charles looked over the collection of perfusion pumps. He thought the designs crude and said so. Matter-of-factly, he told the doctor he could "improve on them."

Then go ahead, replied Dr. Carrel. He offered Charles full use of his facilities.

It was an astounding opportunity for a man who'd barely finished high school and flunked out of college: the chance to work alongside a Nobel Prize–winning scientist in a world-class research facility. Charles immediately accepted.

"THE MYSTICAL AND THE SCIENTIFIC MEET"

While working at the Rockefeller Institute, Charles must have recalled his grandfather Land's words: "Science is a key to all mystery. With this key, man can become like a god himself."

Charles already felt pretty godlike. The supreme confidence he'd exhibited as a child had only multiplied in the years since he'd taken up flying. He'd done something many thought impossible. His abilities seemed limitless. If anyone could unlock the mysteries of life and death, he believed he could.

But accomplishment did not come without work. To become a full partner in this quest, he needed to take part in all Carrel's experiments, understand every procedure. And so he began putting in long hours at the lab, skipping lunch and often leaving past midnight. He used his two-hour commute "for contemplating . . . the phenomenon and rationality of death."

In the incubator room, a textbook at his elbow, he peered for hours through the microscope at "young and pulsing" cells. Was it possible that "with proper care they could live and pulse forever?" He even examined his own sperm, marveling at the sight. "[E]ach one of them myself, my life stream," he exclaimed, "capable of spreading my existence throughout the human race, of reincarnating me in all eternity."

While his work with the microscope forced him to contemplate cellular immortality, his time in the operating room led him to question the border between life and death. Here in the eerie, closed-off world of darkness and silence, Charles felt "the mystical and the scientific meet." Everything in the room was black—the floors, the windowless walls, the operating table. Only the beams from the surgical light overhead and Dr. Carrel's white cap (to distinguish him from his black-clad assistants) broke the gloom. "The animal on the operating table brought my eyes to focus on elements of life—breathing lungs, pulsing arteries, glistening skin, seeping red blood," recalled Charles. "Life sometimes merged with death so closely I could not tell them apart—click of scissors, cleave of scalpel, the surgeon's nimble fingers tying knots in silk—black figures manipulating flesh and organs, preserving them, fragmenting them . . . trying to learn life's limits and capabilities . . ."

When did life end and death begin? Carrel's scalpel might have killed the cat on the table, but parts of its body remained alive—a piece of its carotid artery (a major blood vessel found in the neck) refrigerated in petroleum jelly just above freezing would go on functioning for months; the white blood cells being drawn from its body with a glass tube called a cannula would continue to thrive in petri dishes.

So why couldn't entire organs live likewise?

"If I could design a better perfusion pump," Charles told himself, "I could keep those organs alive long after the body . . . had entered the state called 'death.'"

At his workbench, he drew and redrew plans for his perfusion pump. Within weeks he had an idea for a simple enclosed spiral glass device with two chambers, one for the liquid nutrient and the other for oxygen. When the device was placed on a motorized base that gently rocked back and forth, the fluids inside would mix and perfuse the organ.

In March 1931 Charles passed the design on to the institute's glassblower, and within weeks the men had a Pyrex perfusion pump. Dr. Carrel took a piece of a chicken's carotid artery and inserted it into the device's organ chamber. To their delight, the artery survived for days without infection. But it wasn't good enough. Success required that it survive for months, even years. Charles went back to the drawing board. He made one unsatisfactory model after another.

Carrel, for his part, put each device to the test. The scientist was highly impressed with his protégé, despite the failures. Charles, he claimed, was "original in his ideas, skilled with his hands, utterly dedicated to his work and persistent. Stubbornly persistent."

He wished he could tell people outside the institute about Lindbergh. But he'd promised Charles he wouldn't whisper a word about the pilot's working in the lab. And Dr. Carrel was very good at keeping secrets.

THE PERFECTION OF MANKIND

Secretive though he was, Dr. Carrel was a dazzling talker. He could spin theories as fast as he could construct sentences, and he cited all sorts of weird and obscure data to back up his beliefs. In an hour's lunchtime, he might bloviate about the "difficulty of teaching a camel to walk backwards," discuss the "relative intelligence of dogs and monkeys," or give a longwinded account of a "[French] peasant hypnotizing animals."

He was also outspoken and definite when it came to his opinions about genetics, ethics, race, and biology:

"The white race is drowning in a sea of inferiors."

"There is no escaping that men [are] definitely *not* created equal . . . despite what democracy says."

"Instead of encouraging the survival of the unfit and the defective, we must help the strong; only the elite makes the progress of the masses possible."

Dr. Carrel mused on sunlight's effect on race. "We must not forget that most highly civilized races—the Scandinavians, for example—are white, and have lived for many generations in a country where [sunlight] is weak during a great part of the year . . . The lower races generally inhabit countries where light is violent and the temperature warm."

He riffed on race purification: "Perhaps it would be effective to kill off the worst of [us] and keep the best, as we do in the breeding of dogs."

And once, he provided what he believed was a reasonable and unsentimental approach to solving society's ills. "Those who have murdered, robbed while armed . . . kidnapped children, despoiled the poor of their savings, or misled the public in important matters, should be humanely and economically disposed of in small euthanasic institutions supplied with proper gases. . . ."

Carrel often pointed to his mousery to underscore his opinions. While the deaths of the weak mice seemed cruel, they were necessary, he said. Culling the weak moved the species—generation by generation—closer to genetic perfection.

And perfection of mankind was Carrel's most important scientific goal. This could only be achieved, he insisted, through eugenics.

Charles, of course, already viewed eugenics favorably. Hadn't he practiced the pseudoscience when choosing a wife? But Carrel wasn't advocating the run-of-the-mill brand of eugenics so many middle- and upper-middle-class white Americans believed in. His was a radical brand widely disregarded by the scientific community that openly endorsed imprisonment and euthanasia. "Why preserve useless and harmful human beings?" he asked. He even floated the idea of culling human babies, "like puppies." These harsh measures, he insisted, were the only way to guarantee that white civilization would prevail.

Leaning in and listening closely, Charles learned from his mentor. And his academically untrained mind filled with radical theories about the improvement of the white race.

STILL FLYING

Anne was reluctant to go. "I would have been content to stay home and do nothing else but care for my baby," she wrote in the spring of 1931.

Despite his absorbing work at the Rockefeller Institute, Charles was planning another flying adventure—finding the shortest route from New York to Japan to link the countries by air. And he expected Anne to take her place as his crew member when he took off in July.

Torn between motherhood and her husband, Anne found that her devotion to Charles eventually won out. "Oh, how she loved her Lindy!" recalled the baby's nurse, Betty Gow. "She'd have gone anywhere and done anything for him . . . even leave that beautiful little baby behind."

And little Charlie *was* beautiful, with his silky golden hair and enormous blue eyes. Sometimes, Anne turned up the radio and danced through the house with him. She adored his scrunched-up smile and the way he held out his pudgy hands for his toy lamb, then "strangles [it] affectionately around the neck." Playing patty-cake and piggy toes, she could not have imagined "such joy as this with Charlie." In May, when Charlie was eleven months old, she noted with special pleasure how the baby used his father's knees to pull himself up. Said Anne, "Charles [Sr.] begins to be interested in him."

It wasn't that Charles didn't love his son, but he believed in a more detached approach to fatherhood. Children should not be coddled, he insisted.

On July 30, 1931, Anne climbed into the cockpit of their black Lockheed Sirius seaplane and waved to the little boy in his nurse's arms. Charlie chirped bye-bye, his fingers curling. He was Betty Gow's baby now. Along with Betty Morrow, she would keep him safe until his parents' return.

The Lindberghs flew across Canada, slipping through cloud banks that hovered over the Arctic ice pack and landing in out-of-the-way places with names like Moose Factory and Aklavik in the Northwest Territories. After piloting through a lashing rainstorm, they arrived in Point Barrow, Alaska, where they joined the entire town in a potluck dinner of reindeer meat, wild goose, and canned celery. From there they flew to Nome before crossing the Bering Sea to the Russian island of Kamchatka. It took expert flying through thick fog to get them to their next destination, Hokkaido, Japan, but they didn't stop to rest. On they pushed to Tokyo, arriving one month after they'd left the United States. For the next two weeks, there were "bouquets, cameras, reporters, crowds . . ." Charles inspected Japanese air bases; Anne attended tea ceremonies. And in mid-September they pointed their plane toward China.

All the while, Anne missed the baby. She dreamed about him almost every night, but she didn't say a word to Charles. It seemed like "such poor sportsmanship—when this *is* a marvelous experience," she said.

※

Back at the Morrow estate, Charlie crawled over the lawn with his blocks and played with the dogs. He stuck close to his "Grandma Bee" and Betty Gow, who sang to him and read him stories. He got his first haircut, too. Grandma Bee saved every "snip of gold." Happy and well loved, he called his nurse *and* his grandmother Mummy.

※

In China, Charles decided to fly home by way of Africa and South America, a route that would add another six weeks to their trip. Anne, who had her heart set on being home by October, couldn't bring herself to argue with her husband. But secretly she kept asking, "*When* will we get home?"

The answer came unexpectedly and unhappily. On October 5, Anne received a telegram from her sister Elisabeth. Their father, Dwight, had died in his sleep from a stroke. Charles immediately canceled their plans. After crating their plane, they took the first ship back to the United States.

Nineteen days later, they arrived in New Jersey. Despite the loss of her father, Anne was glad to be home. "And oh, the baby!" she gushed. "He is a boy, a strong independent boy swaggering around on his firm little legs."

Charlie did not recognize his parents, but he didn't act afraid when they swooped down on him. Charles was pleased by his sixteen-month-old's lack of fear. He couldn't conceive of his son being anything less than confident, bold, and independent. "He began to take such an interest in the baby . . . ," exclaimed Anne, "spoiling him by giving him cornflakes and toast and sugar and jam off his plate in the morning."

Playing a game called "ceiling flying," Charles tossed the boy into the air.

"Den!" ("Again!"), screeched the toddler, arms outstretched.

The boy, admitted Charles, was "good looking" and "pretty interesting."

Life settled down. As the house they were having built neared completion, they began spending weekends there. Sitting with Charlie on the terrace, Anne imagined the flowers she would plant in the spring.

Charles returned to his work with Dr. Carrel (with occasional side trips for TAT and Pan Am). He looked forward to seeing his son at the end of his workday. "Hi! Buster," he would call whenever he saw Charlie. "Hi! Hi!" the toddler would happily screech back.

And Anne nestled back into being a full-time mother. By February, her son was calling her Mummy again.

PART FIVE
KIDNAPPED

"He was twenty months old, blond,
blue-eyed, and just beginning to talk."
—*Charles Lindbergh*

CHAPTER FIFTEEN

"THEY HAVE STOLEN OUR BABY"

TUESDAY, MARCH 1, 1932

At about 8:25 p.m., Charles drove up his narrow, mile-long driveway through darkness and past wind-tossed trees. It had been a longer-than-usual ride from Dr. Carrel's laboratory. Blustery wet weather, combined with the unpaved country roads leading to their new home, had made him late.

Gravel skittered under his tires as the Hopewell house came into view. The Lindberghs' new ten-room, two-story structure made of whitewashed fieldstone lacked the grandeur of the Morrows' estate, Next Day Hill. But every inch belonged to him and Anne. And it felt safe. The couple had grown so comfortable they rarely closed their curtains at night. They'd even fired the guard who once stood at the gate.

So far the Lindberghs had stayed here only on weekends, arriving Saturday afternoons and leaving Monday mornings. But this past weekend had been different. Little Charlie had come down with a cold. When the family awoke to sheeting rain that Monday, Charles insisted they stay another night. Why take the feverish, sniffling baby out into the damp?

Anne had agreed. Telephoning Next Day Hill, she let her mother know there'd been a change in plans. Then she spent the day rocking and cuddling the baby and rubbing Vicks ointment on his chest. She hoped to return to her mother's house on Tuesday.

The next morning, although Charlie felt better, Anne had awoken with a scratchy throat and runny nose. Looking out at the damp day, she decided to call Next Day Hill and ask the chauffeur to drive Betty Gow to the Hopewell house.

Charles had approved of her decision. Not many people knew it yet, but Anne was three months pregnant.

Now he honked his horn to alert the staff, then drove around to the garage.

Inside the house, Ollie Whateley, the butler, and his wife, Elsie, the housekeeper, got up from their chairs in the servants' sitting room and went into the kitchen to finish preparing the Lindberghs' dinner. They left Betty behind to finish her meal alone.

Charles found her there moments later. He asked after "Buster."

He felt much better, Betty reported. She recounted how the rascally toddler had galloped into the sitting room a few hours earlier, babbling and pointing and chasing the family's fox terrier, Wahgoosh (named after Charles's childhood dog). Still, as a precaution against the cold's return, Charlie had been put to bed with a layer of chest ointment. Betty had even made a little undershirt earlier that evening from an old flannel petticoat. She had put it on beneath the baby's pajamas so the ointment wouldn't stain. The twenty-month-old had been sleeping safe and sound for almost an hour, since 7:30.

Satisfied, Charles went into the living room, where Anne curled in the corner of the sofa, notebook in hand. He was glad to see her writing. Putting words on paper, he knew, was her lifeline. Lately, she'd begun forming her notes about their flight to China into a narrative she hoped might grow into a book.

On seeing her husband, Anne closed her notebook. The two chatted for a few minutes, then went in to dinner. Afterward, they returned to the living room. Sitting beside the fireplace, they were sharing the events of their days when Charles's head suddenly jerked up. "What was that?" He'd heard a splintering noise, like the slats of a wooden box falling to the floor.

Anne shook her head. She hadn't heard a thing. A few minutes later, exhausted from her cold and caring for Charlie, she went upstairs to bathe and read.

And Charles went into his study. After settling into his desk chair, he opened a biology book.

It was 10 p.m. when Betty Gow burst in on him. "Colonel Lindbergh," she cried, "have you got the baby?"

"Isn't he in his crib?"

"No!"

Leaping up, Charles took the stairs three at a time to the nursery. In the crib he found nothing but the imprint of his son's head on the pillow. On the windowsill he saw an envelope. Grasping the implications instantly, he brushed past Anne, who stood frozen in the doorway, and charged into their bedroom. He grabbed a rifle from the closet.

Back in the nursery, he stood over the empty crib, the gun clutched in his hands. "Anne," he said, "they have stolen our baby."

Charles strode downstairs to his study and telephoned the police. Then, still holding his rifle, he went out into the night. He would have taken a flashlight if there'd been any in the house. Instead, he searched with only the glow from the windows illuminating his way. Around back, directly below Charlie's window, he discovered footprints. Not far from there he found a homemade wooden ladder in three parts. Later, in the daylight, he would see that one of its side rails was broken and would remember the unusual splintering sound he'd heard. Could that have been the cause? Nearby lay a carpenter's chisel he assumed was used to pry open the nursery window.

Charles started off toward the woods, but the pitch blackness stopped him. As he turned back, he heard someone shouting the baby's name.

It was Anne.

She'd flung open their bedroom window and was leaning out into the night, eyes wide, ears straining for her son's cries. Her head swiveled in the direction of the woodpile. What was that noise?

"Only a cat," the housekeeper, Elsie Whateley, said. She led Anne from the window.

And Charles, touching none of the evidence he'd found, returned to the house.

※

The local police arrived a little before 11 p.m., followed by the New Jersey state troopers commanded by Colonel H. Norman Schwarzkopf, a barrel-chested man wearing a tailored suit instead of a uniform. After displaying the badge he carried in his wallet, he asked for details.

Charles showed him the evidence he'd found on the grounds, then led a group of investigators up to the nursery. Charles appeared in complete control as he pointed toward the envelope on the windowsill. How had he kept himself from ripping it open? Even now, with police present, he refused to let anyone touch it until a fingerprint expert could examine it.

Not until after midnight was the envelope brushed, revealing nothing but a useless finger smudge. A state trooper sliced open the envelope and handed over the note for Charles to read:

> *Dear Sir*
> *Have 50000$ ready 25000$ in 20$ bills 1500$ in 10$ bills and 1000$ in 5$ bills. After 2-4 days we will inform you were to deliver the mony.*
> *We warn you for making anyding public or for notify the police.*
> *The child is in gut care.*
> *Indication for all letters are singnature and three holes.*

The signature was unusual: two blue, overlapping circles. Inside the oval shape created by the interlocking circles was a solid red circle. And a square hole had been punched through each part of the design—three holes in all.

Charles looked around at the grim faces crowded into the room. The note had warned him not to call the police, but he'd done so before he'd read it. Would the kidnappers hold it against him? Could he keep the police from interfering? Nothing, he decided, must prevent him from paying the ransom. In the depths of the Depression, $50,000 dollars (about $850,000 nowadays) was a fortune, but it was worth every cent to have his son back.

WEDNESDAY, MARCH 2, 1932

The next day, as police searched the house and grounds, a massive manhunt was getting under way beyond the Lindberghs' property. Agents from the Bureau of Investigation (it would not be called the Federal Bureau of Investigation, or FBI, for another three years), along with the Secret Service, the Postal Inspection Service, and even the Internal Revenue Service, were put on the case. They joined the New Jersey State Police, as well as dozens of detectives from New York City, Trenton, Newark, and Jersey City. The coast guard monitored the nation's waterways. And the assistant secretary of war placed the entire US Army Air Corps (renamed from the previous Air Service) at Charles's disposal.

As if that weren't enough, the head of the Boy Scouts of America called on its current and past members—almost a million men and boys—to keep a close eye out for the toddler. The head of the American Federation of Labor did the same, urging its members in the New York/New Jersey area to form search parties. So vigilant were AFL members that they searched not only woods and fields, but also hotels and boardinghouses. They even stopped baby carriages on the street. Radio stations repeatedly broke into their scheduled programs with updates, as well as a description of the twenty-month-old. And the front page of every newspaper in the country carried a photograph of the baby. Wrote one reporter, "The world dropped its business, that day, to search for the Lindbergh baby."

Despite all these resources, Charles decided to take control of the investigation himself. Drawing on the same single-minded determination that had gotten him across the Atlantic, he resolved to remain levelheaded and methodical. He had conquered the sky. He could conquer this.

It was easy to assert his authority. The newly formed New Jersey State Police had practically no experience in kidnapping cases. Most of the troopers had done little more than write speeding tickets. Awed by the presence of the greatest hero of their time, they naturally looked to him for direction. Schwarzkopf, too, gave Charles free rein. Charles appeared so confident and sure. Who could doubt his competence?

Charles turned the house into the investigation's headquarters. Within hours, a twenty-line switchboard had been set up in the three-car garage. Manned around the clock by policemen, it rang with tips, along with crank calls from people who just wanted to hear their hero's voice. Anyone who sounded reasonable was patched through to Charles. Hundreds of false leads came in, but he insisted every one be followed up.

More police sifted through the mail. Starting the day after the kidnapping, about seven hundred letters a day poured in. As with the telephone calls, no reasonable-sounding lead was ignored.

Every scrap of information was reported directly to Charles while hundreds of police officers went in and out, tracking mud over the carpets. The ground floor was turned into a sort of dormitory for them, with blankets and mattresses strewn across the living and dining rooms. In the downstairs hallway, tables were set up for the mountains of sandwiches being made and delivered by Betty Morrow's staff at Next Day Hill.

Charles did one more thing that day. He called his banker, a partner at J. P. Morgan, and asked him to secretly gather together the ransom money.

Meanwhile, Anne stayed out of the way. Sequestered in her bedroom, she wrestled to remain calm, focusing on the comforting fact that Charles was in charge. She trusted him completely, had given her baby's life over to him. If he couldn't bring little Charlie home, who could?

Midmorning on the day after the kidnapping, Anne dragged herself to her window and looked out. Having heard the news, crowds had begun to stream into the area, bringing traffic along the narrow country roads to a standstill. Not to be deterred, the curious hiked through woods and adjoining farms to the Lindberghs' estate. As they did, they trampled underbrush and left trails of footprints, cigarette butts, and trash, obliterating any clues that might have existed. Unable to get near the house because of the police guards, they settled for having their pictures taken beside Charles's car, now parked in the driveway to make room for the switchboard in the garage. Meanwhile, a private plane roared above, giving passengers an aerial view of the crime scene for just $2.50 a head.

And then there was the press filling the grounds around the estate with newspaper reporters, photographers, newsreel cameramen, and radio commentators. One news service assigned its entire staff to the story, completely ignoring the rest of the world news, including reports of a war between Japan and China, and Congress's attempt to repeal Prohibition. Another news organization fitted out two ambulances with temporary darkrooms so photographs could be developed as the vehicles raced, sirens screaming, back to the news office, where the photos could be rushed into print. In the three weeks after the kidnapping, the *New York Daily Mirror*, a tabloid, would provide its readers with 160 photographs, diagrams, and other illustrations; another tabloid, the *Chicago Daily News,* would publish more than 200. Even the venerable *New York Times* would run as many as eight articles a day on the crime. And if any especially riveting disclosures emerged between a paper's morning and evening issues, special editions were hastily printed and hurried to newsstands.

Every facet of the crime, as well as the irresistible glimpse it provided into their hero's private life, fascinated the public. In 1932, the darkest year of the Depression, the Lindbergh baby kidnapping took their minds off their own troubles. But America's obsession went deeper still. Millions were struggling to keep their families together, which, for many, was impossible. That year, twenty thousand children were left in New York City orphanages alone by parents who were unable to feed or shelter them. In little Charlie's separation from his parents, Americans saw a grim truth. If heroic, handsome, wealthy Charles Lindbergh couldn't keep his family safe, who could? Recalled one reporter, "Little Lindy was everybody's other baby. Or if they had none, their only child. . . . Kidnapped? The Lindbergh baby? Who would DARE?" And they clamored for every detail of the case. At a time when most people had to scrape together the two cents it cost to buy a copy of the *New York Times,* newspaper sales rose 20 percent, resulting in a huge windfall for publishers who'd been hard hit by the Depression. The Lindbergh kidnapping meant big profits.

THURSDAY, MARCH 3, 1932

The police had not turned up any feasible leads. And even though Anne insisted Charles was acting like "a general managing his forces with terrific discipline . . . but great judgment," nothing was under control. The truth was, Charles had no idea what to do. Behind his façade of confidence lay a desperate father.

Schwarzkopf offered his opinion about the case. The crude ransom note, he said, along with the abandoned ladder and the lack of any quick payoff, pointed to a gang of amateurs. In fact, he believed the kidnapping was an inside job. It seemed obvious that the kidnappers, knowing they couldn't get past the guards and fences at Next Day Hill, had decided to do the job there. And he believed someone—probably a servant—had helped. Schwarzkopf asked permission to interview everyone who worked for the family at both the Hopewell house and the Morrow estate.

Charles put his foot down. The servants, he insisted, would never betray him in that way. He was confident his instincts regarding people were impeccable; he *knew* Betty Gow and the others were good and decent. He would not allow police to humiliate them with prying questions.

Besides, he had another theory: an underworld gang. Just that morning he'd read a statement mobster Al Capone had made to the press from the Chicago jail cell where he was being held for tax evasion. Capone claimed one of his own gang members had planned the kidnapping. He offered to recover the baby in exchange for his freedom.

Charles called Secretary of the Treasury Ogden Mills. Could anything be done about Capone's offer? After promising to look into the matter, Mills sent for Elmer Irey, the head of Treasury's Intelligence Unit, the same unit that had caught and jailed Capone. Mills suggested Irey go out to Hopewell, talk with Lindbergh, and help in every way he could—but make clear they would not release Capone.

Irey met with Charles that same afternoon, methodically laying out his reasons for not believing the gangster. "Capone doesn't know who has the child, Colonel Lindbergh," Irey concluded. "He is simply trying to get out of jail."

Though Charles was convinced it wasn't Capone, he still believed his son had been taken by the Mob. What he needed was a person with firsthand knowledge of underworld criminals, someone who could negotiate with them. Minutes after Irey left, he picked up the telephone and asked his Wall Street attorney, Henry Breckinridge, to find him a gangster.

FRIDAY, MARCH 4, 1932

It took Breckinridge less than twenty-four hours to locate one: Mickey Rosner, a "New Jersey bootlegger, con man and sometimes stool pigeon." By the afternoon, Rosner was sitting in the Lindbergh study, claiming he had definite proof mobsters had stolen the baby.

Could he get in contact with them? Charles asked. He desperately wanted to pay the ransom, but the kidnappers hadn't provided any information about how to do that.

Rosner assured him he could, but it would require the help of his associates, a couple of hoodlums named Salvy Spitale and Irving Bitz. Rosner had close ties to crime syndicates, and he and his associates could act as go-betweens. He was "ready to open up negotiations with the underworld," he said, and guaranteed the baby's safety.

Incredibly, Charles not only gave the gangster $2,500 for expenses, but also moved him into the Hopewell house. Installed in the study, Rosner slept on the couch at night and pretended to make phone calls to his intermediaries during the day. He repeatedly assured Charles that it would take "just a little more time" to establish direct contact with the kidnappers.

Frustrated that he hadn't been consulted about this move, Schwarzkopf was helpless to stop it. He knew Rosner and his associates were nothing but petty thieves preying on Charles's naiveté.

His doubts growing about Charles's leadership, Schwarzkopf

now gave the okay for one of his lieutenants, Arthur Keaten, to quietly begin questioning the Hopewell servants. He ordered his men to review even the vaguest anonymous tips and to once again search the property for clues. And he gave one of the troopers manning the switchboard the covert task of listening in on Rosner's telephone calls. It was time, Colonel Schwarzkopf decided, to defy America's hero.

SATURDAY, MARCH 5, 1932

Just after breakfast, Charles and a young attorney named Robert Thayer joined policemen in sifting through the day's mountain of mail. Suddenly, Thayer gave a shout. Inside a plain white envelope, he'd found a letter bearing the kidnappers' unmistakable signature. Breckinridge, Schwarzkopf, and several policemen gathered around as Charles read it aloud.

"We have warned you note to make anyding Public also notify the Police," the note began. Because of all the trouble Charles had caused, they were raising the ransom price to $70,000. Why had he gotten the whole world involved? the kidnappers demanded. Now they would have to "keep the baby for a longer time," until "everything is quiet." There were no directions on how to exchange the ransom for the child, although they claimed he was in "*gut* health."

The message changed Charles's demeanor. "The first two days," Anne wrote, "he looked like a desperate man—I could not speak to him. I was afraid to." But with the letter's arrival, he became "buoyant and alive." The baby *would* be returned, he believed. All he had to do was "mak[e] the right moves and . . . pla[y] fairly."

And then days passed without another word.

CHAPTER SIXTEEN

"JAFSIE" AND CEMETERY JOHN

WEDNESDAY, MARCH 9, TO SATURDAY, MARCH 12, 1932

On the evening of March 9—eight days after the kidnapping—a man called the switchboard. He had a message for Colonel Lindbergh, he told the trooper who answered. He'd been instructed to give it to no one else.

The trooper patched him through to the house. Robert Thayer came on the line. But the caller still refused to reveal why he'd telephoned. He identified himself as Dr. John F. Condon, a seventy-two-year-old retired school principal, athletics coach, and Doctor of Pedagogy. He added that he was deeply patriotic and, as such, outraged by what had happened to America's hero. That was why he had placed a letter in the *Bronx Home News,* his neighborhood newspaper, volunteering himself as a go-between. In addition, he'd offered his entire life savings of $1,000 on top of the already de-manded ransom, "so a loving mother may again have her child and Col. Lindbergh may know that the American people are grateful for the honor bestowed upon them by his pluck and daring."

Another crank, thought Thayer.

Then Dr. Condon told him he'd received a reply to his ad—a sealed letter addressed to Colonel Lindbergh.

Still skeptical, Thayer handed over the phone.

Charles got right to the point. "Kindly open [the letter] and read it to me," he said.

Condon did.

The letter, littered with misspellings and grammatical errors, began:

"Dear Sir, Mr. Condon may act as go-between." The letter reminded Charles what kind of bills the kidnappers had previously specified and warned him again not to notify the police.

Was that all? asked Charles.

No, said Condon. At the bottom of the note appeared some odd circles. "Is it important?" he asked.

It was. The strange signature from the original ransom note had never been divulged to the press. And now here was Condon describing the very same signature. The note had to be from the real kidnappers. Charles insisted the doctor drive out to Hopewell immediately.

It was a two-hour ride from the Bronx, and Dr. Condon did not arrive until after midnight. He was shown into the Lindberghs' bedroom. With policemen everywhere, this was the only remaining private space in the house. When Charles saw the old man, he was doubtful. Dr. Condon looked like a charlatan to the flier, with his walrus mustache and his old-fashioned suit. But once Dr. Condon had repeated his story and handed over the note, Charles quickly changed his mind.

After a brief discussion with Breckinridge, Charles agreed that Condon should act as go-between and place the message "money is ready" in the *New York American* as the kidnappers had instructed. Additionally, he felt it important to hide Condon's identity from the press. It was the old man's idea to use the pseudonym Jafsie, based on his initials, J.F.C., to sign the message.

With Charles now focused on these new developments, Lieutenant Keaten took the opportunity to question the servants in the Morrow household. (He'd already spoken to and cleared those at the Hopewell house.) He knew he'd have to keep things light and informal, more a chat than an inquiry. Insisting his questions were just routine, he talked with the butler, the housekeeper, the personal secretary, and others. He cleared all of them as suspects until he got to the downstairs maid, Violet Sharpe. Tense and evasive, she made it clear that she resented his questions. "You have no business prying into my private life!" she shouted. Finally, defensively, she crossed her arms over her chest and refused to say another word.

Her uncooperative behavior aroused Keaten's suspicions. For the time being, though, he decided to leave her alone. He would wait and see if events with Dr. Condon panned out.

The requested message ran on Friday, March 11. That night someone claiming to be one of the kidnappers called Condon at home. In a heavy German accent, he said he had seen the message and would contact Condon again soon. Before the doctor could ask any questions, the man hung up.

The next evening, a note arrived at Condon's house. It instructed him to go to a deserted hot dog stand on Jerome Avenue, where he would find a stone on its porch. Beneath the stone would be further instructions.

Like a character in a cloak-and-dagger novel, Condon followed the notes from his home to the hot dog stand and eventually to the main entrance of Woodlawn Cemetery. He stood there, uncertain what to do next. The heavy gates were locked. He looked up and down the dark, empty street. Had he gotten the instructions wrong? He shifted nervously. That was when something white flashed between the bars of the fence. A handkerchief. It was signaling him from inside the cemetery. The doctor approached.

"Did you got it, the money?" a man asked.

Condon explained he wouldn't bring the money until he saw the child.

Before the man could reply, footsteps came along the sidewalk. It was just the cemetery guard, but the man believed Condon had called the police. He vaulted over the fence and began running down the street.

Despite his age, Condon ran after him. "Come back here! Don't be cowardly!"

Incredibly, the elderly doctor caught up with the man in a nearby park. After grabbing his arm, Condon led him to a stone bench. Even more incredible, the two sat and talked for almost an hour. Condon noted that the man was muscular and clean-shaven and kept his hat pulled down and his coat collar flipped up to hide his face.

His name, he told Dr. Condon, was John, and he represented a gang of three men and two women who'd been planning the kidnapping for a year. The baby, he added, was being held on a boat five or six hours away by air. Suddenly, he interrupted himself. "[W]hat if the baby is dead? [W]ould I burn if the baby is dead?"

Condon went cold. Was the baby dead? he asked.

"The baby is all right," John said.

But Condon felt wary. He insisted on proof that John actually had the child.

John agreed. He promised to send the old man a token—"the sleeping suit from the baby." In return, and to prove to his gang leader that he'd tried to convince Condon to give him the money, he asked that Condon take out another ad in the *Bronx Home News*. It should read, "Baby is alive and well. Money is ready."

The men shook hands. Then "Cemetery John," as Condon now called him, vanished into the darkness.

SUNDAY, MARCH 13, TO
TUESDAY, MARCH 15, 1932

Colonel Schwarzkopf fumed. Why, he demanded, hadn't he been told about the secret negotiations with the kidnappers? He was aware he'd been cut from those whispered strategy meetings between Charles and Henry Breckinridge. But *this,* he believed, was nothing short of obstructing justice. They'd had the kidnapper in their sights. And what had they done? They'd let him stroll away scot-free. It was outrageous.

The colonel's anger merely confirmed Charles's belief that his interests conflicted with those of the authorities. They wanted to catch the kidnappers. But his only concern was the safe return of his son. He demanded Schwarzkopf say nothing to his troopers about the secret negotiations. He intended to play by the kidnappers' rules, he told the colonel, and keep his side of the bargain.

〜

That same day, March 13, gangster Mickey Rosner—who'd been asked to leave the Lindberghs' house because Charles no longer believed him—suddenly announced to the press that he'd heard from his underworld contacts. The baby was safe and healthy. Nobody else believed him, either.

His associates, Spitale and Bitz, truly *had* been putting out feelers from their base in a New York City speakeasy. But so far, they'd come up empty-handed. In fact, Spitale didn't think the kidnapping *was* a gangland snatch. This one, he said, "was pulled by an independent."

Rosner never relayed this opinion to Charles.

〜

Out in the Bronx, Dr. Condon did as instructed. He placed the ad in the *Home News.*

The kidnappers didn't answer.

On March 14, he ran another: **MONEY IS READY. NO COPS. NO SECRET SERVICE. NO PRESS. I COME ALONE LIKE LAST TIME . . . JAFSIE.**

There was still no reply.

Had something frightened off the kidnappers?

On the fifteenth, an anxious Condon placed yet another ad in the paper, its tone begging: **I ACCEPT. MONEY IS READY. . . . YOU KNOW YOU CAN TRUST JAFSIE.**

WEDNESDAY, MARCH 16, 1932

That morning, the mailman delivered a brown paper bundle to Dr. Condon. The handwriting on the address was unmistakable. The old man immediately called Henry Breckinridge at his Manhattan law office.

Breckinridge arrived within the hour. As Condon watched, the lawyer untied the knotted string and peeled back the paper. Inside was a freshly laundered gray sleeper, size 2.

Breckinridge telephoned Charles. Could he come to the Bronx and identify it?

It was 1:30 in the morning before Charles reached Condon's house. He removed his disguise—a hunting cap and a pair of large glasses—then carefully examined the sleeper. "It looks like my son's garment," he finally said.

After directing Condon to place an ad in the newspaper, he telephoned Anne and told her about the bundle. Then, with the little sleeping suit in hand, he headed back out into the night.

〰

Anne waited for the sound of her husband's car in the driveway. When at last he arrived, he handed her the sleeper and she pressed it to her chest.

Anne knew almost nothing about the negotiations. Instead, she waited for news, cocooned in her bedroom. At times the endless waiting overwhelmed her, but she made sure to hide her tears because Charles insisted she not cry in front of him. "I have a sustained feeling—like a high note on an organ that has got stuck—inside me," she wrote Elisabeth. "The time since [March 1] has been all in one mood or color, no variation, no come and go. . . . It is just that night elongated."

She forced herself to eat, sleep, and look to the future for the sake of her unborn child. And she clung to the belief that her Charles—her hero—would bring their baby home.

Betty Morrow, who'd been staying at the Hopewell house, thought it best *not* to tell Anne about the black crow that had flown in through the nursery's open window the morning before to perch on the baby's crib.

CHAPTER SEVENTEEN

THE RANSOM

THURSDAY, MARCH 17, TO THURSDAY, MARCH 31, 1932

Another week passed. Nine days. Eleven. Fourteen.

Fourteen days since they'd received the baby's sleeper. Fourteen days with only one additional communication from the kidnappers, scolding Charles for following "so many false clues." Obviously, they had read newspaper coverage of the aviator's association with Mickey Rosner, and they didn't like it. "[Mr. Lindbergh] knows we are right party," their letter stated. "But if [he] likes to fool around for another month, we can't help it."

Mr. Lindbergh most definitely did *not* want to wait any longer. He directed Condon to place yet another ad in the paper. Simple and direct, it appeared in the *Bronx Home News* on March 31 and read: **I ACCEPT. MONEY IS READY. JAFSIE.**

Days earlier, Charles had directed his banker to have the ransom money ready. Now he telephoned Treasury Agent Elmer Irey in Washington, DC, to help with bundling it to the kidnappers' exact specifications.

On the evening of the seventeenth, Irey had met with Charles, Henry Breckinridge, and two partners from J. P. Morgan to discuss his plans for the money. Not only would every bill's serial number be recorded, but the bundles would also include several gold certificates. Gold certificates looked like ordinary bills except for the round gold seal on their fronts—which made them easier to spot if used. Irey reminded the men that once the baby was returned, police would pursue the kidnappers.

Charles argued stubbornly against it all. He'd given his word to the kidnappers to play fair. And a promise was a promise—even one made to a criminal.

Irey pushed back. "Colonel Lindbergh," he said firmly, "unless you comply with our suggestions . . . we shall have to withdraw from the case. We cannot compound a felony."

Charles narrowed his eyes and tightened his lips.

Irey walked out.

But the next morning, Charles agreed to the agent's plan. "I am just desperately anxious that [nothing] bungle this," he explained, apologizing.

That same day, under Irey's watchful eyes, Morgan bank tellers put together the ransom money, following the agent's instructions exactly.

All they needed now was a message from the kidnappers.

FRIDAY, APRIL 1, 1932

That message came the next evening. Was Condon ready to proceed? If so, the kidnappers wanted him to place an ad reading **YES. EVERYTHING O.K. JAFSIE** in the *New York American*.

After telephoning Charles with the news, the doctor hurried to comply.

In Hopewell, Colonel Schwarzkopf begged to be allowed to follow the doctor. Charles refused. No police. No traps. The Lone Eagle intended to do this on his own.

SATURDAY, APRIL 2, 1932

In the early afternoon, wearing his hunting cap disguise, Charles drove to the Bronx, the ransom money in a wooden box beside him on the front seat. Beneath his jacket in a shoulder holster, he carried a small handgun . . . just in case.

Breckinridge was already at Dr. Condon's house when Charles arrived. Sitting in the doctor's front room, the men waited. Charles was tense but in control. Time crawled. Hour after nerve-wracking hour passed. No one spoke. At 8 p.m., the doorbell rang, shattering the taut atmosphere.

It was a note, delivered by messenger, directing Dr. Condon to a greenhouse on Tremont Avenue. There he would find another note with further instructions.

Charles drove. At the greenhouse, which was closed for the night, Condon discovered another note on a bare display table just outside the door. Back in the car, the two men read it by the dashboard lights.

The kidnappers instructed Condon to walk across the street and into St. Raymond's Cemetery. Another graveyard! Cemetery John's nickname seemed especially apt.

Charles began to get out of the car, but Condon stopped him. The note, he pointed out, specified he come alone. After leaving the money in the car with Charles, the doctor approached the shadowy graveyard.

"Hey, Doctor! Here, Doctor! Over here!" shouted John in a voice loud enough for Charles to hear.

Condon threaded through the tombstones, stumbling a bit in the gloom as he headed in the direction of the kidnapper's voice. Eventually, he came to a tall hedge. There stood John. This time he hadn't bothered to cover his face. The dim light provided concealment enough.

They had a sharp, brief bargaining session. Then Cemetery John went to fetch a note with directions to the baby's whereabouts. And Dr. Condon returned to the car for the ransom.

Minutes later, Condon handed over the box of money.

And John handed over an envelope. "Don't open that note [yet]," he warned. Not for six hours. Then he hoisted the wooden box onto his shoulder and disappeared among the tombstones.

Condon hurried back to the car.

"The baby—where is the baby?" exclaimed Charles.

The doctor handed over the sealed envelope and relayed John's warning.

Charles nodded firmly. "We'll keep our end of the bargain," he said.

Condon, however, couldn't stand it. John, he pointed out, had said *he* shouldn't open it. He hadn't said anything about Charles.

Charles considered this a moment. Then he tore open the envelope. The familiar handwriting met his eyes. The baby, he read, was on a twenty-eight-foot boat called the *Nelly,* cruising in the waters of Vineyard Sound in Massachusetts.

As planned, the two drove to the Morrows' apartment in Manhattan. There they met Breckinridge, Irey, and some others. While Condon described Cemetery John for a sketch artist from the Treasury Department, Charles arranged to have an amphibious airplane waiting at the airport in Bridgeport, Connecticut. The plane would be perfect for putting down beside the *Nelly* once Charles spotted it from the air. Then Charles raced around the apartment, gathering up Charlie's favorite blanket and toys, some diapers, and a bottle. Only a few more hours . . .

SUNDAY, APRIL 3, 1932

At dawn, Charles, Breckinridge, Condon, and Irey climbed aboard the plane. The rising sun glinted off the water as they soared up into the brightening sky. Hopeful and in good spirits, they headed toward Vineyard Sound. No one spoke but Condon. Above the engine's roar, he shouted dramatically, "To be, or not to be; that is the question." The old man had never flown before, and the recitations helped soothe his nerves. Recalled Irey, "When [Jafsie] wasn't reciting *Hamlet,* he was reeling off biblical quotations by the hour." Soon the men were scouring the area between Martha's Vineyard and the Elizabeth Islands. Sometimes they dove so low, observers thought the plane was about to land. Then it would swoop up, turn wide, and come in low again to scan the boats below.

By noon, their good spirits evaporated. Charles's face grew pale and taut. Condon fell silent.

By midafternoon, desperation set in.

As their plane crisscrossed the waters of the sound, they inspected anything afloat. Their eyes ached from looking so keenly. Searching . . . searching . . . until night fell.

There was nothing to do but return to the airport.

Back on the ground, Charles turned to his companions. "We've been double-crossed," he said, his voice sounding bitter and anguished.

No one replied. What was there to say? It dawned on Dr. Condon that the pilot hadn't been prepared for this outcome. Naively, he'd trusted the kidnappers and played by their rules. But now all his hopes had come "crashing down in the space of a few terrible hours." Charles didn't know what all this meant, and he had no idea what to do.

After tossing the baby's things into the trunk of his car, he got behind the wheel. Empty-handed, he drove home.

He pulled up to his house hours later. He could see that Anne had gotten things ready to welcome the baby. How had she known? He hadn't told her about the drop-off. He could only assume his mood had given him away, that and his disappearance since Saturday night. He looked up at the nursery window. No lights had burned there since the kidnapping, but now they glowed brightly, casting a golden halo on the dark ground.

Anne came expectantly to the door.

Charles's expression said it all.

At the bottom of the stairs, she put her arms around him.

He leaned into her. "I'm sorry," he said.

CHAPTER EIGHTEEN

SEARCH'S END

MONDAY, APRIL 4, TO WEDNESDAY, MAY 11, 1932

"All the newspapers here lately say that there is an 'air of great optimism' etc. and predict a speedy return of the child," Anne wrote her mother-in-law in early April. "I don't know where they get that from. . . . We are now living from day to day but realize we must look forward to weeks."

The changed atmosphere frightened her. Just days earlier, all had been frenzied busyness as dozens of detectives, inspectors, and state troopers worked to bring the baby home. But now the house had fallen quiet, and the investigation had taken on a feeling of resignation. The switchboard in the garage was still operative but received less than a hundred calls per day. The mail, too, had fallen off. And hordes of police no longer camped out downstairs. The few troopers who remained had made a shooting range in the woods behind the house to pass the time. Charles often joined them for target practice. They were starting over, Anne realized, but "with a worse start than we had six weeks ago."

In hopes of finding a lead—*any* lead—Colonel Schwarzkopf reviewed his thick piles of investigation notes. He asked his men to sift back through all the mail received since the baby's disappearance, some thirty-eight thousand letters. And he once again cast an eye toward the servants. Perhaps there was more to be learned from them.

Then, a tall, gray-haired man with a solemn face arrived at the Lindberghs' house. John Hughes Curtis, a bankrupt shipbuilder from Norfolk, Virginia, had met Charles before. Weeks earlier, on March 22, he'd finagled his way into the Lindbergh study with an astonishing story. The kidnappers, he claimed, had contacted him and asked him to be their go-between. At the time, Charles, deep in secret negotiations in the Bronx, had dismissed Curtis. But now here he stood once more with an updated version of his story.

Charles led him into his study, then asked Schwarzkopf and Keaten to join them. All three men listened intently as Curtis told how he'd continued to be in contact with the kidnapping gang. He claimed it was the same gang Charles had paid off earlier. After the ransom drop, however, the kidnappers had gotten scared. What if Lindbergh brought the cops when he collected the baby? They'd decided to lie low for a while, but now they were ready to keep their end of the bargain. And they still wanted the shipbuilder as their new go-between particularly since they wanted to hand over the baby at a remote, at-sea location.

Schwarzkopf and Keaten didn't believe a word of Curtis's story.

But Charles changed his mind. What other leads were there? Against Schwarzkopf's advice, the desperate father agreed to accompany Curtis in search of a boat called the *Mary B. Moss,* upon which the baby was now supposedly being held.

For the next two weeks, the men battled storms and high seas off the coast of Virginia, but they didn't find the *Mary B. Moss.* Curtis's explanations for this were complicated and detailed. He spun a good tale. And Charles accepted his word.

Anne, however, believed Curtis was a liar. "I have, of course, great confidence in [Charles's] judgment but I do not dare hope too much, especially in the face of the tremendous body of evidence which seems to say, 'Don't trust these people.'"

On May 7, Curtis relayed a messaged he claimed to have received from the kidnappers. The boat with the baby on board was near

Cape May off the coast of New Jersey. The gang had agreed to rendezvous at a spot called Five Fathom Bank in two days' time. There they'd hand over the child.

Elated, Charles chartered a boat sturdy enough for the rougher northern waters—an eighty-five-foot ketch named the *Cachalot*. Then he and Curtis sailed toward the rendezvous point. So certain was Charles of retrieving his son that he'd arranged a radio code to send to Schwarzkopf when he had the boy safely in his arms. But after six hours of crisscrossing the spot in rising wind and mounting seas, the two men turned back; it was obvious the rendezvous had failed. Curtis went ashore, ostensibly to find out what had gone wrong, while Charles stayed aboard the rocking ship.

Curtis returned with good news. He'd made contact with the kidnappers, he said. They still wanted to turn the baby over, but the bad weather had slowed them down. Curtis had agreed to return to the rendezvous spot once the storm had passed.

It took almost thirty-six hours for the wind to die down enough for the *Cachalot* to safely leave port, and on the morning of May 12, the men finally put out to sea. Charles's hopes were so high he barely noticed the cold, steady drizzle.

THURSDAY, MAY 12, 1932

The windshield wipers on William Allen's pickup truck beat rhythmically as he and his friend Orville Wilson drove along the road that wound past the Lindbergh place. It was 3:15 in the afternoon, and they were two miles from the house when Allen pulled over. Nature called. So after scrambling through thick brush, he ducked under a low-hanging branch—and stopped in his tracks.

A tiny human foot protruded from a drift of rotting leaves and dirt.

〜

By 3:45 a team of police officers and detectives stood over the gravesite . . . if one could call it that. "It really wasn't a grave," County Coroner Walter Swayze noted. "It was more like a depression someone had shallowed-out by kicking the ground with his foot."

A tiny body lay half-buried, facedown. Badly decomposed and blackened, it was missing its left leg from the knee down, as well as the right arm from below the elbow and the left hand. Investigators surmised animals had eaten them.

One of the police officers gently lifted the corpse from its shallow grave and turned it over. Despite the body's bad shape, there was still enough of the face for them to recognize the baby. The men fell silent. The only sound was the pattering of cold rain as they gazed down at the curly golden hair, the high, prominent forehead, the deep-set dimple beneath a still sweetly tender lower lip. One of the officers choked back a sob as Inspector Harry Walsh knelt down for a closer look at the shreds of cloth clinging to the body. It was the flannel undershirt Betty Gow had made the night of the kidnapping.

The search for the Lindbergh baby was over.

※

Two hours later, Colonel Schwarzkopf and Betty Morrow went upstairs to the Lindberghs' bedroom. Wordlessly, they stepped over the threshold.

Anne looked up from the letter she was writing.

Betty moved toward her. "The baby is with [your] Daddy," she said.

※

The news of his son's death was radioed to Cape May, but Charles didn't receive it. He was still out at sea, battling wind and rain, searching for the boat carrying his son.

※

In his New York office, Henry Breckinridge paced the floor. Soon the whole world would know that the Lindbergh baby was dead. What a terrible irony if this happened while his father was still out searching for him. Breckinridge picked up the telephone. Someone had to drive out to Cape May. Within minutes, Lieutenant George Richard of the Norfolk Naval Air Station, along with businessman E. B. Bruce, had been dispatched to deliver the news.

〜〜

It was growing dark when the *Cachalot* slipped back into Cape May Harbor after another failed rendezvous. Charles was disappointed but not discouraged. Tomorrow it would happen. He was sure of it. Tomorrow he'd have his son back.

He was on board doing his usual chores when Bruce and Richard approached.

"Colonel," said Bruce. "I have a message for you. They have found the baby."

"Found—?" cried Charles.

"He is dead."

Charles rubbed his forehead. His eyes were bloodshot, and for a second he looked a little unsteady. Then he glanced around the cabin. "I'm going home" was all he said.

Alone, he drove through the darkness toward Hopewell.

〜〜

Meanwhile, the baby's body arrived at Swayze & Margerum, Funeral Directors, in Trenton, New Jersey, which doubled as the Mercer County morgue. Investigators had spent the previous hours collecting evidence—photographing the corpse and methodically shifting through the surrounding underbrush. They found a burlap bag with several strands of golden hair stuck to it, bits of the baby's clothing, a tiny toenail, and four delicate metatarsal bones from his left foot.

The little body was laid on the stainless steel autopsy table, and

Mercer County physician Dr. Charles H. Mitchell closely examined it. It was his job to discover the cause of death. Even though the corpse was badly decomposed, he could tell the child had died from a "fractured skull due to external violence" sustained two or three months earlier. It appeared the baby had been dead since the night of the kidnapping.

～∿～

Charles arrived home at two in the morning. He found Anne in bed, weeping uncontrollably, her body jerking with spasms of emotion. Memories of Charlie flooded over her—"every incident, every act, every word." Each one brought more grief, more tears.

Sitting beside her in a chair, Charles stayed with her that long night. He didn't sleep, just watched her. He said almost nothing. He didn't shed a tear. "His terrible patience and sweetness and silence—terrifying," Anne wrote in her diary the next day. His grief, she knew, was deep and roaring. But he could not express his emotions—even now.

As dawn broke, he touched her hand and said, "I hoped so I would bring that baby back."

FRIDAY, MAY 13, 1932

The next afternoon, Charles drove to the funeral home to identify his son's body, even though Colonel Schwarzkopf had told him it was unnecessary. Both the baby's pediatrician and Betty Gow had confirmed that it was Charlie. But Charles needed to see his son. It was the last thing he could do for Buster. He would not shirk his responsibilities as a father.

The blocks around the funeral home had a carnival atmosphere. Onlookers packed the streets, and vendors sold hot dogs and souvenirs. The night before, while Charles was en route from Cape May, a press photographer had somehow gotten into the morgue and taken pictures of the dead baby. Too gruesome for most newspapers, the photos were being sold on the street for five dollars apiece. Deeply wounded, his privacy violated, Charles would never forgive the press this.

To avoid the crowds, he drove around to the back door and went inside, accompanied by Colonel Schwarzkopf. There lay the little body. Charles nodded and the coroner's assistant pulled back the sheet.

What did Charles feel as he gazed down at the pitiful remains of his baby?

His stone-faced expression provided no clues.

Bending over the body, he looked into his son's mouth and counted the teeth. Sixteen in all—eight on top and eight on the bottom.

He lifted the small right foot and noticed how the second toe overlapped the big one.

He checked again.

Sixteen teeth.

Overlapping toe.

Methodically. Conscientiously. He would not allow grief to cloud his judgment. Only the truth could comfort him now, so he had to be sure. It was, his daughter Reeve wrote many years later, "the truest and the most intimate measure of the father he was."

Sixteen teeth.

Overlapping toe.

At last, he straightened. Turning from the table, he walked into the adjoining room where the county prosecutor waited. "I am perfectly satisfied that it is my child," he said.

PART SIX
BLOWN OFF COURSE

"We are starting all over again—no ties,
no hopes, no plans."
—*Anne Morrow Lindbergh*

CHAPTER NINETEEN

REBUILDING

STUDIES IN RESTORING LIFE

How does a parent recover from such a tragedy? How does a family rebuild its life? Anne turned to her diary. By committing everything she felt—pain, grief, fear—to its pages, she was able to mourn. On paper, she discovered, she could re-create Charlie—play with him, sing to him, feel his pudgy hands on her cheeks.

Anne tried to talk with Charles about it all. She hoped to make sense of her emotions, share her grief. But he brushed her off. "I went through it [once]," he said. "I can't go through it again."

He'd already begun picking up the threads of his old life. Back at Carrel's laboratory two weeks after the baby was found, he studied cells under his microscope, scribbled notes on a nearby pad, and redesigned the flasks Dr. Carrel used for his living tissue cultures. Completely absorbed, Charles worked with almost wordless concentration. Human death was more than an abstraction now. It was the enemy. And he intended to vanquish it.

RECONSTRUCTING A MURDER

The investigation into his son's murder also absorbed Charles. He grew obsessed with catching the criminals and insisted on staying in close contact with Colonel Schwarzkopf. On friendlier terms now, the two worked on the case incessantly. "They talk and talk, conferences, discussions," said Anne. "To reconstruct his murder, to try to understand."

Six days after the body was discovered, detectives put a replica of the kidnappers' ladder up to the nursery window. Carrying a flour sack the same weight as the child, a policeman climbed out the window. With a groan, the ladder's rung snapped in exactly the same place as the original. The sack thudded sickeningly to the ground.

Inside, Anne covered her ears.

But outside, standing at the ladder's bottom, Charles unemotionally put together the facts. Since no blood was found near the gravesite, he theorized Charlie had died when the ladder rung broke. The baby must have been dropped just as the reenactment showed. Schwarzkopf agreed. Both men optimistically believed the baby's death had been instantaneous, that he'd never known confusion or fear.

At the same time, state policemen dragged Dr. Condon from police station to police station to look at mug shots. Was this Cemetery John? Was this? Time and again, the old man shook his head.

John Curtis, the shipbuilder who'd claimed to have been in contact with the kidnappers, confessed. His story had been a cruel hoax. He'd made it all up, he told the police, because he'd been "insane on the subject of the Lindbergh matter." But he was well now, he added, and deeply regretted the "inconvenience" he'd caused the Lindberghs. New Jersey prosecutors eventually found him guilty of obstruction of justice. The judge fined him $1,000 and sentenced him to a year in jail.

Mickey Rosner, the bootlegger, stuck to his story when police interrogated him. He claimed he'd been telling the truth when he gave that March 13 press statement. "[I] had every reason to believe I was dealing with the kidnappers and the baby was alive and safe," he said, and he would testify to that in court. Schwarzkopf was convinced he'd made up the entire underworld story to bilk the Lindberghs and bask in the national spotlight. But without evidence to the contrary, Schwarzkopf had no choice. He let the con man go.

Detectives also returned to the servants, in particular the evasive and uncooperative Violet Sharpe. During their second interview, they asked about her whereabouts on the night of the kidnapping.

She'd gone to a movie, she replied.

What was the movie called? they asked. What was it about?

Violet claimed she couldn't remember. Then, abruptly, she changed her story. No, she hadn't gone to a movie, she'd really met someone named Ernie (she couldn't recall his last name) and they'd gone to a bar.

When detectives returned to interrogate her a third time, she fainted, ending the questioning. Detectives believed she was faking it.

But there was no faking the change in her physical appearance since the night Charlie had been taken. Once plump and rosy-cheeked, Violet was now pale and gaunt. She'd lost forty pounds in a few months' time.

On the morning of June 10, police telephoned the Morrow estate to let Violet know they'd be coming by to escort her to the police station for yet another round of questioning. Hysterical, Violet poured poisonous cyanide into a glass (she used the stuff to clean the Morrows' silver), filled it with water, and gulped it down. Then she stumbled down the stairs and fell to the kitchen floor, dead.

The Morrow butler screamed. One of the other servants rushed to the phone to call the doctor. And Anne's brother, realizing the maid was dead, carried her body upstairs to her room and placed it on the bed.

That was when Charles walked in. Hours earlier, he'd taken the pitifully small urn that held his son's ashes and flown—by himself—out over the Atlantic. A warm sun. An endless blue horizon. To

Charles's mind, there could not have been a more fitting resting place for his Buster. He opened the plane's window and poured the ashes into the air, watching as they spiraled away.

Now, returning to the Morrow home, he found yet more "death and horror," Anne would write to her sister Elisabeth. "Oh, what a terrible train of misery and sorrow this crime has pulled behind it. Will the consequences never never cease?" But though everyone in the household was shaken, Charles remained outwardly calm. If internally he was distraught, he left no record of these feelings. "[He] has hold of things," Anne wrote.

Police viewed Violet's suicide as an admission of guilt. Schwarzkopf continued to believe that more than one person had carried out the crime, and that Violet was their contact inside the house. But the day after her death, a bus driver named Ernie Miller came forward, stating that he did, indeed, have a date with Violet the night of the kidnapping. His story matched hers. There was no evidence linking her to the crime.

With that, the case went cold.

"MY LITTLE RABBIT"

On August 16, 1932, Anne gave birth to her second son. The healthy baby boy weighed seven pounds, fourteen ounces, and had a nose "just like Grandma Morrow" and a dimple in his chin like his father's. When the doctor pronounced him perfect, both parents felt relieved. They'd worried that the strain of the past months on Anne might have harmed him.

They called him Jon, although his mother preferred "my little rabbit." Charles chided Anne that she'd wear the baby out, gazing at him so much. But she loved to look at him, "stretching his mouth, wriggling, and his nostrils quivering with a yawn."

Charles immediately issued a statement to the press in hopes of dousing the publicity sure to surround the baby's arrival. He begged the press to allow his family "to lead the lives of normal Americans."

Charles and Anne couldn't imagine returning to the Hopewell house. In fact, they hadn't lived there since June. Though they told themselves it was because of the ghoulish sightseers who kept coming around, the truth was, the place to them felt blighted. "I don't believe I can ever live in [that] house in freedom and sanity," said Anne. "That window, that side of the house, the approaches—I shall always be trying to know just what happened in terror and curiosity and misery." And Charles claimed he would "never be able to go away to work—leave [you] and the children there without armed protection."

And so they moved back in with Betty Morrow at Next Day Hill. With its guards and tall fences, it felt safe. But Charles needed more than safety. He needed to feel relaxed and easy again.

FLYING TO FORGET

As the anniversary of Charlie's death rolled around on March 1, 1933, Anne could not stop the flood of dark thoughts. She obsessed over the last minutes of his life: "I want to know—to know just what he suffered—I want to see it, to feel it even." She longed for death so "the distance between [the baby] and me will be nothing." And one morning, as she sat on a Manhattan subway, trying not to cry, she found herself staring at the faces around her. "Horrible horrible-looking people," she wrote bitterly in her diary. "I wanted to say, 'And which of you killed my boy?'"

She was "terrified of a smashup," she wrote, on the verge of a nervous breakdown. Still, she hid her despair as best she could, knowing Charles had little patience for displays of emotion. She cried silently at night, or out walking the fenced grounds of Next Day Hill, while her diary entries howled her pain: "I will never accept it—*cannot* accept it or get used to it or get past it. . . . It is not a 'normal' sorrow. Back of it is always 'It need not have happened' and that is torture. It will . . . always be there, and always hurting, like something in your eyes . . . you are always conscious of it."

Perhaps that was why she agreed to accompany Charles on another long-range survey flight to establish air routes for Pan Am. This time they would fly across the Atlantic Ocean, first to Greenland and Iceland, then to the European continent. From there they would fly south across Africa and return home by way of South America. Planning to leave in July, Charles estimated the trip would take five months.

Yes, they would miss the baby's first birthday, he told Anne. But if all went as expected, they'd be back in time to celebrate Christmas with him.

She must have done the math. Jon would be sixteen months old by then, and his parents would have missed almost a third of his life. And yet Anne—still despairing over the loss of her first son—didn't hesitate to leave her second.

Her going wasn't just to please Charles. Flying, like writing, claimed Anne, "cut her free from the strings of memory." With her mind on Morse code and radio transmissions, she'd have little time to dwell on loss and grief.

The Lindberghs took off on July 10, 1933, a pale, colorless morning, from the Morrows' summer house in Maine. Just as they'd done two years earlier, they left their baby in the care of Grandma Bee and Betty Gow. As they rose into the sky, Charles's attention was focused on the direction of the wind and the tilt of his Lockheed Sirius's wings. Behind him in the navigator's seat, Anne's heart ached.

It ached through the entire trip—29,781 miles.

Summer turned to fall. In Maine, servants closed the Morrow house for the season and Betty Gow returned with Jon to Next Day Hill, while in Europe, Charles and Anne took in Finland, Holland, Spain, and Portugal—all potential airline stops.

Fall edged into winter. At Next Day Hill, Betty Gow pulled Jon on his little sled through the snow-covered garden, while on the Azores Islands, Charles plotted the route to Brazil, and Anne longed for home. How much longer? she asked Charles. How much farther?

He was indifferent to her unhappiness. "My time is my own," he coldly replied.

By the time they returned to Next Day Hill on December 19, Jon no longer remembered them.

CHAPTER TWENTY

ORDEAL BY TRIAL

EVIDENCE

On September 19, 1934, while Charles and Anne were enjoying a pleasant and sunshine-filled day in Los Angeles, the telephone rang. It was Colonel Schwarzkopf. Police had arrested a German-born carpenter named Bruno Richard Hauptmann for the kidnapping and murder of their baby, he told Charles. He believed without a doubt Hauptmann was their man. And they now believed Hauptmann had acted alone.

Charles hung up the phone. He dreaded telling Anne. When they'd returned from the Atlantic trip, she'd tried to stop dwelling on what they'd lost and had begun looking forward to what would come—making a home with Charles, mothering Jon. She'd even begun working on her book again. They'd rented an apartment in Manhattan, started accepting the occasional invitation to dinner, tried to live a normal life. Even the press furor died down. As time passed with nothing more to report about the crime, the Lindberghs fell off the front page, and Anne felt as if she could breathe again. Life on the ground had begun to feel stable.

Charles went outside to where she sat with her sister in the shade of a tree on the lawn. Thin and listless, Elisabeth was growing weaker every day. It was the reason they'd come to Los Angeles—to spend some time with her. Charles knelt before his wife and broke the news.

"Oh, God!" Anne cried when he'd finished. "It's starting . . . again."

"Yes," he replied matter-of-factly, "but they've got him at last."

They flew back east the next day and took refuge at Next Day Hill. Once again, their names made headlines as the frenzied press printed story after story about the suspect.

The day after their return, Schwarzkopf brought Charles into his headquarters in Trenton, New Jersey, and laid out the evidence against Hauptmann.

Charles examined it closely. An investigation had been done by Arthur Koehler, the country's preeminent expert on wood identification. He'd analyzed the ladder left behind on the night of the kidnapping, tracing the ponderosa pine of its rungs to the mill in South Carolina where it had been planed. A slight, unique dimple—detectable only under a microscope and made by one of the planer's blades—allowed him to follow the wood from the mill to a lumberyard in the Bronx. It was the same lumberyard where Hauptmann bought wood.

And there was more.

One of the ladder's side rails—made from a low-grade sapwood—matched the plank floor in Hauptmann's attic. Koehler believed Hauptmann had run out of wood when building the ladder and had sawed a piece from his attic floor. Impressed by Koehler's scientific approach, Charles found this evidence compelling.

But it was the other clues gathered by police that convinced Charles of Hauptmann's guilt. Since the ransom drop sixteen months earlier, the bills with which Charles had paid had been turning up in the New York area with regularity. Unfortunately, law enforcement had been unable to trace them to the person who'd originally used them. But that changed when a ten-dollar gold certificate with a serial number matching the Lindbergh money turned up at a Manhattan bank. Someone had written a license plate number on the bill. It hadn't taken New York detectives long to trace the plate to a Bruno Richard Hauptmann of 1279 East 222nd Street in the Bronx—

an address within blocks of the cemetery where the ransom had been left.

Police swooped down to search Hauptmann's apartment. Not only did they find road maps of New Jersey, binoculars, and a drawing in Hauptmann's hand of the ladder, but they also discovered something written on a wall inside a closet. The words had been wiped off, but investigators still managed to make out "2974 Decatur." That was Dr. Condon's home address. Written just below it was Jafsie's phone number. Additionally, in Hauptmann's tool chest, officers found a set of carpentry tools, complete except for a quarter-inch chisel like the one left behind at the crime scene. And in Hauptmann's garage, hidden in various places, they discovered over $14,000 with serial numbers that matched the ransom money.

Charles agreed with Schwarzkopf. It appeared to be an open-and-shut case. Still, he had to be absolutely sure.

Days later, Charles pulled a hat low over his forehead, donned a pair of lensless eyeglasses, slipped into a Bronx courthouse, and listened to Hauptmann call out, "Hey, Doctor! Here, Doctor! Over here!"

Charles didn't have a shred of doubt. That was the voice of the man who'd collected the ransom. That was the man who had killed his son.

"THE TRIAL"

On January 1, 1935, the day before the trial began, sixty thousand sightseers descended on the little town of Flemington, New Jersey (population twenty-seven hundred), causing backups for ten miles in every direction. The town's two policemen were completely overwhelmed by the crowds who swarmed into the third-floor courtroom to pose for pictures in the judge's seat. The police even had to nail down the witness chair after one souvenir hunter tried to steal it.

Meanwhile, technicians strung thousands of feet of wire and

cable along telegraph and telephone poles in preparation for the approximately one million words that would be transmitted each day during the Hauptmann trial, by the more than seven hundred reporters covering the event. Already, the press was calling it "the greatest courtroom drama in history." Radio stations and newspaper publishers sent special correspondents—gossip columnist Walter Winchell, Pulitzer Prize–winning novelist Edna Ferber, renowned newspaperman Damon Runyon—to the trial, in hopes of capturing the poignant, the shocking, and the tragic for listeners and readers all around the world.

Townspeople rented out their attics and parlors at sky-high prices, and Flemington's only hotel was booked solid for six weeks. The hotel restaurant—which served nearly a thousand meals a day during the trial—added "Lindy" ice cream sundaes and "Lamb Chops Jafsie" to its menu.

Vendors hawked everything from the phony to the macabre— ladies' lapel pins shaped like miniature ladders and forged photo-graphs of Charles and Anne. One enterprising teenager even clipped his own blond curls, put them in wax envelopes, and advertised them as locks of the dead baby's hair. At five dollars an envelope, he made a fortune, although by the end of the trial he looked like a sheared sheep.

Into this circuslike scene drove Charles Lindbergh on January 2. With Schwarzkopf beside him, he parked two blocks from the court-house, then walked—with a sure stride and a resolute set to his jaw—through the jostling, pointing, shouting crowds to the court-house. His purpose was obvious—to remind people what all this was *really* about: his son.

The courtroom was packed. People had been lined up before dawn to get one of the two hundred seats available to the public. Charles took his place behind New Jersey state attorney general

David Wilentz's table. Schwarzkopf sat down beside him as observers buzzed with excitement. The hero, they noted, was just a few feet away from where Hauptmann sat at the defense table. With his chin resting on his hands, Charles leaned forward in his chair and listened intently. He would be in court every day of the trial, whether his presence was needed or not.

Anne did not appear until the next day. Called to the stand, she resolved not to break down. While she gave her evidence, she kept her eyes fixed on a patch of blue sky she could see through the window. She would not allow herself to look toward Hauptmann. Having reminded herself not to "disappoint [Charles] at the Trial," she described the baby, the fact that he had been able to walk and talk, that his hair had been curly. Her voice quivered when she identified the sleeper sent by the kidnapper and the undershirt sewn by Betty Gow that had been found on the body. And she blinked back tears as she relived the night Charlie was taken. When she finished, defense attorney Edward J. Reilly declined to question her. "The grief of Mrs. Lindbergh," he said, "requires no cross-examination."

Pale but showing no emotion, Anne stepped down from the witness stand. She would not return to court again except on the day her mother testified. Instead, she remained cloistered at Next Day Hill, refusing to read or listen to anything about the trial. Whatever she learned about it came from Charles. And he told her very little.

Charles also took the stand that second day. When Wilentz called his name, he strode to the witness stand, also without a glance toward Hauptmann. After taking the oath, Charles sat down, crossed his legs, and placed his elbows on the arms of the witness chair. Then, concisely, convincingly, and with absolutely no emotion, he told the court about the first hours of the search, spying the ransom note on the windowsill, and the evidence he'd discovered below the nursery window.

At dinnertime, the court adjourned. The following morning, Charles returned to the stand to describe the night the ransom money had been handed over. He had heard a voice, he testified, "very clearly coming from the cemetery."

"Whose voice was it, Colonel?" asked Wilentz.

Charles turned from Wilentz and for the first time looked directly at the accused. "That was Hauptmann's voice," he said firmly.

A murmur ran through the courtroom.

From the defense table, Hauptmann stared right back at Charles, his expression, reported the *New York Times,* was "stone-cold."

The trial continued. The prosecution presented a good circumstantial case. Among the seventy-eight witnesses Wilentz called to the stand over the next three weeks was Amandus Hochmuth, an elderly Hopewell resident who testified he'd seen Hauptmann with a ladder in his car near the Lindberghs' house on the afternoon of the kidnapping. Two other neighbors also testified to seeing Hauptmann in the area. Dr. Condon, in a thundering and melodramatic voice, identified Hauptmann as Cemetery John, the man who'd taken the ransom money. There was handwriting expert Albert Osborn, who testified that in his opinion Hauptmann had written all the ransom notes. There was even an agent from the Department of the Treasury who had calculated Hauptmann's finances between the date the ransom was paid and the day he was arrested. According to the agent, the accused's income had increased by more than $44,000—during a time when he was unemployed. On January 24, the prosecution rested its case.

WITNESSES FOR THE DEFENSE

Now it was the defense's turn. Defense attorney Edward J. Reilly, once a top criminal lawyer, was past his prime. Flamboyant and pompous, he was also an alcoholic, and it was commonly believed he'd taken the case because of the publicity it would bring him. In fact, he'd become Hauptmann's lawyer only after the defendant's wife, Anna, had agreed to a proposal from the Hearst newspaper organization to pay Reilly's big legal fees in exchange for exclusive rights to her story. She'd been impressed by Reilly's track record of getting his clients acquitted in difficult homicide cases. But she had made a terrible mistake. Reilly didn't seem particularly interested in mounting much of a defense. He called a motley parade of poorly prepared witnesses whose testimonies were easily discredited by Wilentz on cross-examination.

Among these witnesses was bootlegger Louis Kiss, who claimed to have seen Hauptmann drinking coffee at a bakery on March 1, the night of the kidnapping. How could Kiss be certain of the date? asked Wilentz. Easy, Kiss replied. One week earlier, on Washington's Birthday, he'd rushed his son to the emergency room because of a kidney ailment. Nodding, Wilentz handed him a calendar and pointed out that 1932 had been a leap year. Therefore, one week after Washington's Birthday, the prosecutor explained to the court, would have been February 29, not March 1.

Another alibi witness was August Van Henke, a Manhattan restaurant owner, who testified to seeing Hauptmann at a gas station on the night of the crime. On cross-examination, Van Henke admitted he also went by the name August Wunstorf. When pressed further, he confessed that his name was actually August Marhenke, and his restaurant was, in truth, a speakeasy and brothel.

Others who testified for the defense were Lou Harding, an ex-con who'd served time for assault and battery; Sam Streppone, a psychopath who'd been committed to mental institutions four separate times for hallucinations, as well as once for shooting his wife in the leg; "professional witness" Peter Sommer, who made his money by testifying in courtrooms for a price; and handwriting expert John Trendley, who asserted that Hauptmann did not write the ransom notes. This opinion came, he said, after poring "day and night" over photographs of the documents. On cross-examination, however, he admitted to having "just looked them over casually."

So shady and disreputable were most of these witnesses that at one point Hauptmann looked over at Lloyd Fisher, one of the members of the defense team, and said in disgust, "Where are they getting these witnesses? They're killing me."

Hauptmann's own testimony didn't help his case, either, and Reilly left him largely undefended. Incredibly, of the seventeen hours Hauptmann was on the stand, eleven of them were under cross-examination by Wilentz. The prosecutor's hard-hitting questions brought out the worst in the accused. His chin jutted. His eyes smoldered with anger. He broke into a nervous sweat and repeatedly wiped his face and palms with a handkerchief. Sometimes he shouted out his answers in a burst of anger. Other times, he laughed sarcastically.

"You're having a lot of fun with me, aren't you?" asked Wilentz after one such incident.

"No," replied Hauptmann with a sneer. "Should I cry?"

"You think you are bigger than everybody, don't you?" persisted Wilentz.

"No, but I know I am innocent," retorted Hauptmann.

VERDICT

Charles's thirtieth day in court, on February 12, 1935, was spent listening to the summation of the prosecution's evidence. "We have shown conclusively, overwhelmingly, beyond a reasonable doubt that Bruno Richard Hauptmann is guilty of the murder of Charles A. Lindbergh, Jr.," declared Anthony Hauck, a member of the prosecution's team.

Throughout Hauck's speech, Charles sat rigid and emotionless, his grief tightly bottled. But the trial was obviously taking its toll. The previous morning, he'd exploded at Anne, shouting out months of frustration. Why did she have to cry so much? It was time to grab control of herself. He called her "weak, less, irretrievably broken" for giving in to her grief. Shouldn't her book be done by now? It would be, if she'd quit letting her sorrow consume her. Then, storming from the house, he'd driven to Flemington to spend yet another day in court.

Sobbing, Anne had stumbled into her mother's study and poured out her misery.

Betty Morrow stroked her daughter's head and cooed soothing words. But inside she burned with anger at her son-in-law. "Charles isn't capable of understanding [Anne], the beauty of her soul and mind," Betty wrote in her diary. "He would like to *reform* her—make her over into his own practical scientific mold." Betty longed to give him a piece of her mind, but she could say nothing, "no matter how stupid he is."

Anne's emotions spewed onto the pages of her own diary:

> I must not talk. I must not cry. I must not write—I must not think—
>
> I must not dream. I must control my mind—I must control my body—I must control my emotions—I must finish the book—I must put up an appearance, at least, of calm for [Charles]. I must force myself to be interested in plans, in work, in Jon. I must eat. I must sleep.
>
> But last night lying in bed, shrinking over into my corner,
>
> trying not to cry—or at least cry only inaudibly—not to wake C., trying not to toss and turn, trying to be like a stone, heavy and still and rigid, except for my tears, except for my mind. And the mind wasn't running free; I don't dare let it. Say poetry—think clothes—don't let it run away.

I felt I could understand insanity and physical
violence. I could understand anything.

☙

At eleven o'clock on the morning of February 13, the jury retired to consider its verdict. All through the day—as the jurors remained sequestered in their guarded room and reporters and broadcasters spread speculative stories—tension mounted. Outside the courthouse, a milling crowd of thousands filled the streets. When darkness fell, the mood turned angry. "Kill Hauptmann!" the mob chanted. "Kill Hauptmann!"

In his jail cell, the defendant lay facedown on his cot, his hands pressed over his ears.

Meanwhile, Charles, who'd driven back to Next Day Hill that afternoon, sat down to dinner with Anne, Betty, and a houseguest, the famous author and diarist Harold Nicolson. Because they expected a verdict at any minute, two radios were turned on, one in the pantry next to the dining room, the other in the drawing room. "Thus there were jokes and jazz while we [ate], and one ear strained for the announcer from the courthouse," recalled Nicolson.

After dinner, everyone went into the library, the radio blaring from the drawing room. Betty took out some photograph albums and they all pretended to be interested in them. Around 10:45 the family left Nicolson alone in the library. But moments later, Betty returned. "Hauptmann," she told her guest, "has been condemned to death without mercy."

Nicolson followed her into the drawing room, where Charles and Anne stood beside the radio, listening. "You have heard the verdict in the most famous trial in all history," the announcer cried. "Bruno Hauptmann now stands guilty of the foulest . . ."

Anne trembled. "Turn that off, Charles, turn that off."

They all went into the pantry and poured glasses of ginger beer.

Charles hopped up and sat on the counter. "There is no doubt Haupt-mann did the thing," he said in a calm, detached way. "My one dread all these years has been that they'd get hold of someone about whom I wasn't sure. I am sure about this—quite sure. It is this way. . . ."

Everyone listened as he went over the case point by point. Only once did his feelings leak into his narrative, when he described Hauptmann. "He was a magnificent-looking man," he said, "splendidly built. But his eyes were like the eyes of a wild boar—mean, shifty, small and cruel."

The next morning, Anne wrote in her diary, "The trial is over. We must try to start our life again, try to build it securely—[Charles] and Jon and I."

CHAPTER TWENTY-ONE

LOST FAITH

BREAKTHROUGH

On April 5, 1935, a small group gathered in Dr. Carrel's operating room. The surgical team was clothed in black from head to toe, only their eyes uncovered. But there was no need to see their faces. The tall figure a few paces back from the surgical table was obviously Charles Lindbergh; the man in the white cap was, of course, Dr. Carrel. His assistants moved forward to arrange the lights in the windowless room. Moments later, a pillar of light illuminated what lay strapped to the operating table. A cat.

Earlier that morning, the animal had been etherized and shaved, its blood drained. Now a black surgical cloth covered its entire body except for its throat. Dr. Carrel peered at it through his pince-nez, considering where to make the incision. He held out a gloved hand and was given a scalpel. Deftly, he sliced open the animal's neck. It was the work of just twenty minutes to lift out the dime-sized thyroids—one at a time—along with the carotid artery, the vagus nerve, and surrounding tissue. After handing the cat's left thyroid to an assistant, who lowered it into a flask of formalin, Carrel carefully wrapped the right thyroid, still attached to its artery, in sterile cellophane and placed it on a black-draped surgical tray.

He carried it into the incubator room.

Charles followed. His latest perfusion pump for keeping tissue alive outside the body gleamed—elegant, almost sculptural—on the sterile counter. Here was the real test: to keep an organ alive outside the body. Far more complex than mere tissue, an organ required a delicately balanced environment—sterile, nutrient-rich, with just the right amount of pulsing motion to circulate those nutrients throughout the organ.

Charles believed he'd perfected that environment.

Since returning to the laboratory after the Hauptmann verdict, he'd worked at a feverish pace, calculating and recalculating his designs. He was largely silent during the long hours spent in his work area. Rarely speaking to the others in the lab, he saved most of his comments for his early-morning discussions with Dr. Carrel.

The men had a routine of meeting in Carrel's book-lined office before dawn to talk through ideas and theories. As usual, Carrel did most of the talking, reiterating his radical opinions about racial hygiene. The Hauptmann trial with its grotesque partylike atmosphere had proved that democracy was in a state of deterioration, he told Charles. America had "succumbed to ochlocracy, the rule of the worst, and the reign of the lawless." So festering was society's illness that a radical eugenics program was the only cure. Prisons should be abolished, he asserted, and criminals sterilized or gassed.

Carrel also floated a new idea. His eugenics cure should include the formation of what he called a "higher council of learning," which would be made up of superior humans such as him and Lindbergh, who would govern society using scientific principles. Through sheer intellectual force, these men—and Carrel envisioned *only* men— would teach the rest of the world the proper way to live. Such an organization would be "the salvation of the white race," he added.

And so would their work with organ perfusion. If organs could be kept alive indefinitely, they could be used as replacement parts to keep members of the "higher council" alive forever. Living uninterrupted for centuries, these men could gather knowledge, reach conclusions, and issue edicts telling the rest of mankind how to live.

They would become the "immortal brain" of the white race, creating a perfect social order.

This was why so much depended on their success with the perfusion pump. It was the first step not just toward overcoming death, but also toward perfecting white civilization. Could any experiment be more important?

Charles watched closely as Carrel carefully slid the cat's thyroid out of the cellophane and placed it in the top chamber of the device. (The new, improved design had three chambers stacked on top of each other.) Once he'd attached the organ's artery to the glass feeding tube, he stoppered the chamber.

Charles switched on the electric motor that powered the pump. With a soft hiss, it began to rotate. The nutrient fluid in the bottom chamber—the reservoir chamber—was driven up the glass tube connected to the organ's artery and through the organ itself. After passing through the thyroid, the fluid ran back down into the middle chamber—the pressure-equalizing chamber—then back into the reservoir chamber, where the process repeated itself.

The fluid moved through the pump with a sloshing sound. Charles calculated the pressure—sixty pulses per minute. It was exactly right.

Carrel moved away. The results would not be known for days . . . weeks . . . months. Yet Charles remained, his eyes glued to the pump.

Twelve hours later, long after the other assistants had gone for the day and the rest of the lights had been turned out, he was still there, watching . . . waiting . . . willing the organ to live.

On the eighteenth day of their experiment, Carrel decided to analyze its results. After removing the thyroid from the pump's organ chamber, he laid it in a sterile petri dish. As Charles anxiously watched, the scientist carefully weighed and measured the organ before examining it for infection. He found none. The thyroid, he told Charles, was functioning perfectly. "There is no reason why [we] could not keep organs alive indefinitely," he declared.

Over the next six weeks, the two men performed twenty-six more experiments, perfusing kidneys, hearts, spleens, and ovaries from both cats and dogs. But despite Carrel's claims to the contrary, it soon became obvious that the pump was unreliable. Infection *did* frequently occur. Worse, many organs died during perfusion after microscopic debris from the fluid lodged in their small arteries. Charles quickly modified his design by adding a filter inside the pump. Even so, hearts and thyroids continued to die. They were "dead as a doornail," noted one of Carrel's laboratory assistants.

Nonetheless, the scientists insisted on sharing their work with the world. In June 1935, Charles and Dr. Carrel published an article about their achievements in *Science* magazine, titled "The Culture of Whole Organs." Only two pages long, the article gave few details of the pump's design, and did not include any data or results of the experiments. Mostly it dealt with the device's future possibilities: organ transplants and the harvesting of life-essential substances such as insulin. While the scientific community paid little attention (they wanted to see further data first), the press went crazy. Charles Lindbergh was a scientist? He'd been conducting secret research? Reporters milked the story for every inch of newspaper column space possible.

And as usual they blew it out of all proportion. The press dubbed Charles's invention "the artificial heart," which it wasn't. The *New York Times* declared it the "most sensational [discovery] in the annals of medicine," an enormous overstatement. One tabloid reported that Charles was creating artificial people from the hearts, brains, and lungs of human corpses. Another told its readers he was growing babies in the pump. And a third claimed he was having a "robot heart" transplanted into his own chest so he could live forever.

Worse, the press staked out the institute. Charles felt robbed. He was back to sneaking in side doors and wearing disguises.

FEAR

If frustration now permeated Charles's workplace, fear filled his home.

Afraid to let Jon play freely in the yard, Charles had a secure area built for him—"a big wire entanglement like a tennis court," remarked one visitor. "I suppose they think that people may creep through the trees and snatch him while the nurse's back is turned."

Jon had the added protection of Thor, a German shepherd his parents had bought in the summer of 1932. Gentle and affectionate with the family, the dog was also fiercely protective. Refusing to take his eyes off anyone Charles did not identify as a friend, he stood tense and still, ready to leap at the slightest wrong move.

Charles took other protective measures, too. "I carried a Colt thirty-eight caliber revolver, in a chest holster under my coat wherever I went," he admitted. "A retired detective, with a sawed-off shotgun, stayed close to [Jon] whenever he was out of the house. A night watchman made regular rounds at Next Day Hill throughout the night."

But it wasn't enough to protect the boy. In the fall of 1935, while Jon and his classmates played in the yard at nursery school, a suspicious-looking truck covered with canvas pulled up to the curb. Worried, the teachers hustled the children back inside and called the police. When state troopers approached the truck, they found it full of newspaper reporters who'd been taking pictures of the little boy through slits in the canvas. "No arrests were made," grumbled Charles, "because no clear violation of the law existed. . . ."

A few weeks later, reporters tried again. Jon's teacher was driving him home from school when suddenly a car forced the teacher's vehicle to the curb. Convinced they'd come to steal the boy, she clutched him to her. Jon began to cry—as a photographer jumped out, stuck a camera in the sobbing child's face, and snapped a picture. Then the photographer drove off. The picture appeared on the front page of a tabloid the next day.

Jon never returned to nursery school.

And Charles felt forced to chart a radical new course.

SLIP AWAY

Once again, Charles made secret plans. He compiled a checklist of things Anne should gather up—clothes, books, toys—and ordered her to start packing. She should be ready to leave at any time with only twenty-four hours' notice.

Where were they going? she asked.

Charles remained close-lipped. Only he knew their destination.

His decision angered Anne. Had he even thought to consult her? Here she was, almost thirty years old, and she was still being treated like "Mother's little girl, Daddy's little daughter, C's little wife," she noted in her diary. But Anne kept these feelings to herself and told Charles only what he wanted to hear. She didn't long for anything but a home, she said, a home *anywhere* with him and Jon.

While Anne dutifully packed, Charles flew to Washington, DC, to arrange for the family's passports. Reluctant to travel across the Atlantic on a passenger liner that would carry hundreds of other travelers, he bought tickets on a freighter, the *American Importer.* Meant to transport cargo instead of people, the freighter would carry only three passengers: the Lindberghs. (Since Pan Am had not yet instituted trans-Atlantic passenger flights, flying commercially was not an option, nor was piloting themselves. Nonstop trans-Atlantic flight remained dangerous, and without established airports along the route, the Lindberghs would have been taking a considerable risk with their child.) By mid-December, Charles was *almost* ready. There remained just one last detail.

Charles wanted Americans to know how badly they'd betrayed him, how they'd forced him to leave. So he called reporter Lauren D. Lyman at the *New York Times.* Would Lyman come to Next Day

Hill? Charles had an exclusive for him, something too confidential to discuss on the phone.

Lyman arrived the next afternoon. What was the scoop? Charles promised to reveal all on one condition—that the *Times* hold the story for twenty-four hours. Lyman agreed. Then in words both measured and tinged with anger, Charles described the threats and meddling reporters and tension surrounding their lives as being like "flying in a fog, with hidden dangers all about them." He decried the conditions in his country that made it impossible for them to live here; assured the reporter that he wasn't giving up his citizenship *yet;* and disclosed their destination—England—but did not say exactly where they'd be living. Then, with an insulting swipe at his countrymen, he explained this choice: "The English have greater regard for law and order." He did not plan to come back until conditions in the United States changed.

⋙

In the early-morning hours of December 22, 1935, the Lindberghs' ship slipped quietly out to sea. On strict orders from Charles, no one had seen them off. Instead, Anne's mother and her sister Constance had waved from the front door of Next Day Hill as the limousine had driven out of sight. After arriving at the Manhattan dock, Charles and Anne registered under false names and presented their new diplomatic passports. Even the crew wouldn't know their identities until they were at sea.

Anne carried Jon down the darkened passageway to one of the ship's few staterooms, while Charles lingered on deck. He had grown stony, and his face had a hard maturity to it although he was only thirty-three years old. As the ship navigated past the Statue of Liberty, he saluted.

Twenty-four hours later, Americans woke to the news that their national hero had abandoned his country.

THE FALL

PART SEVEN

LOSING ALTITUDE

"Hitler, I am beginning to feel, is . . .
a visionary who really wants the
best for his country."
—*Anne Morrow Lindbergh*

CHAPTER TWENTY-TWO

SPRING 1936

"[WE] ARE VERY HAPPY IN ENGLAND"

The house, called Long Barn, stood at the far end of the village of Sevenoaks Weald in Kent. "Crooked, rambling [with] tipsy floors and slanting walls," it sat on a hill overlooking gardens, fields, and farms. The Lindberghs "laugh[ed] for joy" when they saw it. "It'll do," said Charles.

At first, after landing in Liverpool, the family had headed to Wales, where they spent two secluded weeks in a private country manor just west of Cardiff. Then they moved to the Ritz Hotel in London, with its "carnations, gilt door handles, satin curtains, mirrors and the telephone . . . and the sense that anyone may drop in at any moment," wrote Anne. It was a luxurious base from which to search for a suitable home in the surrounding countryside. But house hunting hadn't gone well. "When you get to the country, there are only thatch-roofed farms—no in between, no lovely old house," Anne complained in her diary. "I have a headache from peering at signs and the long drive."

A month later, they were still at the hotel. That was when Harold Nicolson, the friend who'd been with them the night of the Hauptmann verdict, offered to lease them Long Barn, his country house.

"We have been bothered very little," Anne wrote to her mother, "and seem to be left quietly, alone here, both by people [and] press." No one grabbed at Charles, or demanded an autograph when he walked through the village. No reporters lurked in the bushes or hung around the front door.

After hiring a small staff—a cook, a maid, a personal secretary for Charles, and a nurse for Jon—the Lindberghs settled down to English country life. At Long Barn, Anne wrote and rewrote her next book. Her narrative about their trip to China, *North to the Orient,* had just been published and had become a bestseller, as Charles had known it would. When she wasn't writing, she took long walks down country lanes and through pastures speckled with sheep.

Three-and-a-half-year-old Jon climbed fences and collected pigeon feathers, threw stones in the pond, and chased the cat. One day Charles hung a tree swing for him. As the boy held tight to the ropes, his father turned the swing around and around, then let it spin.

"Merry-go-round!" hooted Jon.

"A darn fast one," said Charles.

"A darn fast one," repeated Jon.

His parents didn't worry about their son here. No longer did guards with sawed-off shotguns follow him around, although Thor still tromped beside him. (The German shepherd, along with Skean, a Scottish terrier, had come over separately.)

From a far wing of the house came the muffled squeaking of caged mice and guinea pigs. Claiming this space for his laboratory, Charles had set up his pumps and gas canisters and microscope. Dr. Carrel had been one of the few people who'd known in advance about the Lindberghs' departure, and he'd given his protégé a new problem to solve while away: the development of a mechanical kidney.

And so Charles worked on designs at Long Barn. He was constantly in touch with Carrel and sometimes wrote him as many as ten times a week. They both believed Charles was making progress.

THE FIRST RUMBLINGS OF WAR

At noon on March 7, 1936—two months after the Lindberghs' arrival in Europe—Adolf Hitler, the Nazi dictator of Germany, stepped to the rostrum in the Reichstag, his country's parliament. Six hundred men in brown uniforms and heavy boots—all personal appointees of Hitler—leaped to their feet. Their right arms rose in the Nazi salute as they screamed, *"Heil Hitler!"*

Hitler put up his own hand for silence. "Men of the Reichstag," he said in a deep, resonant voice.

Complete silence instantly fell over the room.

Today he had taken the first step in restoring Germany's greatness, he informed them. Just before dawn a troop of German soldiers had marched into the Rhineland—a slice of Germany lying west of the Rhine River and bordering France, Luxembourg, Belgium, and the Netherlands—on his orders. He had purposely flouted the Treaty of Versailles.

Signed in June 1919 by Germany and the Allies (France, Britain, and the United States), the Treaty of Versailles had officially ended World War I. Additionally, it imposed stiff and punishing peace terms on the defeated Germans by including clauses that forced them to take full blame for the war and to pay steep financial reparations. But it was the clauses that dealt with disarmament that humiliated Germans most, reducing their army to just a hundred thousand volunteers and prohibiting them from building warplanes and tanks. The navy, too, was slashed, forbidden to manufacture submarines and large ships. Particularly frustrating was the classification of the Rhineland as a demilitarized zone. In other words, even though Germany had economic and political control of this area, Germans could not do as they wanted there; all German military installations, activities, and personnel were barred. These terms, the Allies believed, would permanently cripple the German army and create a military-free area between Germany and France that would ensure future peace.

But almost as soon as the treaty was signed, the Germans secretly began to rebuild their military. Manufacturers were put to work building submarines, tanks, and warplanes. Gunmakers went back to producing rifles and bullets. And scientists found a way to make synthetic rubber and gasoline, two materials no modern war could be fought without. Soon, these products were being produced and stockpiled in four underground factories.

By 1935, France and Britain knew about Germany's secret rearmament—but they did nothing to stop it. The Great Depression had forced them to deal with problems within their own borders.

French and British lack of will to enforce the Treaty of Versailles was the reason behind Hitler's orders that morning. He was convinced he could get away with it.

Upon hearing that Germany had occupied the Rhineland, the men of the Reichstag yelled and cried louder. Reported one American journalist, "Their hands raised in slavish salute, their faces now contorted with hysteria, their mouths wide open, shouting, shouting, their eyes, burning with fanaticism, glued on their new god, their Führer, Hitler."

A charismatic leader and mesmerizing speaker, Hitler had been the leader of the Nazi Party since its establishment in 1920. He had a passion for German nationalism and a burning hatred of democracy, communism, and Jews. He believed that God had chosen Aryans (white people), and most especially Germans, to be the master race. And he envisioned a "Greater Germany"—a vast new empire that would include all the German-speaking Aryans in Europe. Of course, this new empire would require space. Therefore, Germany needed to expand east under a policy called *Lebensraum,* or "living space"— the proposed conquest of Central and Eastern Europe, as well as the Soviet Union. The people already living in these places would simply have to make way for the Germans. As the master race, they would have dominance. All this would be run, declared Hitler, by a dictator, with an array of lesser leaders taking orders from above and giving them to those below.

At first, Hitler's views had not struck a chord with the Germans. Before 1930, the Nazi Party had been considered a fringe group on the radical right of Germany's political spectrum, and it had received just 2 percent of the national vote in the 1928 elections. But then the Great Depression struck. Almost overnight, three million Germans found themselves out of work. Many lost their homes and their savings. And they blamed their government—a parliamentary republic established by the Treaty of Versailles—for the downturn.

Out of want came fear, and out of fear came fury. Hitler tapped into these feelings. His promises to put people back to work and shake off the remaining shackles of the Treaty of Versailles; to restore German cultural values, bring the Jews (who he claimed had all the money) to heel, and make the German army great once more, appealed to the people. Nazi Party membership doubled, then tripled. By 1932, it was the biggest political party in Germany. And Hitler, through a series of complicated intrigues and political maneuverings, using cunning, intimidation, and violence, seized power. By August 1934, he'd made himself dictator. All government power rested in his hands.

Standing at the rostrum, his head lowered as if in humility, he now waited out the exuberant pandemonium of the Reichstag. With one bold gesture, he had scrapped the Treaty of Versailles. No longer would the German people be humiliated by the nations of France and Britain. His voice still low, choking with emotion, he uttered a final promise. "[I] swear to yield to no force whatever in restoration of the honor of our people."

NEWS FROM THE STATES

On the afternoon of April 3, 1936, Charles headed into the village. It had stopped raining and three-and-a-half-year-old Jon begged to come along. As they walked—the boy splashing through every puddle—Charles pointed out the rain beads on the outside of the lupine leaves. Didn't they look like stars?

A cable was waiting for him at the post office: . . . WOULD LIKE TO OFFER FULL FACILITIES OF THE UNITED PRESS OF AMERICA IF YOU SHOULD DESIRE TO MAKE ANY STATEMENT WHATSOEVER IN CONNECTION WITH HAUPTMANN'S EXECUTION.

More than a year of complicated legal wrangling had passed since Hauptmann had been found guilty. This included his lawyers' appeal to the US Supreme Court (which had refused to review the case), as well as the intervention of New Jersey governor Harold Hoffman, who expressed doubt about the verdict. "I am worried about the eagerness of some of our law-enforcement agencies to bring about the death of this one man," he told the press, "so the books may be closed. . . ." Convinced Hauptmann had accomplices, and wanting answers to the many still-unresolved questions, Hoffman took the unprecedented move of launching his own investigation into the case. When no new evidence turned up, the governor tried to bargain with Hauptmann. He would commute the prisoner's death sentence to life imprisonment in return for a complete and detailed confession. But Hauptmann swore he was innocent. He couldn't confess to something he hadn't done. By the end of March 1936, all legal avenues had been exhausted. Despite doubts that linger even today, authorities decided to proceed with the execution.

And so in just a few hours' time, Bruno Richard Hauptmann would be strapped to the electric chair in the state prison at Trenton, New Jersey. At 8:44 p.m., the electricity would be turned on. Three minutes later he would be dead.

Charles believed that Hauptmann would be getting what he

Evangeline Land Lindbergh poses with her infant son, Charles Augustus Lindbergh, in 1902.

Minnesota Historical Society

Congressman C. A. Lindbergh and his eight-year-old son, Charles, in 1910.

Minnesota Historical Society

Charles attended this demonstration of aircraft at Fort Myer, Virginia, in 1912. A Wright biplane flies overhead.

Library of Congress

Dogs were always Charles's preferred companions. Here the eleven-year-old poses with Dingo in 1913.

Minnesota Historical Society

During Charles's first weeks at the University of Wisconsin in Madison, Evangeline snapped this photo of her smiling eighteen-year-old son as he flipped through his scrapbook in the bedroom of the apartment they shared.

Minnesota Historical Society

Charles in front of the plane in which he learned to fly—a Lincoln-Standard J-1—with another pilot at the Nebraska Aircraft Corporation around 1922.

Library of Congress

Charles's first plane, a Jenny, after a crack-up in a Minnesota pasture, June 1923.

Minnesota Historical Society

Cadet Lindbergh poses on the Kelly Field bomb range in 1924 with Booster, the dog he adopted during basic training.

Minnesota Historical Society

Charles loads mail into a Robertson mail plane around 1926. It was while flying one of these that he conceived the idea of making a nonstop flight to Paris.

National Archives and Records Administration

Cross Section of the
Spirit of St. Louis

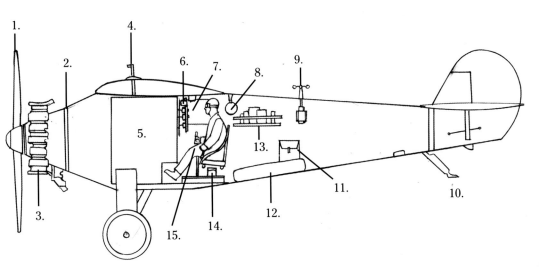

Eric Rohmann

1. Metal Propeller	9. Generator
2. Firewall	10. Tail Skid
3. Wright J-5C Whirlwind Radial Engine	11. Knapsack
4. Air Vent	12. Life Raft
5. Gasoline Tank	13. Rack for Map, Flashlight, and Notebooks
6. Periscope	14. Bag of Sandwiches
7. Instrument Panel	15. Control Stick
8. Canteens	

Charles tinkers with the *Spirit of St. Louis*'s Wright J-5C Whirlwind radial engine in his hangar at Curtiss Field on Long Island in May 1927. (The propeller and spinner have been temporarily removed.)

Library of Congress

After refusing reporters' demands to kiss goodbye, mother and son pose uncomfortably for the press, 1927.

Library of Congress

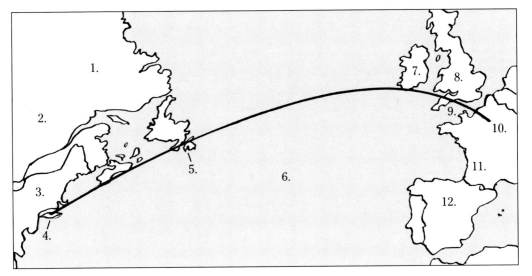

This map shows Charles's route from New York to Paris. He flew a great circle route, one that takes into account the curvature of the earth, thus tracing the shortest possible route between two points on the globe.

Eric Rohmann

1. Laborador
2. Canada
3. United States
4. Long Island, New York (Roosevelt Field)
5. St. Johns, Newfoundland
6. Atlantic Ocean

7. Ireland
8. United Kingdom
9. English Channel
10. Paris (Le Bourget Field)
11. France
12. Spain

Looking solemn and overwhelmed, the hero rides up Broadway on June 13, 1927, through a blizzard of ticker tape and confetti. Beside him is New York City mayor James J. Walker.

Library of Congress

A grinning Charles and a dazed-looking Anne are caught by a photographer just weeks after the world learned of their engagement in 1929.

Bettman Archives/Getty Images

Newlyweds Charles and Anne, looking awkward and uncomfortable, promote commercial air travel for Transcontinental Air Transport (TAT).

Library of Congress

Anne holds the Lindbergh's first child, Charles A. Lindbergh, Jr., in June 1930.

AP/Wide World

DR. ALEXIS CARREL   5761-10

Dr. Alexis Carrel, the man who influenced Charles's thinking about both medicine and the perfection of mankind.

Library of Congress

Dr. Carrel talks while Charles leans in and listens closely over lunch in the Rockefeller Institute's dining room in 1935.

The "first couple of the air" posing in front of the Lockheed Sirius seaplane in which they would fly to Japan in 1931.

While Charlie and his nurse, Betty Gow, were out for a walk on August 30, 1931, tabloid photographers startled them by leaping out and snapping this photograph. Riding with the boy in the baby carriage is Skean, one of the Lindberghs' Scottish terriers, while the other, Bogey, follows behind.

AP/Wide World

Charlie celebrates his first birthday on June 22, 1932.

New Jersey State Police Museum

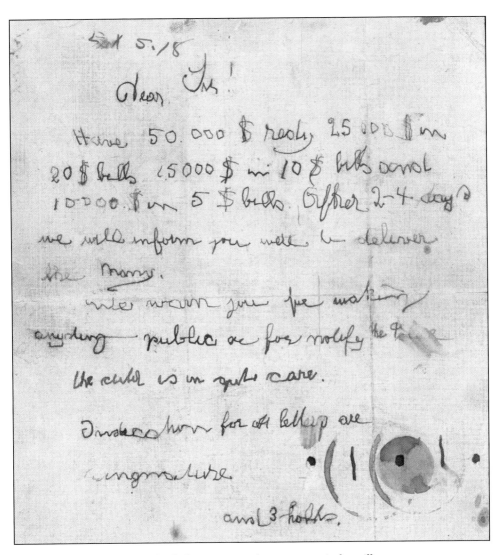

The ransom note left by the kidnappers on the nursery windowsill.

New Jersey State Police Museum

The Lindbergh home near Hopewell, New Jersey, in March 1932. After repositioning the ladder left behind by the kidnapper, state police climbed into the baby's window in an attempt to reenact the crime.

New Jersey State Police Museum

Banned from the Lindbergh property, the dogged press found creative ways to scope out the crime scene. Here reporters climb a tree bordering the estate.

Jersey City Free Public Library

WANTED

INFORMATION AS TO THE WHEREABOUTS OF

CHAS. A. LINDBERGH, JR.

OF HOPEWELL, N. J.

SON OF COL. CHAS. A. LINDBERGH

World-Famous Aviator

This child was kidnaped from his home in Hopewell, N. J., between 8 and 10 p. m. on Tuesday, March 1, 1932.

DESCRIPTION:

Age, 20 months   Hair, blond, curly
Weight, 27 to 30 lbs.   Eyes, dark blue
Height, 29 inches   Complexion, light
Deep dimple in center of chin
Dressed in one-piece coverall night suit

ADDRESS ALL COMMUNICATIONS TO
COL. H. N. SCHWARZKOPF, TRENTON, N. J., or
COL. CHAS. A. LINDBERGH, HOPEWELL, N. J.

ALL COMMUNICATIONS WILL BE TREATED IN CONFIDENCE

March 11. 1932

COL. H. NORMAN SCHWARZKOPF
Supt. New Jersey State Police, Trenton, N. J.

Wanted posters like this one were distributed nationwide.

New Jersey State Police Museum

Dr. John F. Condon, "Jafsie," demonstrates for state police how "Cemetery John" wore his hat and collar to disguise his face the first time the two men met, 1935.

New Jersey State Police Museum

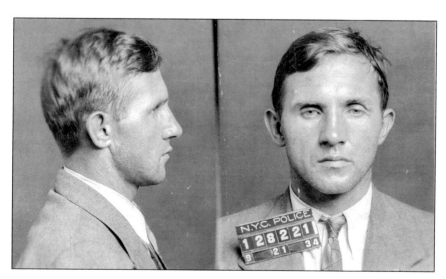

Mug shot of Bruno Richard Hauptmann, the man accused of the kidnapping and murder of the Lindbergh baby.

New Jersey State Police Museum

Five hundred people crammed into Flemington's tiny courtroom each day for the trial. The tight space forced the prosecution and defense teams into uncomfortably close proximity, as shown here. (A) Charles Lindbergh, (B) Colonel H. Norman Schwarzkopf, (C) lead defense attorney Edward Reilly, (D) New Jersey attorney general David Wilentz, (E) defense team attorneys Egbert Rosecrans and (F) Lloyd Fisher, and (G) Bruno Richard Hauptmann.

Library of Congress

Looking strained but composed, Anne appears in court to testify on January 3, 1935. When she entered the room, spectators murmured her name, and some stood for a better look, forcing Judge Thomas W. Trenchard to rap his gavel for quiet.

AP/Wide World

A calm and methodical Charles finishes his testimony on the third day of the trial, January 5, 1935.

Library of Congress

Children (the top one wearing a leather flying helmet just like Lindbergh's) peek through the bars of the Flemington jail to get a look at Bruno Hauptmann.

New Jersey State Police Museum

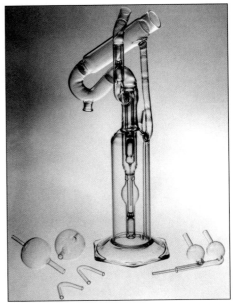

Hauptmann signed this photograph to one of his attorneys, Lloyd Fisher. Despite being on trial for kidnapping and murder, he appeared to enjoy his celebrity.

New Jersey State Police Museum

After five years of redesigning, building, and testing, Charles finally created this perfusion pump.

Minnesota Historical Society

Anne, Charles, and three-year-old Jon arrive in Liverpool, England, on December 31, 1935.

AP/Wide World

Looking happy and relaxed after seventeen months in England, Anne and Jon pose in front of Long Barn with their dogs Skean and Thor in May 1937.

Minnesota Historical Society

Charles shows four-and-a-half-year-old Jon how to use a bow and arrow at Long Barn in May 1937.

Minnesota Historical Society

Berlin as Charles and Anne saw it for the first time in the summer of 1936. Swastikas and Olympic flags fluttered everywhere, while all evidence of the Nazis' anti-Semitic policies had been temporarily swept away.

National Archives and Records Administration

Charles is driven to the opening ceremony of the Olympics on August 1, 1936, in a car full of Nazi officials.

United States Holocaust Memorial Museum

Leaving the White House after his meeting with President Roosevelt on April 20, 1939, Charles is besieged—and obviously annoyed—by reporters.

Charles speaks at an America First rally in Fort Wayne, Indiana, in 1941.

Constantly traveling, Charles rarely appears in family photographs, like this one with Anne, taken in the backyard of their Bloomfield Hills, Michigan, home in 1943. From left to right are three-year-old Ansy, one-year-old Scott, eleven-year-old Jon, and six-year-old Land.

Lindbergh Picture Collection, (MS 325B), Manuscripts and Archives, Yale University Library

A Holocaust survivor shows a US soldier the crematorium ovens used to burn corpses in Dora-Mittlebau on April 11, 1945. Just eight weeks later, Charles would have a similar tour of the same camp.

United States Holocaust Memorial Museum, courtesy of Arnold Bauer Barach

Three more Lindbergh children in 2005: Astrid Bouteuil and her brothers, Dyrk Hesshaimer (left) and David Hesshaimer (right). They did not come forward until after their mother, Brigitte Hesshaimer, had died.

AP/Wide World

Charles faces old age with optimism and confidence in 1969. He would live five more years.

Minnesota Historical Society

deserved. What bothered the flier was the fact that the American press knew the Lindberghs' whereabouts. Charles certainly would *not* be making a statement. And he was surprised that so many Americans believed he would come home after Hauptmann's death. "There has never been any question in our minds about returning to America," he wrote a colleague at the Rockefeller Medical Institute. ". . . [Anne and I] are very happy in England."

In response to the cable, Charles had nothing to say.

᠅

Spring became summer, and the flowers outside Charles's laboratory window bloomed. While taking a walk across the field one evening, he caught a rabbit. He carried it into his sleeping son's bedroom.

Slowly, the boy opened his eyes. He blinked and a smile spread across his face. "What is it—a mouse?" he whispered so as not to frighten the creature.

Charles encouraged him to pet it.

Oh so gently, Jon's little fingers stroked the rabbit's soft fur.

Then Charles took it back outside and let it go in the garden.

Afterward, he and Anne went out onto the grass and counted the stars.

FLYING IN EUROPE

Charles didn't completely bury himself in the English countryside. Aviation still fascinated him. So not long after moving into Long Barn, he took a weekend and visited some nearby aircraft manufacturers.

He was appalled at what he found. Much of Britain's aviation industry had been allowed to simply rust away since the end of World War I. Charles didn't understand it. How could the English be so shortsighted? Didn't they see the importance of an air force?

Still, he found some cause for hope. Just that year, the government had begun producing the Vickers Spitfire, a single-seat fighter that was sleek, swift, and maneuverable. Still, there weren't yet enough of them to provide much fighting power. He wondered what other countries were producing.

He soon got the chance to find out. At the end of April he borrowed a small airplane and flew to Paris. Dr. Carrel had put him in touch with a biophysicist with whom he could discuss his work on the mechanical kidney.

Little about Paris impressed Charles. Almost a decade earlier, he'd landed in a vibrant city, its people wild with excitement over his trans-Atlantic flight, but now Charles observed that Paris looked run-down and shabby. Buildings were boarded up. Roads and bridges needed repair. Parisians suffered from fuel shortages and labor strikes and weak leadership. "There is an air of discouragement and neglect . . . and people seem to be waiting almost from day to day for something to happen."

The airplane factory he visited was also down at the heels, "inefficient by American standards." The manufacturer used cheap materials, and its "mechanical designs were behind the times." While it did have a warplane prototype, the Morane-Saulnier M.S. 406, engineers predicted it would be another two years before it could be put into production.

"What amazed me was the fact that . . . France did not have a single modern fighter available for defense!" Charles wrote.

MEANWHILE, IN GERMANY . . .

On a Sunday morning in May 1936, Major Truman Smith, military attaché to the American embassy in Berlin, sat down to breakfast with his wife, Kay. As he buttered his toast, she flipped through a copy of the *New York Herald*'s Paris edition. A front-page story caught her eye: Charles Lindbergh had visited an aircraft factory in France.

Kay pointed it out to her husband. Wasn't that marvelous? Obviously, the Lindberghs again felt safe enough to leave their son behind with servants in England.

Major Smith also thought it marvelous, but for a different reason. The article had sparked an idea. He wondered if Lindbergh might be willing to visit German aircraft factories, too. If so, it could be the answer to one of Smith's stickiest problems—ascertaining the strength of the Luftwaffe, the Nazi air force.

Everywhere Smith looked he saw airfields being built and barracks and factories springing up. As attaché, he was in charge of army and air intelligence; and it was his job to compile data and statistics for the United States about Germany's rearmament. He felt sure that faster, more modern aircraft were being built, and he was deeply concerned that the day was not far off when fast-flying airplanes with powerful new weapons would appear in the sky. What exactly were the Nazis building? Despite his well-cultivated connections inside the Reich, his information remained sketchy.

But a visit from a man of Charles Lindbergh's stature, well, that would surely unlock a few Nazi secrets, especially if Smith promised the hero's attendance at Opening Day of the 1936 Summer Olympics in Berlin.

And Hitler was making elaborate preparations to showcase the Nazi regime. With the world spotlight on Germany, it was his chance to extol the virtues of the Third Reich, cast himself as a strong, sane, and tolerant leader, and prove that Germany had crawled out of the economic ditch of the Depression. Most importantly, he wanted to show off the Fatherland's athletes. Two years earlier, he had instituted an "Aryans-only" policy throughout the country's athletic organizations that effectively barred German Jews from competing in the Olympic games. Now he touted the German Olympic team as the stars of the Aryan race, not because of their athletic training, but because of their pure genetic makeup. The Olympics would be "the symbol of conquest of the world by National Socialist doctrine," remarked one American embassy staffer working in Berlin. In short, it was a propaganda bonanza.

As part of this propaganda, the Nazis hoped to attract celebrities from all over the world to the Games. And who was a bigger celebrity than Charles Lindbergh?

Major Smith presented the Nazis with his idea. Recalled Smith, "It was [my] impression that the German Air Ministry would like nothing better than to gain favor with Hitler by presenting the world-famous flier as a special guest of the Luftwaffe at the Olympics."

Smith was right. Eager to strike a deal, Air Minister Hermann Goering agreed to show Charles factories, research facilities, and combat units in return for his very public appearance at the Games.

Two months before Opening Day, Smith wrote to Charles extending Goering's invitation. "I consider that your visit here would be of high patriotic benefit," he added. "I am certain that they will go out of their way to show you even more than they will show us."

Smith was appealing to Charles's sense of duty. Although he'd abandoned his country, the pilot still retained the rank of colonel in the Army Air Corps Reserve, and he had no doubt he was being asked to go on a military mission. Clearly excited about the prospect, he wrote back immediately. He'd be happy to visit Germany with his wife, he replied. All he asked was that he be treated like any other private citizen—no press conferences, parades, or special honors.

Charles didn't express any concern over the darker side of Nazi Germany. Just eight months earlier, Hitler's government had passed a series of "racial purity" laws stripping German Jews of their citizenship and designating them as "subjects." Other laws already on the books barred them from public office, the civil service, journalism (or any mass media), farming, or teaching in German universities. These laws weren't passed in secret, and newspapers around the world had given them front-page coverage. In fact, in March 1934—on a day Charles was working at the Rockefeller Institute—twenty thousand Americans had jammed into nearby Madison Square

Garden to protest worsening human rights in Germany. Eyewitness after eyewitness had detailed the terror and misery they'd suffered at the hands of Nazis. The crowd, in a mock trial, had even convicted Hitler and his regime for "crimes against civilization." The event made national headlines.

It is doubtful Charles could have missed all this. And he certainly could not have overlooked the cable he received just before leaving for Germany. It was from Roger Straus, cochairman of the National Conference of Christians and Jews in the United States, an interfaith organization dedicated to ending religious persecution. Straus urged the Lindberghs not to go. I AM CONVINCED THAT THE GERMAN PROPAGANDA DEPARTMENT WILL TRY TO INTERPRET YOUR VISIT AS AN APPROVAL OF THEIR REGIME, he warned.

Charles ignored Straus's entreaty. His trip was about aircraft, not politics. How, he wondered, could his appearance possibly "give aid to anti-Semitism?"

CHAPTER TWENTY-THREE

"HITLER IS UNDOUBTEDLY A GREAT MAN"

TEN "THRILLING" DAYS

Charles and Anne took off from Penshurst airfield in a borrowed monoplane, leaving Jon behind with his nurse. The Kent police had promised to keep an eye on their house. As they circled over Long Barn, Jon ran out onto the green grass, waving a large towel and doing a little dance. His parents waved back.

Then they flew over the English Channel, following maps and landmarks, until they landed in Berlin four hours later.

A row of officials from the Air Ministry greeted them with a click of their heels and a thrust of their right arms. *"Heil Hitler!"* An officer stepped forward. Handing a bouquet of red roses to Anne, he relayed greetings from General Hermann Goering. Then he briskly escorted Charles to an open car. Charles and Major Smith climbed in beside the officer. Anne found herself in the backseat of a second, closed car with Kay Smith.

It was, of course, ridiculous to think the Nazi propaganda machine would abide by Charles's request not to publicize his visit. The publicity value of the famous aviator's visit was the whole point. And so Berlin gave him an official welcome as he drove into the city. Unlike those at similar events in other cities, however, these crowds were controlled. There was no pushing or shoving, no one breaking

through barriers and running up to the hero's car. They were ador-
ing yet polite.

Charles responded with a surprised, shyly pleased smile. He nodded at the people. He even waved occasionally. He almost seemed to
be enjoying himself.

Behind him in the second car, Anne gazed out the window and
marveled at the "neatness, order, trimness, cleanliness [of the
streets]." There was no sense of poverty. Berlin looked untouched by
the Depression. Filled with cars and bicycles, the city's boulevards
felt alive with optimism. Everyone looked healthy and well-dressed.
She was especially delighted by the city's "sense of festivity, flags
hung out, the Nazi flag, red with a swastika on it, *everywhere. . . .*"

Neither she nor Charles realized that in order to put its best face
to the world, Berlin had been cleaned up. Under Hitler's orders, the
omnipresent JEWS NOT WELCOME signs had been removed from hotels, restaurants, and other public places. Nazi police were warned
not to take any action against Jews, and to be unfailingly courteous
to everyone. Even the virulent anti-Semitic newspaper *Der Stürmer*
had temporarily ceased publication. Additionally, all "undesirable
persons," including eight hundred members of the Sinti and Roma
tribes, had been rounded up off the streets and interned in a special
detention camp eighteen miles outside the city. The goal, recalled
one Nazi official, was to give Berlin the appearance of a "perfectly
normal place in which life went on as pleasantly as in any other European country."

The Lindberghs stayed with the Smiths at their apartment. Major
Smith marveled at Charles's knowledge of mechanics, while Kay admired his vitality and confidence. Neither, however, was impressed
by his knowledge of history or government. He was, admitted Kay,
"a naïve political thinker." And when it came to understanding post–
World War I Europe, his mind was "an empty void." Both Smiths
warned him not to be taken in by Berlin's façade. But Kay doubted

Charles would be able to separate Nazi propaganda from the truth.

※

The Lindberghs spent much of this visit apart. Charles's days were filled with drives to various aeronautical sites. One morning he flew two German planes: the Junkers Ju 52, the centerpiece of the Luftwaffe's new bomber force; and an experimental plane that had four of the biggest engines Charles had ever seen. Afterward, he visited a Junkers factory, where he saw engines far more sophisticated than he'd expected. Another day, he went to two Heinkel factories, where he saw their latest bombers, fighters, and observation planes—all, he concluded, superior to anything being built in the United States. Another visit took him to a research facility, where he talked with scientists about their technological advances. He even got to meet pilots from the Luftwaffe's elite fighter squadron.

Why were the Nazis so eager to share their secrets?

Neither Charles nor Major Smith seems to have asked this question.

By the end of his time in Germany, Charles's respect for German aircraft was matched only by his awe at their national pride and discipline. There was, he wrote, "a spirit in Germany which I have not seen in any country. There is a great ability, and I am inclined to think more intelligent leadership than is generally recognized. A person would have to be blind not to realize that they have already built up tremendous strength."

While Charles shuttled from factory to airfield, Anne marveled at how Hitler's government kept the press at bay. In Berlin she was left alone to shop and dine and stroll through parks and museums as she pleased. Perhaps she'd been wrong to believe that "dictatorships are of necessity wrong, evil, unstable, and no good can come of them," she admitted. After all, she concluded, "there is no question of the power, unity, and purposefulness of Germany."

Charles was rethinking his opinion of dictatorships, too. Despite how newspapers in England and America depicted Hitler, he knew what he saw. "The organized vitality of Germany was what impressed me," he wrote. "The unceasing activity of the people, and the convinced dictatorial direction to create the new factories, airfields, and research laboratories." To him, the country concretized his values: "science and technology harnessed for the preservation of a superior race." Charles was beginning to think that the "strong central leadership of the Nazi state was the only hope for restoring a moral world order." No matter that it came at the cost of democratic institutions, individual liberties, and a free press. All that freedom, Charles believed, just led to irresponsibility and moral decay. But here in Germany, Hitler had restored moral order to Western civilization. Wasn't this exactly what he and Dr. Carrel had always talked about?

⋙

On August 1, 1936, a hundred thousand people streamed into the newly built Olympic stadium for Opening Day. As one, they raised their arms and hailed the Führer. A few seats away from Hitler, Charles Lindbergh sat ramrod straight, while next to him Anne enthusiastically applauded the spectacle of it all—the band playing *"Deutschland über alles,"* the blond-haired little girls offering bouquets of roses to the dictator, the lighting of the Olympic torch and the release of five thousand pigeons. Time and again, Anne touched her husband's arm and exclaimed, "Look, Charles! Look!" Leaving the stadium later that day, Charles told reporters that he was "intensely pleased" by all he'd seen while in Germany.

Also present at Opening Day, American reporter William Shirer overheard people in Nazi circles boast about their success in "making Lindbergh 'understand' Nazi Germany."

Upon leaving Germany, Anne wrote that she'd found her ten days there "thrilling . . . Hitler is a very great man, like an inspired religious leader . . . not scheming, not selfish, not greedy for power," she gushed, "but a visionary who really wants the best for his country."

Charles was also impressed. "Hitler is undoubtedly a great man," he said, "and I believe he has done much for Germany." The British and Americans, Charles believed, had "a very distorted and incomplete picture" of the Nazis. Hitler's government would be a "stabilizing factor" in Europe.

Charles wondered: Was a democracy truly superior to a dictatorship? Modern Germany challenged that notion. So had Dr. Carrel when he talked of rule by elites, and his higher council. Now Charles's experiences and ideologies coalesced. New ideas emerged with clarity. *Are we deluding ourselves when we attempt to run our governments by counting the number of heads, without a thought of what lies within them?* he asked himself. It now seemed to him that democracy—which allowed everyone, even those obviously "unfit," an equal say in national decisions—would soon become obsolete. The future—"the only hope for restoring a moral world"—lay in the hands of a strong, smart dictator like Hitler.

NEW EYES

Back in England, Charles found the country suddenly exasperating. Having witnessed Nazi "virility" and "efficiency," he felt that the British people's "softness" and "stupidity" were obvious in comparison. England "saw not the future, but the past," he testily wrote in his journal.

Months earlier, he'd had a plane designed and built especially for him—a Miles M.12 Mohawk. With its powerful engine, the lightweight, low-winged aircraft could fly an impressive 1,400 miles without refueling, at a top speed of 200 miles per hour. Charles once more had wings, and he took to the air, in part to escape his irritation.

In November he flew alone to Ireland, where he inspected a new airport. And in February 1937 he and Anne headed off on an eight-week trip to India (still a British colony), where he swore he could see "the early symptoms of the breakup of the British Empire."

As they flew along the coast of Greece, Charles looked down on the ancient ruins and saw a metaphor for modern Europe. "The Greek city-states were in constant disagreement, and the extraordinary civilization they had developed gave way to [chaos and destruction]."

He worried this would happen to European civilization if another war on the continent ever erupted. Fighting with itself, Europe would self-destruct. And what would be left behind?

But it was the sights, sounds, and smells of India with its "ragged, hungry people . . . filthy streets . . . [and] scabby, thin-legged children" that confirmed for him one of Dr. Carrel's core beliefs—that real civilization meant *white* civilization. In India, human life had sunk to levels he'd never seen before. How had this country once produced "a civilization of art and architecture and religion?"

Charles grew alarmed. What if modern Western civilization destroyed itself through war or politics? Perhaps he should move his family to some "distant white men's frontiers" like Australia or New Zealand. The future of the white race, which had once seemed "secure beyond the need of questioning," was now in peril. "We whites [were] so accustomed to dominating that it was difficult to realize that we were a minority in a world of yellow, brown and black."

Charles felt as if his eyes were being opened.

A SECOND ENGLISH SPRING

Another spring at Long Barn. It was good to be back with Jon; good to see Anne working on her book again; good to be in his lab. But this second April in Kent was not as idyllic as the first. Charles could not stop dwelling on Germany's "magnificent spirit." It was as if his unhappiness with England was growing in direct proportion to his admiration for the Third Reich.

The English spring did bring one joyous event. On May 12, 1937, Anne gave birth to their third child—a boy with blue eyes and "Grandma Morrow's nose—just like the others."

Not until the day before Anne's (and little Charlie's) birthday did they finally register the baby's name—Land Morrow Lindbergh, after Charles's maternal grandfather. "As we couldn't agree on any first names, we have taken a last one," Anne wrote her mother.

The next morning, June 22, "when I was thinking of all my other birthdays, sitting on my bed, remembering little Charles, [the new baby] gave me the most beautiful *real* smile. . . . A real one that fills his whole face . . . and the blue eyes trying to talk, too. I was so happy—so happy to have on this birthday my two little boys."

DAYS IN MUNICH

Anne and Charles flew through a thick London fog before heading south across the English Channel to France. Soaring above hilltop castles and the spires of cathedrals, they followed a tributary of the Rhine River until they finally landed in Munich. It was October 1937, and Charles had gotten the wish he'd repeatedly expressed in letters to Major Smith. The Air Ministry had invited him to return to Germany. They said they wanted to show him some planes no one outside the Luftwaffe had seen yet.

While Anne rambled through Bavarian villages, Charles went on a unique round of sightseeing. With German general Ernst Udet as his escort (Goering requested that Smith remain behind), he visited a secret aircraft installation in Pomerania. There he examined the seven airplanes lined up on the airstrip for inspection, including Junkers and Messerschmitts. Udet allowed his guest to sit in the planes' cockpits and even let him test another new model, the Fieseler Fi-156 Storch liaison plane. They did not, however, go inside any of the dozens of gigantic hangars.

That day, Charles left the airstrip firmly believing that Germany was "once more a world power in the air," a sentence he included in a four-page memorandum he collaborated on with Major Smith. The memorandum was eventually sent to the United States War Department, and not only detailed all Charles had seen, but also estimated the strength of the entire Luftwaffe. Charles was convinced that strength was awesome, easily outstripping the French and British air forces, and quickly closing in on the United States.

It was exactly what Goering wanted him to report. Since Charles's first visit to Germany, his amiable Nazi hosts had been feeding him inflated numbers and exaggerated readiness reports. His naiveté about Nazi propaganda made him easy to fool, claimed one Luftwaffe official. Lindbergh's "willing self-deception simply refused to see what his eyes saw," admitted Lieutenant General Heinz J. Rieckhoff years later. "Instead, [Lindbergh] insisted on assuming that there was still more hidden behind it. He had no way of knowing that the hangars he was being shown were completely empty or filled with ancient dust-covered aircraft."

Charles's second stay in Nazi Germany also confirmed his earlier, personal impressions. Any fanaticism he glimpsed was offset by the Germans' "sense of decency and value which in many ways is far ahead of our own."

And this second visit deepened his annoyance with the British. He even found their constant tea drinking irritating. "The whole idea seems a little effeminate to me," he said.

During dinner with his friend and landlord, Harold Nicolson, the following spring, Charles prattled on about the German air force. "[It] is ten times superior to that of Russia, France and Great Britain put together," he said. "[Your British] defenses are futile. . . . [You] should just . . . make an alliance with Germany."

Nicolson never invited the Lindberghs to his home again. Not that they cared. They had already decided to abandon "crumbling, backward England" and move to a tiny, windswept island off the coast of Brittany. Taken up almost entirely by a weather-battered, three-story stone house lacking heat, electricity, or plumbing, Illiec, as the island was called, was scenic, private, and, best of all, just a ten-minute rowboat ride from Dr. Carrel's summer home on the nearby island of Saint-Gildas. Charles purchased the place sight unseen in March 1938, choosing not to wait until renovations on the run-down house were completed. He wanted to leave England as soon as possible.

ANSCHLUSS

For months, the Nazi Party in Austria—funded by and taking directions from Berlin—had been stirring up trouble, rioting, setting fire to buildings, brawling in the streets. Then, on March 11, 1938, Nazi tanks and armored cars rolled across the border Germany shared with that country.

That same day, the Austrian government had appointed a Nazi politician, Arthur Seyss-Inquart, as chancellor, in hopes of appeasing the party and putting an end to the violence. As soon as he was sworn in, however, Seyss-Inquart—following Hitler's orders—cabled Berlin and begged for Germany's help in restoring order. It was a ruse, of course, an excuse for a German invasion of Austria.

The troops arrived in Vienna the next morning. No one tried to stop them. Instead, the majority of Austrians—seven million of whom were ethnic Germans—welcomed them as heroes. Twenty-four hours later, on March 13, Chancellor Seyss-Inquart signed the document that would end Austrian independence. Called *Anschluss,* meaning "union," it allowed the Third Reich to annex the entire country. It was the first step in Hitler's grand scheme to unite all

German-speaking people. And he'd done it without firing a single shot.

British and French leaders barely whimpered when they heard the news. France, its own politics in turmoil, was in no position to oppose the annexation, while Britain did not have the political will. Besides, Anschluss didn't appear to threaten their security. And since Austria and Germany spoke the same language, why shouldn't they unify?

Few people, including Charles, seemed to realize that with Anschluss, Hitler had added seven million people and an army of a hundred thousand to the Reich. He'd seized important resources like steel and iron ore. He'd tipped the balance of power in southeastern Europe in Germany's favor. And Czechoslovakia was bordered on three sides by the Nazis.

LAST DAYS AT LONG BARN

The gardens at Long Barn seemed to bloom before Anne's eyes: the red roses on the trellises, the lilac bushes, the wrinkling pink poppies. She wished she had time to soak it all in, to impress the place on her memory. But she was too busy. Their last days in England had been crowded with closing accounts, shopping for supplies to send to the island, and packing, endlessly packing.

Charles packed in a methodical and tedious manner. Before being wrapped and put in a box, every single item—every article of clothing, every book, every package of rubber bands, every packet of tinsel for the Christmas tree—had to be listed. Then the list was typed and glued to the inner lid of the box before it was sealed.

Today, though, the Lindberghs put aside their work for a few hours. It was May 12, Land's first birthday, and while Jon sang at the top of his lungs, Anne settled the one-year-old on her lap. The baby made a grab for his cake. It was decorated with a single candle and silver button candies that spelled out his name. Anne pulled back his plump hand. Land cried. And Charles, making silly noises in the hope of getting his son to smile, snapped his picture.

Later, after the cake had been eaten and Land had opened his present (a toy duck), the nurse took both boys upstairs for baths and bed, and Charles and Anne walked in the garden as the light faded. Anne ached with sadness at the thought of leaving. She knew her husband had no sentimental attachment to Long Barn. But she loved it "as if it were mine, a part of me," she confessed in her diary. "I feel dimly that I shall look back on this period as the happiest in my life—the two years in this house."

AFTER THE ANSCHLUSS

In May 1938, while the Lindberghs were still packing, Adolf Hitler was sizing up Czechoslovakia, with all its valuable raw materials. He considered invading. But if he did, France, obligated by treaty, might come to the Czechs' aid. So, too, would Britain, which was treaty-bound to France. Hitler doubted France or Britain, who'd barely said a word about Anschluss, would fight. But why take the chance? So he settled on a different course of action and set his sights on the Sudetenland.

Before World War I, this small section of western Czechoslovakia had belonged to Germany, but under the terms of the Treaty of Versailles, the territory had been given to Czechoslovakia. A majority of the Sudetenland's inhabitants remained ethnic Germans, and many of them genuinely wanted to return to German rule. Using their desire as pretext, Hitler demanded the Sudetenland be handed over to him. He expected the Czechs, like the Austrians, to fold quickly. But the Czech government dug in its heels. It appealed to France and Britain for help.

As the weather warmed, tensions heated up. While French prime minister Édouard Daladier and British prime minister Neville Chamberlain desperately searched for ways to avoid a fight with Germany, Hitler grew angrier and more strident, and the Czechs grew even more stubborn. By June, it had become a war of nerves, with Nazi groups in the Sudetenland, under Hitler's direction, staging violent demonstrations and launching terrorist attacks. By July, armies all over Europe were put on a war footing. And by August, things looked so bad that US President Franklin Delano Roosevelt cabled a personal message to the leaders of Czechoslovakia, Britain, France, and Germany. He urged the four countries to find a peaceful solution. Additionally, and privately, he told France and Britain that America could not help if they chose to go to war. Both Daladier and Chamberlain assured the president of their commitment to reason rather than armed conflict.

Hitler, however, insisted that if the Sudetenland was not handed over, he would resort to force.

CHAPTER TWENTY-FOUR

LINDBERGH REPORTS

A MAN ON HIS ISLAND

It was the first day of summer, June 21, 1938, when the Lindberghs arrived on Illiec. From the moment he set foot on his tiny island, Charles loved everything about it—the salty smell of the sea, the steeply slanted beach of storm-ground stones, the way the tide receded so far out that twice a day he could walk on the exposed sea bottom. He knew that buying the French island had been foolhardy, understanding "only too well that conditions in France are bad." The country was in economic and political chaos, and war clouds loomed.

The island's main attraction, however, was its proximity to Dr. Carrel. That summer, over breakfasts of black bread and oatmeal, during walks along the wave-pounded shore, in the flickering shadows cast by Carrel's fireplace, the two talked about the precarious state of civilization and race betterment. Both men blamed England and France's "degeneration" on democracy. It was time, they agreed, for the "construction of civilized men" who would rebuild a world "suited to *their* needs," the start of "a new social order organized according to biological worth."

Despite having built a primitive lab in the courtyard of Carrel's house on Saint-Gildas, Charles did little serious work on his perfusion pumps and mechanical kidney. He hadn't lost confidence in the projects, but "the problems of civilization and survival towered above [all else]," he later explained. "Why spend time on biological experiments when our very civilization was at stake, when one of history's greatest cataclysms impended?"

On August 2, a cable arrived on Illiec from Colonel Raymond Lee, an American military attaché in London. He urged Charles to fly to the Soviet Union and inspect their air force. Eager to "see enough of Europe to be able to think intelligently about the problems which exist here," Charles agreed.

It was a bad time to leave the island. The plasterers and painters hired to patch up the long-neglected house had only just finished, and while they'd made the place safe to live in, it remained anti-quated. The only light came from kerosene lanterns, and the water had to be drawn from a well. Unable to produce edible meals on the wood-burning stove, their English cook had quit and returned to Kent. So had the nursemaid, who couldn't abide the isolation or the outhouse.

And then there were the children. Charles had no qualms about leaving Jon with the local help Anne had quickly hired. The boy had taken to the island almost immediately, fishing on the beach with a net and collecting pocketfuls of stones. But fifteen-month-old Land was a different story. He cried often, not just because he was teeth-ing, but also because the chaotic new household left him feeling anx-ious. Charles, however, never considered going without Anne. And although she dreaded the trip, she never considered staying behind. *I must go,* she told herself. *I must be a part of [Charles's] life.*

For weeks, they toured Kiev, Odessa, Rostov, and Moscow. The Soviets were not as eager to show off their air force as the Germans had been. Allowing Charles access to just a handful of aviation sites, the communists padded the Lindberghs' schedule with visits to two museums, a ballet, a new subway, a collective farm, and even an ice cream factory. Charles concluded the Soviets had nothing worth showing. Even their best airplanes were pitiful, as were their research facilities and their pilot training schools. In no way would Soviet military aviation be a match for the Luftwaffe.

He spoke even less admiringly of Russian life, with its "secret trials and executions," its "[lines] in front of stores and the scarceness of goods," its "control of information and suppression of free speech." Even as he lauded Hitler's Nazism, he declared the communist system unworkable.

It is likely that Charles's utter distaste for the Soviet Union stemmed from his belief in eugenics, which placed Russians in the "nonwhite category." (The "infusion of Mongol blood," eugenicists believed, had resulted in the Russians' racial characteristics being more Asian than European.) Whenever Charles spoke of the "yellow race," which he definitely thought was inferior, he was including the Russians. "Asia presses towards us on the Russian border," he warned a year later. "We must . . . build our White ramparts . . . [and] guard our heritage from the Mongol and Persian and Moor."

SEPTEMBER 1938

The boys were already tucked in for the night when Charles and Anne returned to Illiec on September 10. Eager to see their children after being gone for a month, the parents poked their heads into the boys' bedroom. A grinning Jon quickly sat up in the dark. He showed them his new flashlight and his toy boat. Land woke, too, standing up in his crib and crying until Anne played patty-cake with him.

Charles tried to relax back into his island routine. But he took little pleasure in his early-morning swims or his long talks with Carrel. Over all of it hung the threat of war.

Eight days later, despite the sudden drop in temperature and the lashing rain, Charles and Anne took their motorboat to the fishing village of Buguélès, where they'd garaged their car. The news coming from Eastern Europe wasn't good. The Czechs had ordered the mobilization of troops to the border, and the French were drawing up plans for an attack on Germany. War could erupt at any moment. After climbing into the front seat of the car, Charles turned the radio dials, searching for the latest news. Dripping wet, their breath fogging the windows, they strained to hear the crackling voices from London.

"There is still hope," one British minister assured radio listeners.

"Nothing is desperate," said another.

But it sounded desperate to the Lindberghs. Discouraged, they boated back to Illiec in the rain.

Two days later, a cable arrived from America's ambassador to England, Joseph Kennedy. Would Charles come to London immediately? Kennedy wanted the flier to write a report about military aviation in Europe. Charles's comments, Ambassador Kennedy promised, would be wired to government officials in both Washington, DC, and London.

The Lindberghs hurried to their bedroom to pack. Jon followed. They told him about going to London. "But not for long . . . only for a day or two," said Anne. "We'll be back the end of the week."

"When will that be?" asked Jon, who'd recently celebrated his sixth birthday without them. Then, after plopping onto the floor, he played with his seashell collection and stayed underfoot until his parents left.

"Without doubt the German air fleet is now stronger than that of any other country in the world," Charles's report for Ambassador Kennedy began. "Her air strength is greater than that of all European countries combined." He believed Germany had "the means of destroying London, Paris and Prague if she wishes to do so," and "England and France together could do nothing about it because they did not have enough planes for either defense, or a counterattack."

It was, he continued, "essential to avoid war in the near future at any cost," or risk "the loss of European civilization."

It was a devastating report. The world's foremost aviation expert was saying Germany could wipe Britain and France off the face of the earth.

The Lindbergh Report, as it came to be called, quickly circulated. In France, it stunned Prime Minister Édouard Daladier. Peace must be preserved, he was overheard to say, or French cities would be destroyed with no means of defense.

In England, Prime Minister Chamberlain was handed a copy of the report as he boarded the plane that would take him to Bad Godesberg, Germany, for a round of delicate negotiations with Hitler over the Sudetenland crisis. Charles's dire predictions merely confirmed the prime minister's belief that appeasement was the only possible choice.

〜〜

On September 28, Charles and Anne dropped by the American embassy in London. Ambassador Kennedy waved them into his office. "There's some good news coming in," he said.

An agreement had been concluded between Britain, France and Germany. The Sudetenland would be ceded to Hitler. In return, the Führer promised not to invade any other countries. War had been avoided . . . for the time being.

Confident his report had played a part in this compromise, Charles was "not surprised [by the outcome]," but was "very much relieved."

Some, however, were less than confident about the Lindbergh Report. Remarked one military expert working with the British diplomatic corps in Paris, "the Führer [has] found a most convenient ambassador in Colonel Lindbergh." And John Slessor, soon to become marshal of the Royal Air Force, wondered how much of Charles's views were "due to German propaganda and carefully staged arrangements to impress him." He warned British officials to take the report's estimates "with a pinch of salt."

Slessor was right to be cautious. What Charles didn't know was that the Luftwaffe's superiority in the late 1930s was limited to its ability to support German ground troops. It had not yet developed a long-range bomber fleet with the capacity to launch raids on London or any other target distant from Germany. In fact, in August of 1938 (two years *after* Charles's first visit), generals informed Goering that German air attacks on Britain would amount to "pin pricks." As late as May 1939, Luftwaffe Chief of Staff Hans Jeschonnek warned the German High Command, "Do not let us deceive ourselves, gentlemen. Each country wants to outstrip the other in air armament. But we are all roughly at the same stage."

Completely duped by the Nazis, Charles had passed on false intelligence to leaders and military personnel in the United States, Britain, France, and Czechoslovakia. They, in turn, had factored in his fake report when deciding how to respond to Nazi aggression. Not once had Charles attempted to verify what he'd been told, and he used no other data beyond what the Germans gave him.

Certainly, he wasn't the only aviator fooled by the Germans. But Charles Lindbergh's views carried more weight than others'. And while most historians do not believe the Lindbergh Report was a major factor in the decision by England to appease Hitler (Chamberlain, after all, had *never* wanted to go to war over Czechoslovakia), it no doubt bolstered the belief that it was better to give Hitler the Sudetenland than to plunge into a war for which the British were not ready.

CHAPTER TWENTY-FIVE

NO PLACE LIKE HOME

HOME, SWEET GERMANY

Anne couldn't stop smiling in such beautiful weather. She and Charles had arrived in Berlin on October 11, 1938, a day when the sun shone warm and golden and trees along the wide boulevards blazed red and orange. Ostensibly, they'd returned to Germany to attend an aeronautics conference. But in truth, Charles wanted his family to spend the winter there. This trip would really be about doing "some groundwork on homes, nurses, households, etc." As Anne and Charles walked along the Tiergartenstrasse to the American embassy for tea, she caught sight of her reflection in a shop window. She was surprised to see how happy she looked. Beside her, Charles appeared happy, too. The city, Anne decided, was a delight.

Neither Charles nor Anne commented on all the signs and posters. They were hanging practically everywhere, and declared JEWRY IS CRIMINAL and JEWS NOT WANTED. Even though neither of the Lindberghs read German, they could not have mistaken the hook-nosed caricatures that accompanied the words. Evidence of Germany's persecution of the Jewish people was obvious.

Just six days before their arrival, Hitler's government had passed a decree ordering Jews to carry special identification cards, and their passports were marked with a large "J" so Nazi authorities could easily identify them. (It would be another year before they were required to wear a Jewish star on their clothing.) These latest laws had been widely reported in both European and American newspapers, but neither Anne nor Charles commented on any of it. Instead, both chirped about Berlin's appearance of prosperity. "The shops [are] luxurious," gushed Anne.

Two days later, the couple attended a dinner at the Fliers Club. Dressed in evening clothes, they floated through a sea of jeweled and uniformed guests. Everyone admired Charles, spoke politely, saluted or shook his hand. Again, he was struck with how comfortable he felt, how completely at home. Both he and Anne agreed with Prince Kinsky, a Sudetenland German and head of the Austrian Aero Club, that a controlled press like Germany's was preferable to the free press of the United States or Britain. Kinsky even sounded a lot like Charles when he launched into his view that the British Empire could not withstand another war. "It would break to pieces," the prince said, "and that would be a great loss to civilization and the white race."

Anne was seated beside Kinsky during dinner, and at first she found him amusing. But over dessert, he launched into a vicious tirade against Jews, calling them "creepers" and "parasites." He suggested that they all be "expelled to Madagascar since they could not be *used* even by our civilization."

Anne could not believe what she was hearing. Her Nazi hosts had—up to now—been careful to insulate the Lindberghs from that kind of talk. "I was depressed," she admitted.

But not depressed enough to stop house hunting. She looked at several homes. One particularly lovely cottage was located in an idyllic Berlin suburb with a big sign posted at its city limits that read JEWS ARE NOT WANTED HERE.

Again, Anne felt "depressed." But still she kept looking. A few days later, the couple walked through a large, heavily furnished house in Wannsee. Its large garden extended downhill to a river with swans. "It would be an excellent place for Jon and Land," said Charles.

But when Charles spoke with officials in the German Air Ministry about signing the lease, they talked him out of it. "There seemed to be something strange about the transaction," said Charles.

Eventually, it was revealed that the house belonged to a Jewish family who'd fled the country. Officials did not think it would do for such distinguished guests to live there. The Lindberghs should pick someplace else. Architect Albert Speer, who would later become Hitler's minister of armaments and war production, even offered to help. He would be glad to build them a house on any site they liked.

Even this incident did not shake Charles's resolve to live in Berlin. He viewed the "Jewish Problem" as an internal German problem, unimportant to the larger political and military situation. Besides, he wrote in his journal, the Jews were apparently to blame for Germany's ruinous economy after World War I. While the rest of the country starved, they "obtained the ownership of a large percentage of property in Berlin and other cities—lived in the best houses, drove the best automobiles, and mixed with the prettiest German girls." Of course, all this was vile propaganda perpetrated by the Nazi government. Did Charles accept these lies as truth? Later actions would suggest he did.

A GERMAN EAGLE FOR AN AMERICAN ONE

The American embassy's ballroom looked magnificent on the evening of October 18, 1938. Elaborate floral centerpieces decorated the silver- and crystal-laden table, and an orchestra played softly. American officials mingled with German military advisers. A "men's dinner" hosted by Ambassador Hugh Wilson was being given in honor of both Charles and Hermann Goering, who had recently been promoted to field marshal general. Wilson, newly appointed to his post, hoped the event would help him get to know both men better.

Goering arrived last. Pushing his way through the guests, he approached Charles, who stood at the back of the room, and thrust a red leather box at him. Then Goering launched into a speech.

A member of Wilson's staff stepped forward to translate. Goering was presenting the pilot with the Service Cross of the German Eagle with Star—the highest decoration the Reich could bestow on a foreigner—given "by order of the Führer."

Charles opened the box. Gleaming inside was a white enamel cross bordered by four small swastikas and hung on a red ribbon. The citation accompanying the medal explained it was being awarded for service to the Reich.

Charles, according to an army officer standing next to him, seemed surprised.

Then the guests applauded and everyone sat down to dinner. Charles appeared to think little more about it. And in fact, he never spoke about the medal publicly.

He did, however, send this note to Goering:

> I want to thank you especially for the honor which you conferred on me . . . I hope that when the opportunity presents itself, you will convey my thanks to the Reichs-chancellor [Hitler]. It is difficult for me to express adequately my appreciation for the decoration, and for the way in which you presented it that evening. It is an honor which I shall always prize highly.

BROKEN GLASS

At the end of the month, the Lindberghs headed back to Illiec to pack and collect the children. Although no lease had yet been signed, they felt sure German officials would find them a suitable home.

Less than a week later, on the nights of November 9 and 10, 1938, violent mobs surged through the streets of Germany, Austria, and the newly annexed Sudetenland. Shouting *"Judenschwein!"*—"Jewish pigs!"—they burned over two hundred and fifty synagogues, looted and destroyed more than seven thousand Jewish businesses, desecrated cemeteries, and vandalized homes, schools, and hospitals. Afterward, more than thirty thousand Jewish men were rounded up and transported to concentration camps. Afterward, Propaganda Minister Joseph Goebbels—who'd incited the violence—remarked coldly, "We shed not a tear."

Reading an account of the event, which became known as Kristallnacht, "The Night of Broken Glass," in the newspaper, Charles was confused. "I do not understand these riots on the part of the Germans," he admitted in his journal. "It seems so contrary to their sense of order and their intelligence. . . . They have undoubtedly had a difficult Jewish problem, but why is it necessary to handle it so unreasonably?"

But the news horrified Anne. Finally, she seemed to grasp the hellishness of Germany's treatment of the Jews. "How *can* we go there to live?" she asked.

With its lack of heat and electricity, Illiec was impossible in the winter. America remained out of the question. And Charles felt nothing but disdain for Britain nowadays.

He was still pondering choices, and hadn't completely eliminated Germany, when the *New York Times* published a front-page article revealing the Lindberghs' "plan to move to Berlin." Remarked the reporter sarcastically, "the recent abandonment of many Jewish homes might make available apartments for rent."

Other publications jumped on the story. "With confused emotions we say goodbye to Colonel Charles A. Lindbergh who wants to go and live in Berlin, presumably occupying a house that once belonged to Jews," wrote E. B. White for the *New Yorker* magazine. "If he wants to experiment further with his artificial heart, his surroundings there should be ideal."

And several editorial cartoons published in newspapers across the country portrayed Charles proudly wearing his Nazi medal on his chest.

It was Dr. Carrel who finally set his protégé straight. Writing from New York, where he'd returned to his work at the Rockefeller Institute, he explained the growing anti-German feeling in America since news of Kristallnacht. Cancel your plans, he advised. A move to Berlin wouldn't sit well with Charles's fellow Americans.

Already, moviegoers hissed whenever Charles appeared on newsreels. Trans World Airlines, TWA (formerly TAT), removed the phrase "the Lindbergh Line" from its marketing. And Jewish booksellers began boycotting Anne's latest book, *Listen! The Wind.*

Anne fumed at what she called "unfair labeling." Her husband was "not and never has been anti-Semitic." She noted, however, that he was "marvelously untouched" by all the controversy.

At the end of November, the Lindberghs rented an apartment on the Avenue du Maréchal Maunoury in Paris.

And yet Charles's deep admiration for Germany was not seriously dampened. On the contrary, crossing the border from Belgium into Germany just a month later, he was captivated by the fine-looking young German immigration officer whose "air of discipline and precision" was in sharp contrast to the inefficiency of the French. Nazi Germany still offered the striking image of virility and modern technology he prized.

A HARD DECISION

In April 1939, Charles made a hard decision: it was time to return to America. After three years, he still had misgivings about his homeland. But this decision wasn't about him. It was about saving Western civilization.

Weeks earlier, on March 15, Hitler had broken his diplomatic promises and seized the rest of Czechoslovakia, and appeared to be sizing up Poland. A short time later, Prime Minister Chamberlain—at last recognizing the futility of appeasing the dictator—announced that Britain would go to the aid of Poland if invaded. France made a similar pledge.

Charles read Hitler's speech justifying the invasion in the morning newspaper and found the Führer's reason—the Nazi expansionist policy of *Lebensraum*—plausible and well stated. Certainly, it was unfortunate the dictator hadn't kept his word, but what politician did? He'd simply "moved a little faster than other nations have in breaking promises." Obviously, Hitler held "the future of Europe in his hand," Charles wrote in his journal. "Civilization depends upon his wisdom far more than on the action of the democracies." In fact, Charles now believed France and Britain should form an alliance *with* the Third Reich. "It is time to turn from our quarrels and to build our White ramparts again," he said. "Our civilization depends on a united strength among ourselves; on a strength too great for foreign armies to challenge; on a Western Wall of race and arms which can hold back . . . the infiltration of inferior blood; an English fleet, a German air force, a French army, an American nation, standing together as guardians of our common heritage, sharing strength, dividing influence."

But he knew this wouldn't happen, because of the "shortsightedness and vacillation" of British and French statesmen. He could do nothing in Europe to ward off war. But he *could* use his influence back home to keep America out of it.

So on April 8, 1939, Charles again slipped away, this time boarding a ship bound for New York City. He left Anne, the boys, and the dogs behind in Paris. He was, he felt, returning to hostile territory. It was best if he went alone and looked over the situation. He would cable when it was safe for them to follow.

PART EIGHT
AMERICA FIRST

"We [must] band together to preserve that most priceless possession, our inheritance of European blood . . . against . . . dilution by foreign races."
—*Charles Lindbergh*

CHAPTER TWENTY-SIX

AN INFLUENTIAL CITIZEN

THE EAGLE RETURNS

Even though the *Aquitania* had docked, Charles remained locked in his cabin. Someone had tipped off the press that he was on board, and the dock at New York Harbor swarmed with reporters. So did the ship, as soon as the ramp was lowered. They hammered at his door, shouting questions. He wondered how he would ever debark. He was thinking through a plan when a photographer broke down the door from the adjoining cabin and shoved a camera in his face. Flash! The photographer took a picture and ran.

Democracy, Charles fumed. "Where does freedom end and disorder begin?"

At least the trip had been peaceful. He'd spent most of his time reading, writing, and taking brisk walks on the mostly empty decks. Rough weather had kept the others in their cabins. "The steward tells me that most of the Jewish passengers are sick," he noted in his journal. In fact, many of the passengers, Charles noticed, were Jewish refugees fleeing Nazi oppression. "Imagine the United States taking these Jews in in addition to those we already have," he wrote. "There are too many in places like New York already. A few Jews add strength and character to a country, but too many create chaos. And we are getting too many."

He put on his hat. Pulling it low over his eyes and flipping up the collar of his coat, he pushed open the cabin door. Cameramen lined the corridor. After stepping into a blaze of flashbulbs, he fought his way onto the deck and down the gangplank behind a wedge of policemen. Then he dove into the backseat of his waiting car. With cameras still flashing and hands beating at the window, Charles was driven away. It was, he said, a "barbaric" return to his country.

BUSY DAYS BACK

The next day, before Charles even had a chance to settle, General Henry H. Arnold, chief of the Army Air Corps, summoned him for a meeting. It was now six months after the Lindbergh Report, and military officials still didn't know how wrong Charles had been about German air power. As far as they were concerned, he had provided valuable intelligence and was an important asset on the eve of a European war. Now General Arnold invited Charles—still a colonel on the corps' inactive reserve list—back to active duty effective immediately, so he could tour and assess American air bases.

Charles didn't hesitate to accept. Believing US foreign policy should be one of strength and neutrality, he was eager to help build up a strong military defense. And he was eager, too, to get back to his first passion: flying.

That night, after his meeting with General Arnold, Charles returned to his hotel room with a stack of aeronautical reports to study. But first he sent two cables. One was to Dr. Carrel at the Rockefeller Institute, letting him know he'd visit as soon as possible. The second was to Anne in Paris—it was safe for the family to join him. For the time being, he'd decided, they would once again live with Betty Morrow at Next Day Hill.

Five days later, on April 20, Charles was informed that President Franklin D. Roosevelt wanted to thank him personally for returning to active duty. Ushered into the Oval Office, Charles found FDR sitting behind his desk. This was the first time the two men had ever met, although they had dueled politically five years earlier.

It had happened in 1934 when Roosevelt suddenly canceled all commercial airmail contracts between the government and thirty airlines, including TWA (formerly TAT, "the Lindbergh Line"). Going forward, he ordered, the Army Air Corps would carry the mail.

Charles had been infuriated, and fired off a 275-word telegram to the White House that Anne helped him write. At the same time, he leaked it to the press. The rebuke, defending commercial mail carriers, appeared on the front page of every American newspaper. At first, most Americans sided with charming, savvy President Roosevelt. But after Charles testified before the congressional committee that was investigating what the press had begun calling the "Air-Mail Fiasco," public opinion turned. Reported the *New York Times,* every time Charles "flashed [his] familiar, winsome smile, a murmur of approval ran through the hall. He still seemed to be one of the world's most fascinating figures." Three months later, mounting public pressure forced Roosevelt to order Postmaster General James A. Farley to reinstate commercial airline contracts. For the first time, Charles had harnessed the power of his fame for political purposes. And President Roosevelt recognized a political foe.

Despite the friendly way he leaned across and clasped Charles's hand now, the president was deeply distrustful of his visitor. He knew about Charles's trips to Nazi Germany, as well his decoration from Adolf Hitler and his brief desire to live in Berlin. Was the hero up to something else? That was the real reason FDR had invited Charles to this meeting. A shrewd judge of character, he wanted to get a sense of the younger man. The last thing he needed at this pivotal time was a man of Lindbergh's stature getting involved in politics. Roosevelt remembered all too well what had happened the last time they'd clashed.

Charles hadn't forgotten, either. He smiled genially, knowing full well he was being scrutinized. "Roosevelt judges his man quickly and plays him cleverly," he wrote that night in his journal. "There was something I did not trust, something a little too suave, too pleasant, too easy. Still, he is our President, and there is no reason for antagonism between us in the work I am doing now." It was better, Charles told himself, "to work together as long as we can, yet somehow I have a feeling that it may not be for long."

⥳

A physical exam, a parachute fitting, and an intelligence briefing were all it took for Charles to be back in the Air Corps. He climbed into his assigned Curtiss P-36A Hawk, the most advanced fighter plane in the service, then took off for the first stop on his inspection tour. But the cloudless sky invited him to play first. Climbing to fifteen thousand feet, he did wingovers, stalls, dives. He had to admit that the plane "handles better than the [Germans']," then added, "even if it is not as fast."

Charles's return to active military duty helped mend his frayed reputation. Many citizens took it as proof of his patriotism. How could the Lone Eagle possibly be a Nazi if the reason he'd come home was to inspect air force bases and suggest ways of making America the leading air power in the world? they asked. The *New York Times* concurred. "[C]riticism of any of his activities—in Germany or elsewhere—is as ignorant as it is untrue," it wrote that spring. Lindbergh, the newspaper went on, had been on military missions in Berlin, gathering vital information for the US government. This work had "earned him some personal unpopularity. But any [poor opinion] founded on [the] belief [that] he has not been a patriot . . . is ill-founded indeed."

Over the next three weeks, Charles made twenty-three inspections. At every air base on his hectic schedule, he told servicemen that the Germans were "superior in the air and probably unstoppable on the ground." The United States, he warned, had lots of catching up to do. Additionally, he described the "vibrant, new [Nazi-infused] spirit" he'd found in Germany and compared it to the weakness of Britain and France. It was "imperative," he said, "for the sake of Western civilization that America stay out of Germany's way as [it] guarded against the West's true enemies." These, he explained, were the "Asiatic hordes" of Russians, Chinese, and Japanese.

He also suggested to Air Corps brass that they use eugenic measures to screen both their candidates *and* their potential spouses. He even advised that they be given the final say in those marriages. Wisely, the Air Corps chose not to act on this recommendation.

RETURN TO DR. CARREL'S LAB

Dr. Carrel leaped out from behind his desk to embrace the tall figure before him. It had been so long since Charles had been at the medical institute's lab—more than four years. Ignoring the younger man's embarrassment at this show of affection, Carrel grasped his arm. He insisted they take a tour.

In the steam room, the chicken heart cells still beat, alive after twenty-seven years. And in the perfusion room, a dozen pumps sloshed away. Ovaries, hearts, kidneys—whole organs from cats and dogs—were being kept alive and functioning outside the body. "The first laboratory approach to enabling man to live indefinitely," Carrel liked to say.

Charles remained silent as they moved on to the mousery. Thousands of rodents still burrowed, fought, and died in its soil. Carrel explained the latest experiments he'd been performing on them, examining the links among mind, body, and diet. Some of the rodents' diets, he said, contained too much salt or sugar. Some had too little fat. Others had coal tar added to their food, or cobalt, or alcohol. And a few underwent regular periods of starvation. It was all part of a new investigation into aging and longevity, he said. How soon could Charles return to the lab?

Charles broke the news. Despite his fascination with their research, he would not be returning. All his energies had to be directed at prolonging the life of Western civilization, not individual people.

While neither man realized it at the time, it was the end of their work together. As for their perfusion pump, it would become a dusty memory.

ANNE'S AMERICA

Anne had felt uncomfortable since her return to America in April. She longed for a simple life, out of the spotlight, a place where she could be alone with her family. That place was *not* Next Day Hill.

The Morrows' estate was too busy and crowded, constantly bustling with Betty's charity activities. Along with the four Lindberghs, Anne's sister Constance and her husband, Aubrey, lived there, as well as Anne's brother Dwight Jr. and his wife, Margo. "The hours spent arranging what nights are free for whose guests and what cars will take who into town, etc.!" exclaimed Anne.

At the end of June they moved to a rented house at Lloyd Neck, Long Island. Land and the dogs loved the place immediately, but Jon whined with homesickness, declaring, "It isn't like Illiec." Soon, though, he found a cherry tree to climb and went swimming in the sound. On that first day in their new home, after the boys were in bed, Anne sat outside as the bell buoy chimed and some nearby sheep baaed. She prayed she could "keep this place as peaceful as it seems to me tonight for [Charles], and that I can accomplish something here."

Summer passed. The war clouds over Europe darkened. And Charles still mulled over his actions should war erupt. He wanted to keep his fellow Americans from getting embroiled in the conflict. But how? He was still considering possibilities when German troops invaded Poland.

CHAPTER TWENTY-SEVEN

THE HERO SPEAKS

WAR IN EUROPE

As Charles strode down Fifth Avenue for his breakfast meeting at New York City's Engineers Club on the sun-drenched morning of September 1, 1939, his mind filled with questions. *Why did England and France get themselves into such a hopeless position? What has happened to "democratic leadership"? Why in heaven's name [fight for Poland]?* Even though Britain and France had yet to declare war, Charles knew it was just a matter of time. There would be no more appeasing Hitler. As they had in World War I, Britain and France were once again forming a military alliance. The war in Europe had unofficially begun.

The first to arrive at the club, Charles went into the dining room and chose a table by the window. *Somebody blundered,* he thought about the invasion of Poland, and in the next instant, *This war will change our lives.* But war was here, so one had to be practical and face it.

He pulled out paper and pen. What action should he take? He'd just jot down a few ideas before his breakfast companions arrived.

Anne spent that day imagining what war meant for the people she knew in Europe. "I saw them tortured, torn, dead, cut off before their time . . . before their work, their dreams are finished—wasted, spilled for nothing."

When Charles walked through the front door that evening, she was sobbing.

"Anne, what *is* it?" he asked. "What is the matter?"

"The war," she answered. "Just the war." She cried some more.

And for once, instead of being stern about her tears, he was kind. "You see it all too clearly, Anne," he said gently.

Later that night, he holed up in his study. For the next two days, he ate lunch and dinner at his desk, working long after Anne and the boys had gone to bed.

He broke away only once, at lunchtime on September 3, to listen to King George VI's speech. Earlier that day, Britain and France had declared war on Germany. Now, in simple and moving words, the king addressed the British people (and the world) over the radio. "In this grave hour, perhaps the most fateful in our history . . . For the second time in the lives of most of us, we are at war," he began in his faintly lisping voice. "But we can do the right as we see the right and reverently commit our cause to God."

Listening to him, Anne felt the world crack around her.

Charles felt galvanized. The next time he emerged from his study, it was with a radio speech he'd written. He showed it to Anne. He would speak directly to Americans about the war in Europe, he told her, make them understand why the United States should never take sides.

"AS IMPERSONAL AS A SURGEON WITH HIS KNIFE"

After arriving at the Carlton Hotel in Washington, DC, on the evening of September 15, 1939, Charles made his way to a private suite upstairs. A row of microphones awaited him. Anne, who'd accompanied him, noticed he looked ghostly white. Nonetheless, he was resolved. He had an urgent message for the American people.

They were eager to hear it . . . or more accurately, *him*. Incredibly, Charles hadn't spoken on the radio since his historic flight twelve years earlier. But now, having been gone from the country for three years, he was bursting back onto the national scene. Was it any wonder millions planned to tune in for his address? And all three national networks would broadcast it.

At 9:45 EST, his high-pitched voice went out across the airwaves.

"I speak tonight to those . . . who feel that the destiny of this country does not call for our involvement in European wars," he began. In a speech more emotional than logical, he raised the specter of unspeakable bloodshed. "We are likely to lose a million men, possibly several million. . . . We will be staggering under the burden of recovery the rest of our lives." After warning that involvement would "lead to the end of Western civilization," he urged listeners to view the war as he did, with detachment. Never allow, he said, "our sentiment, our pity, or our personal feelings of sympathy, to obscure the issue. . . . We must be as impersonal as a surgeon with his knife."

Anne shut her eyes. Although she'd read the speech, these words, when spoken aloud, sounded so terribly cold and uncaring. How could he tell his own countrymen to turn their backs on the suffering the war in Europe was sure to bring? She thought of their friends in France and Britain. *Oh, how* can *they understand?* she wondered.

Letters and telegrams flooded the Lloyd Neck house. Most applauded Charles's speech, claiming he'd "answered a real need, a clear call in the confusion." Few criticized him. This was due to his celebrity. Explained one historian, "The speech became a national sensation, not so much because of what was said, but because of who said it."

In just hours, Charles Lindbergh, a man with practically no knowledge or experience in foreign affairs, had become one of the most controversial figures on the political stage. He'd also become the face of isolationism.

A month later, Charles returned to the airwaves. Though his speech made clear he was against selling weapons to Britain and France, as FDR now advocated, the most striking chords showed his increasing obsession with race. Now he shared them with the American people:

> Our bond with Europe is a bond of race and not of
> political ideology. . . . It is the European race we must
> preserve; political progress will follow. Racial strength
> is vital—politics a luxury. If the white race is ever . . .
> threatened, it may then be time for us to take our
> part in its protection, to fight side by side with the English,
> French and Germans, but not with one against the other
> for our mutual destruction.

It was as if Charles saw the war in Europe as nothing more than an unfortunate squabble between members of the white race.

This time, public reaction was swift and critical.

In Washington, DC, one senator after another lined up to denounce Charles's speech.

The press called him "a somber cretin," "a man without human feeling," and "a pro-Nazi recipient of a German medal."

And across the Atlantic, his old friend Harold Nicolson scathingly wrote, "Charles Lindbergh . . . is and always will be not merely a schoolboy hero, but also a schoolboy."

Anne, who agreed with the substance of her husband's speeches, was stung by the response. Previously, most of the attention she and Charles had received had been practically worshipful. Now, almost overnight, Charles had become a controversial figure. She bemoaned what she called the "backwash" from his speeches.

"Bitter criticism," she wrote in her diary. "Personal attacks. He has [received] two threatening letters: He is a 'Nazi.' He will be punished. Our two children will be taken. . . . I feel angry and bitter and trapped again. Where can we live, where can we go? [Charles] is criminally misunderstood, misquoted and misused."

And then the world fell strangely silent. As fall turned to winter, the warring nations seemed to go into hibernation. No marching troops. No invasions. No battles. "The phony war," Americans called it.

But Charles knew what this truly was—the calm before the storm.

THE GUNS OF MAY

Charles and Anne heard the news on the radio: German troops, tanks, and planes were thundering across Belgium, Holland, and Luxembourg with France within their sights. It was May 10, 1940.

"The Germans are meeting with amazing success," said Charles admiringly. "It is a victory for air power and a turning point in military history."

On that same day, Winston Churchill became Britain's prime minister after Chamberlain lost a confidence vote in the House of Commons. This vote, which meant members no longer supported him as their leader, quickly led to Chamberlain's resignation. Three days later, in a speech before the House of Commons, Churchill declared he had nothing to offer but "blood, toil, tears and sweat." But he promised the British people and the world that he would "wage war, by sea, land and air, with all our might and with all the strength that God can give us." In private, he mourned to a friend, "Poor people, poor people. They trust me, and I can give them nothing but disaster for quite a long time."

Belgium and the Netherlands quickly surrendered, and by

May 18—just eight days after the invasion began—the Germans were a mere forty miles from Paris.

To Americans, Germany's Blitzkrieg, or "lightning war," seemed unstoppable. They no longer felt immune to events in Europe, and the ocean they had once believed protected them no longer seemed inviolable. Would the United States be left standing alone to fight a Nazi Europe? "There is near hysteria in some sections of the U.S.," a British attaché in Washington reported back to London, "and near anxiety in all." In a *Fortune* magazine poll, 94 percent of Americans now said they were willing to spend anything to make US defenses stronger.

With that sort of support, President Roosevelt went before Congress and asked for a staggering $17.6 billion (about $3 trillion nowadays) in new military spending, including a plan to build fifty thousand new planes. In his speech, he warned of the Nazi threat to the Western Hemisphere. If Germany was successful in defeating France and Britain, he told Congress, they would eventually try to invade the United States.

After listening to the speech on his radio, Charles pronounced the president's warning rubbish. An invading army would never manage to get across the protective expanse of the Atlantic and Pacific Oceans. Besides, Nazi Germany did not plan to invade the United States. Roosevelt, he believed, was leading Americans on . . . and into war.

It was time for another speech.

On May 19, the day the *Washington Post*'s headline read **NAZIS SMASH THROUGH BELGIUM, INTO FRANCE**, Charles told millions of radio listeners that it made no difference if Hitler conquered and controlled all Europe. "Regardless of which side wins," he said, "there is no reason . . . to prevent a continuation of peaceful relationships between America and the countries of Europe." The United States could maintain diplomatic and economic relations with *any* government—democratic or Nazi. He scolded Americans for their "hysterical chatter of calamity and invasion." There was no danger of this happening unless the Roosevelt administration incited it by meddling in Europe's affairs.

"There are powerful elements in America who desire us to take part," Charles warned. "They represent a small minority of the American people, but they control much of the machinery of influence and propaganda. They seize every opportunity to push us closer to the edge." He did not name these "elements," although he clearly meant Jews and their control of the press, an often-repeated but completely fictitious claim made by anti-Semites.

After his speech, many critics noted the similarity between Charles and his father. Twenty years earlier, C. A. Lindbergh had hinted darkly at conspiracies and secret forces behind America's entrance into World War I.

〰

Two days later, while lunching with his secretary of the treasury, Henry Morgenthau, President Roosevelt suddenly looked up from his egg salad and said, "I am absolutely convinced that Lindbergh is a Nazi. If I die tomorrow, I want you to know this." He lamented that the thirty-eight-year-old flier had "completely abandoned his belief in our form of government and has accepted Nazi methods because apparently they are *efficient.*"

〰

Dr. Carrel—who'd been at his summer home on Saint-Gildas since the war broke out—returned to New York at the end of the month. He'd barely stepped into his Manhattan apartment before Charles telephoned. He wanted to drive right over.

Carrel agreed. He had lots to discuss with his protégé. Foremost on his mind was an article Charles had written for the *Atlantic*

Monthly titled "What Substitute for War?" Carrel found he strongly disagreed with the piece. In it, Charles contended that Germany had a "natural right" to expand. The substitute for war Charles had called for was a negotiated peace *after* Germany had achieved *Lebensraum.*

His logic was this: countries like England and France were content with the territories in their control and so "desire[d] to enjoy rather than acquire." Germany, on the other hand, desired to "acquire before it could enjoy." The conflict, therefore, boiled down to "differing conceptions of right." The Western Allies championed "the static right of man," while Germany championed the "dynamic forceful right of man." Simply put, Germany should be allowed to seize territory until it satisfied its hunger for expansion. Once full, it, too, would settle into complacency like the Allies.

Certainly, Carrel agreed with his protégé's argument that France and Britain exhibited weakness and moral decay. He also agreed that the true enemies, as Charles stated in the article, were the "Asiatic barbarians." But he could not accept the vision of Nazi Germany as "the West's great protector."

As soon as Charles arrived, the doctor began pacing and waving his arms, his voice growing louder and more excited. *Lebensraum* was a farce. Didn't Charles see that if the Nazis succeeded in their quest, there would be "two very unequal classes in the world: Germans and everyone else?" This would not be "the saving of Western civilization, but its death."

Charles wasn't convinced. "Carrel is still able to discuss the war objectively and sees the causes clearly," he wrote that night in his journal. "On only one major point . . . do I disagree with him. Carrel feels that if Germany wins, Western civilization will fall."

It was the first test of their friendship.

NO FAVORS FOR OLD FRIENDS

On June 14, 1940, Paris fell to the Nazis. The next day, as Panzers rolled past the Arc de Triomphe and the swastika fluttered from the Eiffel Tower, Dr. Carrel picked up his phone in Manhattan and placed a long-distance call to Charles, who was meeting with fellow isolationists in Washington, DC. The scientist had a favor to ask.

Charles came on the line. The two chatted pleasantly about work and Anne's health. The doctor was happy to hear her morning sickness had passed. The fourth little Lindbergh was due in October.

Finally, Carrel got around to his request. In his next radio address, would Charles add a "friendly reference to France?" It would mean so much to the beleaguered French people.

"I [do not] see how I could . . . since it [is] primarily an argument against our entry into war," Charles said.

"But it is the Nazis who are destroying Western civilization!" exploded Carrel.

Charles replied that Carrel was "being irrational." After hanging up, he took a taxi to the NBC studios. His listening audience was waiting.

With lightning directness, he told them that England, now fighting alone, would inevitably fall. Nazi Germany was the strongest military nation in the world, thus the British struggle was futile. He urged Americans to stop the trend toward getting involved and again hinted at "the minority" who were trying to get the country into the war.

He didn't include a single sympathetic word for the embattled French people.

The French army fought on for two more days after Paris's fall, but finally and inevitably it surrendered.

Charles went about with a feeling of finality after he'd heard the news. It was over for France, but at least the killing was over, too. And now the rebuilding could begin, the birth of a new Europe.

"Germany has demonstrated an ability in war that has astonished the rest of world," he wrote to Major Truman Smith, who'd recently retired from his position as military attaché in Berlin and returned to the States. "There will soon be an opportunity for her to show an even more amazing [political] leadership."

SUMMER OF 1940

Now Charles put all his energies into keeping America out of war. What little time he had left he devoted to teaching three-year-old Land how to paddle in the surf, and to swimming out to the lighthouse with Jon, who was almost eight. He took long walks with Anne. But his mind was never on the trees or the clouded sky, as he wished it to be. It was forever on war and chaos, politics and plans. As July turned to August, he decided to try a different approach to reaching the American people.

On August 4, a broiling-hot afternoon, he stepped before a crowd of forty thousand at Chicago's Soldier Field. He'd never given an address in public before, but this promised to be the biggest antiwar rally in the country to date and he wanted to be there. Blinking into the sunlight and clutching his speech with both hands, he began. "In England," he told the crowd, "there was organization without spirit. In France there was spirit without organization. In Germany there [was] both."

As he spoke, the enthusiastic crowd broke in again and again. For a man who detested chaos and spontaneity, he liked the clapping and cheering. The feeling of energy coming off the audience invigorated him. He reveled in it, soaked it in. He decided to do more public speaking.

Not long after the speech, Charles showed Anne a couple of angry telegrams they'd received from close friends. One read, "You have let America down." Read another, "You stand for the atrocities of Hitler."

In Washington, DC, Charles's friend and cousin Jerry Land declared, "I just can't talk about him anymore. I think he has gotten into bad hands, and he's all wrong."

Even Henry Breckinridge, who'd stood by Charles throughout the kidnapping ordeal, told newspaper reporters, "He who spreads the gospel of defeatism is an ally of Adolf Hitler." He never spoke to Charles again.

The abandonment by their friends wounded Anne. She began to think that this was her contribution to the war, her sacrifice: "The giving up of all contacts, associations and friendships . . . or rather the *them* giving *me* up."

But there was something else she felt she could contribute. For Charles. She could pose "a *moral* argument for isolationism."

CHAPTER TWENTY-EIGHT

"THE BUBONIC PLAGUE AMONG WRITERS"

THE WAVE OF THE FUTURE

During those hot August days, while German bombs rained down on London, Anne filled her notebooks. It was "so spontaneous," she told her mother. The writing just "pushed" its way out.

She ended up with a slender book she called *The Wave of the Future: A Confession of Faith.* Explaining the title, Anne admitted her heartfelt "faith" in the transforming power of Nazism—something "not seen, but felt; not proved, but believed; not a program, but a dream."

The book went on to argue that the war in Europe wasn't between good (democracy) and evil (Nazism), but rather between the past and the future. Nazism was "energetic and dynamic," democracy "inefficient and exhausted." Anne claimed that since World War I, the "Democracies" (she consistently put the word in quotation marks, revealing her skepticism about self-government) had fallen into "decay, weakness and blindness." Meanwhile, in Germany a "new conception of humanity and more perfect social order" was struggling to be born. "Because we [in democratic nations] are blind we cannot see it, and because we are slow to change, it must force its way through the [stubborn] crust violently." Such a violent birth, she admitted, might result in a few harmful consequences—Jewish persecution, militarism—"but the greatness [of Nazism] remains, and no price could be too high" to pay for establishing Hitler's government.

Besides, she went on, these bad consequences weren't the future. There were merely the "scum on the wave of the future." Indeed, democracies committed worse sins, "such as blindness, selfishness, irresponsibility, smugness, lethargy, and resistance to change." But make no mistake, she went on, this wave of the future was coming. It was unstoppable.

She urged Americans to leap onto the wave of Nazism. It didn't have to be Hitler's brand. It could be uniquely American, "crisp, clear, tart, sunny, and crimson—like an American apple," or as homespun as "baseball and blue jeans." As one historian later summarized Anne's argument, all the citizens of the United States had to do was "simply skim off the scum of Nazism and let the pure and sparkling waves of fascism wash up on the shores."

When Charles read it, he hugged Anne and declared it a great book.

When Betty Morrow read it, she burst into tears. The book's logic, so splintered and warped, was grotesque. She knew her daughter would be attacked for writing it.

And Anne was. Although the book quickly became the country's number one nonfiction bestseller, it also became one of the most hated books of its time. Critics called her "Lindbergh's mouthpiece" and "Satan's little wife." They called the book "poisonous" and "an outright apology for fascism." Secretary of the Interior Harold Ickes labeled it "the Bible of every American Nazi."

"I am hurt, not by the reviews exactly, but by the growing rift I see between myself and these people I thought I belonged to," Anne wrote in her diary. "The artists, the writers, the intellectuals, the sensitive, the idealistic—I feel exiled from them." Loyalty to her husband, she realized, had "stretched me out of my world, and changed me so it is no longer possible to change back."

It was a new kind of isolation for Anne. No one but family visited the Long Island house now, and she rarely went out. "I am now the bubonic plague among writers," she admitted, "and [Charles] is the anti-Christ."

Just days after the book's publication, the baby arrived, a girl, as they'd hoped. They named her Anne Spencer Lindbergh—Ansy for short. Her birth provided the perfect excuse to hide from critics and reviewers. For more than two weeks, mother and daughter were secluded in the hospital before returning home. Once there, Anne remained withdrawn.

"LEND-LEASE"

On December 17, 1940, President Roosevelt rolled himself in his wheelchair to his spot behind a large desk in the Oval Office. Then he called in the reporters. He wanted to tell them about a bold new aid program he'd devised called lend-lease that would supply the British, who'd been fighting alone since France's surrender six months earlier, with the essential war materials they desperately needed.

As the reporters scribbled his words in their notebooks, the president explained how lend-lease would work by using the analogy of lending a neighbor your garden hose if his house was on fire, thereby keeping the fire from spreading to your own house. "You see?" he concluded. He shot the reporters his famously charming smile.

The next day, Americans across the country read about the president's plan. His homey analogy, suggesting that lending war materials wasn't any more radical or dangerous than loaning a hose to a neighbor, helped win over the public.

So did his explanation that his plan was vital to American safety.

If England was defeated, Germany would control all of Europe. It would, he said dramatically, be "in a position to bring enormous military and naval resources against [us]. . . ." To avert this, the

United States "must become the Great Arsenal of Democracy," sup-
plying Britain with everything it needed. Still, he assured the public,
the main purpose of lend-lease was to keep the country *out* of the
conflict. "There is far less chance of the United States getting into the
war if we do all we can now to support those defending themselves
against attacks by the [Germans]," he said, adding, "Any talk about
sending troops to Europe [is] a deliberate untruth."

Charles burned with anger over the president's plan. Lend-lease
was nothing but a scheme to push the country closer to war, and
he believed FDR had sinister reasons for doing so. "I feel sure he
would . . . like to take the center of the world stage away from Hitler,"
Charles wrote in his journal just hours after the radio broadcast. "I
think he would lead this country to war in a moment if he felt he
could accomplish this object."

Americans appeared to side with their president. A Gallup poll
taken that month showed that 72 percent now believed Germany
did pose a direct threat, despite the protective moat of the Atlantic
Ocean. Short of entering the war, they wanted to help England any
way they could.

"The pall of war seems to hang over us," Charles wrote in his
journal when he heard the poll results. "More and more people are
simply giving in to it."

BITTER AND GLOOMY

As 1940 turned to 1941, everything in Charles's life seemed to be
going wrong. Skean, the little terrier who'd been with them since
just after Charles Jr.'s birth, died from old age, and Thor, the fear-
less old German shepherd, was ailing. Anne remained withdrawn
and depressed about her book. And Dr. Carrel had sailed for France
in hopes of using his prestige to set up a relief network for children
between France and the United States. His protégé, of course, didn't

approve of giving any sort of aid, not even food and medical care, to the war's littlest victims.

If all this wasn't bad enough, Charles came down with chicken pox. While he tossed and turned in bed, trying to find a comfortable position in which to read, the editor of the *Saturday Evening Post* phoned. He couldn't use an article Charles had written opposing lend-lease. It was, said the editor, "a little too late." But Charles wondered if it wasn't "a little too hot." It appeared Congress would approve the act.

Days later, Ansy came down with the chicken pox. Then Jon. Then Land. Oatmeal baths, calamine lotion, and itchy, irritable children made up his days. Charles was trapped in the "uninspired drabness of everyday life."

He took a month with Anne to recuperate in Florida. Swimming. Beach camping. Lying in the sun. By April, he was refreshed and once again ready to take on any and all warmongers—and that included the president of the United States.

But first, the Lone Eagle would join a flock of like-minded isolationists.

CHAPTER TWENTY-NINE

CRASH LANDING

AMERICA FIRST

At the start of the 1940s, isolationists came in all stripes—farmers, union leaders, wealthy industrialists, college students, factory workers, and newly arrived immigrants. There were Democrats and Republicans, socialists, communists, radicals, pacifists, FDR-lovers and FDR-haters. Most isolationists were patriotic, well-meaning, and sincere citizens. And many were members of a movement called America First.

America First was started by a handful of Yale College students in 1940—among them a future president (Gerald Ford), a future Supreme Court justice (Potter Stewart), and the future first head of the Peace Corps (Sargent Shriver). Within months of its creation in 1940, it quickly grew into the nation's most influential isolationist organization. It endorsed three principles: an impregnable defense for America; preservation of democracy at home by staying out of war; and no aid for Britain beyond "cash and carry." Seeking to brand itself as a mainstream organization, it denied membership to communists and pro-Nazis.

But America First had one big problem. Its major goal—to keep the United States out of war—was the same as Hitler's. And so, as the organization grew in size and influence, right-wing extremists flocked to join. They should have been denied membership, but in overworked, volunteer-staffed local chapters (there were four hundred across the nation by 1941), they slipped in through the cracks. Soon, remarked one staffer, America First members became a "hodge-podge of sincere citizens . . . dominated by a core of bigots."

Anti-Semites particularly bedeviled the organization. Some chapter leaders spewed anti-Semitic accusations, while others invited anti-Semitic speakers to address their members. The chairman of the Indiana chapter wrote that "Jews or their appointees are now in possession of our Government," and a Kansas chapter leader pronounced FDR and his wife, Eleanor, "Jewish" and Britain's new prime minister, Winston Churchill, a "half-Jew."

Making matters worse, many local chapters of America First welcomed the support of Father Charles Coughlin, a Catholic priest with a large following on the radio and through his national weekly tabloid, *Social Justice,* who denounced the "anti-Christian conspiracy" of Jews, communists, FDR, and the British. Constantly attacking the president, he spoke admiringly of Hitler and praised Nazi persecution of Jews. "When we get through with the Jews in America," he declared, "they'll think the treatment they received in Germany was nothing." Seeing America First as an anti-Semitic organization, he urged his supporters to join.

They did.

In March 1941, President Roosevelt signed lend-lease into law, and all doubt that England and America were allies vanished. A national course had been set to see the British through to victory. Because of this, many moderates changed their minds about isolationists and dropped their membership in America First. But the anti-Semites and other extremists remained. They became the core of the organization.

That was when Charles Lindbergh decided to join.

ROOSEVELT VS. LINDBERGH

On April 23, 1941, the day the Greek government fled Athens for Crete just ahead of the unstoppable German army, Charles spoke at an America First rally at Madison Square Garden in New York. Once again, he denounced America's aid to Britain. The "United States," he cried, "cannot win this war for England . . . regardless of how much assistance we extend." Germany, he assured the audience, was sure to win, and the Reich's victory should be greeted with America's co-operation, friendship, and trade.

In Charles's tone, many heard a new bitterness and contentious-ness that hadn't been there before. His strident attitude whipped the crowd into a fury. They shouted, stomped, shook their fists in the air so violently it made Anne "curl inside with shock." Even so, her husband awed her. When he spoke, she felt his "great strength and power and I watched that crowd looking at him, with faith, with undivided attention, with trust. . . . He was not using his strength or power *intentionally*. No—it was simply there—*in him*."

Two days later, at a White House press conference, President Roosevelt told reporters that it was just "dumb" to think a Nazi vic-tory was inevitable. Lindbergh, he said, sounded like those quitters at Valley Forge who'd urged George Washington to surrender, argu-ing the British couldn't be defeated.

A reporter raised his hand. Why hadn't Colonel Lindbergh, like so many other reserve officers, been called into active military ser-vice?

The question was a plant. The White House press secretary had tipped off correspondents that if they asked this question, they would get an interesting answer.

Earlier, FDR's secretary had done a little research for him on Civil War copperheads—Northerners with pro-Southern sympa-thies who'd criticized President Lincoln. Now FDR spun a history lesson for the reporters, ending with the Union Army's refusal to call copperheads into military service.

"Are you talking about Colonel Lindbergh?" asked another reporter.

"Yes," said Roosevelt.

His message was clear. Charles Lindbergh was a Nazi sympathizer for whom the American Army Air Corps had no use.

"My Dear Mr. President," a furious Charles wrote on April 27, "Since you, in your capacity as president of the United States and Commander in Chief of the Army, have clearly implied that I am no longer of use to this country as a reserve officer . . . I can see no honorable alternative to tendering my resignation as colonel in the United States Army Air Corps Reserve."

The president gleefully accepted it.

Then he sent out his attack dog Harold Ickes to stir up the press. Wasn't it curious, the secretary of the interior pointed out to reporters, that Lindbergh had "no hesitation about sending back to the president his commission in the United States Army Air Corps reserve . . . ? But he still hangs onto the Nazi medal."

There was much Betty Morrow disliked about her son-in-law. But his refusal to show any sympathy for victims of the Nazi regime particularly rankled her. An ardent supporter of aid to England, she was active in several private organizations providing help to Europeans. Couldn't her son-in-law muster up even a "little revulsion" for the Germans' methods? she asked Anne one day.

Impossible, Anne replied. Charles had to remain an impartial observer, a kind of umpire in the war.

Betty stared at her daughter a moment, then snapped, "I always understood that umpires have whistles and sometimes blow for a foul."

But Anne remained adamant. Later, she would even refuse to

help her mother put together bundles of clothes for refugees. It would be a violation of her "personal neutrality," she said.

An indignant Betty would stomp away.

〰️

And still Charles kept speaking at America First rallies—Chicago, Oklahoma City, Minneapolis, Los Angeles. His words grew angrier. And his crowds grew more raucous. They booed any mention of FDR or Winston Churchill and cheered any reference to British defeat.

During one rally, Charles underscored the need for English surrender by describing the country's bombed-out cities and starving children. At that, the cavernous hall erupted into cheers and applause.

At another rally, when he mentioned the president, the audience chanted, "Hang Roosevelt! Hang Roosevelt!"

"Lindbergh is Hitler's puppet-agent in America," reported the *New York Times* on August 31, 1941, and America First was "merely a cloak for the greatest Nazi propaganda movement that has ever flourished in this country." Across the nation, librarians pulled Charles's book (as well as Anne's books) off their shelves. Streets named after him were renamed. Monuments and plaques were removed. Nine-year-old Jon came home from school, chin quivering, wondering why his parents were traitors. Four-year-old Land began chanting "Nazi-lover," after a car drove by, the passengers screaming it.

So many people called the Long Island house spewing anger and hatred that the family felt compelled to move yet again, this time to isolated Martha's Vineyard, which prompted an avalanche of letters to the FBI. "It is a perfect base for German invasion," warned one. "What is being done to guard this island?" demanded another. "Who is watching this man who so loves the Germans and the New Order?"

Still, Charles kept speaking—louder, angrier—like a man with nothing to lose. He met with so much hostility that police motorcycles escorted his car, and detectives went over his hotel rooms "with a fine-tooth comb," he told Anne. They even "x-rayed the furniture [and] . . . assigned a detective to every door at the meeting hall and had guards in the rooms beneath the speaker's stand!"

And then, on September 11, he went to Des Moines.

FALL FROM GRACE

At the sight of Charles's car, a roar rose from the crowd gathered at the back door of the Des Moines Coliseum—a wild and frightening roar. As the driver steered to the curb, throngs surrounded the vehicle. The police struggled to hold them back, clearing a path. A moment later, the door opened. Hundreds of flashbulbs popped so blindingly that for a moment Charles had to shield his eyes.

"Lindy! Lindbergh for president!" shouted some people.

"Nazi-lover!" shouted others.

Charles responded to neither, moving through the crowd with self-assured purpose. He'd expected this rally to be difficult, considering Iowa's large pockets of pro-British sentiment. Just that morning the editor of the *Des Moines Register* had labeled him "public enemy No. 1." In fact, this city was shaping up to be the least friendly place he'd spoken.

Inside the hall, the crowd—numbered at only seventy-five hundred—was even more restless, and the air felt charged with anger. Everyone seemed to be shouting at once.

"Lindy for president!"

"Nazi!"

"Hang Roosevelt!"

"Go back to Germany!"

Standing tall and full of purpose, Charles approached the podium. He adjusted the microphone, peered out into the crowd.

The mob clapped, stomped, booed, heckled.

But Charles stood unflinching, supported by the stone foundation of his convictions. Unshakable. Implacable. And absolutely sure he was right. Just that day, FDR had issued his "shoot on sight" policy, authorizing the US Navy to fire at any hostile vessel. Now Charles prepared to fire his fiercest salvo back at the war agitators.

In previous speeches, Charles had hinted at the "powerful forces" trying to propel America into war. It was time, he told the audience, for "the naked facts . . . for in order to counteract their efforts, we must know exactly who they are."

He singled out three groups: the Roosevelt administration, the British, and American Jews. And while most of his criticism was directed at the first two, it was when he turned to the third group that he revealed his ugliest beliefs.

He began by saying he understood why Jews wanted America to get into a war with Germany. Nazi persecution was enough to "make bitter enemies of any race." But if this country went to war, American Jews would be the first to feel the consequences because there was certain to be a violent outbreak of anti-Semitism. He didn't clarify these comments further, but to many listeners his implication was clear. If Jews didn't stop lobbying for intervention, they would pay.

"The Jewish races . . . for reasons which are not American, wish to involve us in this war," he went on. "We cannot blame them for looking out for what they believe to be their own interests, but we must also look out for ours. We cannot allow the natural passions and prejudices of other peoples to lead our country to destruction."

Other peoples? Charles was saying that Jewish people living in this country were not Americans, but *others*—a group living within the United States with no allegiance to the nation.

Charles Lindbergh, the greatest hero of the day, a man whose utterances carried tremendous weight, had told those in the hall and millions of others listening on the radio that American Jews were dangerous to the country. He'd called them conspirators, a hostile foreign race, and a people deserving of public condemnation. He'd put them on notice that America's tolerance was tenuous. That if they supported intervention, they would be punished.

He didn't see his remarks as a signal to hatemongers. Nor did it occur to him that there were people—in particular President Roosevelt—who supported England not out of narrow interests, but because they believed freedom for Western Europe was essential to American freedom. He simply wanted to get a few things off his chest before some incident resulted in war, "and I decided if I waited any longer I might not have another opportunity."

AND THE NEXT DAY . . .

On September 12, 1941, state representatives in Texas passed a resolution informing the aviator he was no longer welcome in the Lone Star State.

In Washington, DC, a congressman from Alabama waved a copy of Hitler's *Mein Kampf* in front of his colleagues and declared, "It sounds like Charles A. Lindbergh," before heaving the book to the floor in disgust.

The *San Francisco Chronicle* editorialized, "The voice is the voice of Lindbergh, but the words are the words of Hitler." Practically every newspaper in the nation echoed these sentiments, even the ones that supported isolationism, like the *Chicago Tribune.* It called Lindbergh's address "intemperate," "intolerant," and "repugnant."

Liberty Magazine, a publication advocating religious freedom, labeled Charles "the most dangerous man in America." Before he came along, "anti-Semites were shoddy little crooks and fanatics. . . . But now all that is changed. . . . He, the famous one, has stood up in public and given brazen tongue to what obscure malcontents have only whispered."

And Wendell Willkie, the 1940 Republican candidate for

president, called the speech "the most un-American talk in my time by any person of national reputation."

Only the White House remained silent. With all the public outrage, there was no need to say a word.

This outrage perplexed Charles. "I felt I had worded my Des Moines speech carefully and moderately," he wrote in his journal. Then he added, "It seems that almost anything can be discussed today in America except the Jewish problem."

⋙

America First straggled on for a few more months. Charles—refusing to apologize or take back any part of his address—continued to speak despite the resignation of several key committee members and thousands of canceled memberships. On October 3, he warned an audience in Fort Wayne, Indiana, that FDR was scheming to cancel the 1942 midterm elections. This, of course, was a baseless accusation. And on October 30, at Madison Square Garden, he claimed the British had "one last desperate plan remaining" to win the war—American troops. As he spoke, a peaceful protest took place outside.

Then, with no more speeches scheduled until December, Charles went home to Martha's Vineyard. He walked the beach with arthritic Thor hobbling beside him, and shot at targets with Jon's .22 rifle. He built a tree house with the boys, complete with drawbridge and spyglass. As he hammered nails, he couldn't help but notice the many ships passing by the island. "All . . . are now in dark war paint."

CHAPTER THIRTY

THE LINDBERGHS' WAR

"A DATE WHICH WILL LIVE IN INFAMY"

Charles sat glued to the radio. As news bulletins broke in and disastrous details emerged, he began to get a clear picture of what had happened.

At 7:55 that morning, two waves of Japanese bombers had attacked the US naval base at Pearl Harbor, Hawaii. Some 2,400 Americans had been killed and another 1,000 injured. Additionally, over 1,400 ships and 188 airplanes had been destroyed, making it the worst naval defeat in American history.

"How did the [Japanese] get close enough," Charles kept asking himself, "and where is our Navy?"

Land tapped Charles's arm. The boy wanted to tell his father the Christmas story. Land recited the Bible verses he'd learned in Sunday school. "And the Angel said, 'Fear not, New York!'"

Father turned to look at son. New York? Where had he gotten that?

At lunchtime the next day, the Lindberghs listened to President Roosevelt's declaration of a state of war. "Yesterday, December 7, 1941—a date which will live in infamy . . . ," the president began.

Ansy, in her high chair, was kept quiet by being fed a single grape at a time, and when the shouting on the radio died down, Land—who'd been asked to play silently—tiptoed over. "And more and more angels came," he whispered in his mother's ear, "'Fear not' . . . !"

Four days later, on December 11, Germany and its ally Italy declared war on the United States. Charles certainly did not want to fight the Nazis. But weeks earlier, despite his loud insistence that America stay out of war, he'd admitted to a friend that he had "no misgivings about an all-out war against Japan." In fact, he'd added, "[it] would be entirely 'practical'—we could win it easily." And while he didn't want to be deployed to Europe, he was obviously itching to fly a fighter plane in the Pacific. "I want to do my part," he wrote that night in his journal.

Even though he'd resigned his commission, he wrote to General Henry Arnold of the Army Air Corps volunteering his services. He felt sure the corps, needing his skill and know-how, would reinstate him as a colonel. So he was stunned when the War Department said no. "You can't have an officer leading men who thinks we're licked before we start," explained a White House official. "And that's that."

Charles turned to the commercial airlines he'd helped to form—TWA, Pan American, Ryan Aeronautical. Certainly they would need his expertise now that they were busy designing and building aircraft for the war. But one after the other said no. "Obstacles have been put in our way," explained one executive. Another said hiring him was "loaded with dynamite."

The truth dawned on Charles. The Roosevelt administration had blackballed him.

Now he hung around the house writing letters to people in hopes of rustling up an opportunity. Nobody would hire him. Toward the end of March 1942—just when Charles had given up all hope—he answered the phone and heard a brisk voice say, "Henry Ford wants to talk to [you] about assisting him with the bomber factory."

AWAY AND AT HOME

If there was one man capable of defying Franklin Roosevelt, it was Henry Ford. Despite Ford's vocal support of isolationism (as well as his rabid anti-Semitism), the government needed him. Or rather, it needed his factories, including three main ones in Detroit and sixty branches across the country. Ford's plants were being turned into a war machine, churning out engines, planes, tanks, and jeeps. Now Ford wanted Lindbergh for his aviation operations, and what Ford wanted, Ford got.

A week later, Charles left Anne and the children behind in Martha's Vineyard and became a production executive at Ford's Willow Run factory outside Dearborn, Michigan, testing planes, implementing improvements in aircraft design, and representing the company at meetings across the country. The plant—three square miles of factories, plus hangars and runways—worked around the clock to churn out Ford's quota of one B-24 Liberator bomber an hour.

It was a tall order, and Charles flung himself into his job, rising before dawn and returning to his hotel room long after dark. On weekends, he visited his mother and uncle—whom Charles confusingly called Brother—who still lived in Detroit. He shoveled coal for their furnace, trimmed trees and bushes to let more light into the house, and spent hours oiling some of his grandfather Land's tools. It wasn't what he'd seen himself doing in the war. But it would do . . . for now.

In June, Anne and the children moved into the house Charles had found for them in Bloomfield Hills, north of Detroit. With its satin upholstery, pink, green, and gold wallpapers, and formal, manicured yard, it didn't suit either of their tastes. But it was big— four bedrooms and three acres—and given the housing shortage caused by the war, they felt lucky to have it. Still, it made Anne giggle the first time she stepped over the threshold. "Very Hollywood!" she exclaimed.

It would be a summer of both sorrow and joy.

In August, on a clear, sunny day, Anne found Thor dead beneath a tree in the yard. She buried him by herself, "in the quiet of an afternoon and no strangers around." It was exhausting work for a woman who was now nine months pregnant, but she had to do it this way. "To others he is only a dead dog, while to me he is a life, a faithful friend . . ."

Arriving home very late that night, Charles found his wife in bed crying. "It's all right," he said soothingly. "I wanted him to die, he was so old. . . . It's hard to lose him." Although Anne had never seen Charles cry over his murdered son, he now allowed a tear to slip down his cheek. Later he wrote in his journal, "There is a great empty, lonely feeling in the places [Thor] used to be."

Ten days later, at Henry Ford Hospital, Anne gave birth to their fifth child.

"It is a boy," the doctor told her.

"A *boy*!?" Anne repeated incredulously. They'd both been sure it was another girl. She saw Charles's smiling eyes over his surgical mask. "We'll never be able to name it," she told him.

And indeed, it was almost Christmas before they put a name on the baby's birth certificate. They called him Scott, a name that had been in the Land family for two generations.

In September, Charles heard about a new field of aviation research—high-altitude flying. The latest innovations in aircraft allowed planes to reach forty thousand feet—but could a pilot fly at that altitude without passing out? Civilian doctors at the Mayo Clinic in Rochester, Minnesota, were conducting experiments to find out. Still fascinated by medical science, Charles offered himself up as a test subject.

For ten days that month, Charles climbed into a pressurized steel cylinder, strapped himself into a high-backed chair, and covered his nose and mouth with an air mask. The chamber was set to equal the pressure inside a plane flying at forty thousand feet. Charles performed numerous activities—simulating parachute jumps, mimicking opening a cockpit hatch—all the while measuring his temperature and alertness. More than once, he gasped and choked for breath before passing out. He considered his discomfort a small price. The knowledge gleaned from the experiments would help improve planes' oxygen equipment, ultimately saving countless lives.

Still, he wished he could have shared the details of these experiments with Dr. Carrel. Sadly, the two were no longer in touch. Charles claimed he dared not write Carrel because of the political conditions in France. "A letter from me might [have been] used by his enemies to injure him," he said.

And Dr. Carrel—in German-occupied Paris—never wrote Charles.

FORGIVENESS

Michigan's winter wind howled, and whispers of Nazi atrocities—mass shootings, concentration camps, the cold-blooded murder of Jews—trickled across the country.

Anne recoiled from the rumors, but Charles seemed unperturbed. As they got ready for bed one night, they quarreled about what was happening in Europe and the Pacific. He defended the human suffering that inevitably accompanied war. Dreadful as it was, he said, it was better than civilization's decay.

How could mass shooting in France or the horrific events in Poland be anything but decay? she argued. "It *is* the loss of civilizations."

No, he replied calmly. Suffering and loss are necessary parts of rebirth. Strong nations always subdue the weak. It was natural. Like in Dr. Carrel's mousery.

Exterminating the Jewish race could hardly be natural, she

snapped. She lay back against her pillow, disturbed by her husband's lack of sympathy.

Charles didn't know it, but Anne had changed her mind about their antiwar fight, and especially about her own book *The Wave of the Future*. As the war ground on and the true face of Nazism was slowly revealed, she could not reread what she'd written without deep shame. Sometimes she would wake up in the middle of the night with a sharp awareness of the "pain and hurt and wrong of my book." The knowledge was as piercing as a "point of light from a burning-glass."

The next day she woke very early, unable to sleep.

"I want to be forgiven," she said into the darkness.

"For what? And by whom?" he replied.

"I don't know [by whom], but I feel so strongly that I want to be forgiven." To herself she added, *For our stand, for my book.*

He looked at her. "If you *want* to be forgiven, then you *are* forgiven."

But after Charles had rolled over and gone back to sleep, Anne found herself whispering a prayer she repeated often these days: "Help me to live, to live *right*."

SPIRITUAL DISCOVERIES AT 41,000 FEET

As winter snows thawed and the spring of 1943 bloomed, Charles began to realize that a German victory was far from certain. This worried him, since he still believed a "Russian dominated Europe would be far worse than a German dominated [one]." No matter that the Soviet Union was an American ally. Charles continued to lump the country in with the enemy.

He was busy testing B-24 bombers and P-51 Mustangs. For weeks, he put the new aircraft through rigorous exercises, searching for design flaws and creating emergency procedures. He put himself through rigorous paces, too, updating his license to fly multiengine planes . . . just in case he ever got to see action in the Pacific.

One morning in October, Charles took up a P-47 Thunderbolt for a test flight. As he was descending from forty-one thousand feet he felt a blackout approaching—"a vagueness of mind and emptiness of breath." He recognized these symptoms—he was out of oxygen. And from his experiences in the altitude chamber at the Mayo Clinic, he knew he had about fifteen seconds before he passed out.

He had to drop down to where the air wasn't so thin, where he could breathe naturally.

With his vision already fading and his mind losing focus, he shoved the stick forward and aimed the plane straight down.

His plane went into a screaming dive, but Charles was only dimly aware of the sound. "I'm blind . . . I can't see the [dials] . . . there are no more seconds left . . ."

He fell twenty thousand feet before he came to. Air filled his lungs and awakened his mind. Pulling out of the dive, he leveled the plane. As he did, he was flooded with the "pure joy of existence," as well as a deeper knowledge that came from escaping death. In those moments of free fall he'd become "a part of all things, feeling them, being them, as well as seeing them through my eyes."

Charles was still wrestling with these emotions when he landed and taxied back to the hangar. He glanced at the broken oxygen gauge and felt a "sudden revulsion for . . . needles, instruments, and readings. What fools men were to impress their minds, enslave their bodies, with figures and machines when life lay everywhere around them, free for the taking, unperceived."

Unperceived.

His mind took a leap. He saw it now. *Really* saw it.

Just a few hours before, he had viewed the factory as a feat of engineering. He'd felt proud of the part he played in this scientific marvel. But now the assembly line and the bombers stretching as far as the eye could see seemed "a terrible giant's womb . . . giving birth to [machines] which were killing people by the thousands each day as they destroyed the culture of Europe. Inside . . . were thousands of men and women, sacrificing sunlit hours, home and family, shop and farm, to serve this hellish monster."

His mind took another leap.

The factory was nothing but "a temple of the god of science at which we moderns worshipped." But science was a false god, he now realized, "hypnotizing [man] with its machines, dulling his senses with its knowledge, destroying its culture with its bombs." It blinded him from higher values. It separated him from God.

All his life he had worshipped at this temple. But in those moments of the almost-failed test flight he'd learned that "in worshipping science man gains power but loses the quality of life."

THE WAR ZONE AND THE HOME FRONT

Summer passed . . . and fall . . . and another Michigan winter. But with the spring of 1944 came the winds of change for the Lone Eagle. Word reached Washington, DC, that not only had Charles Lindbergh improved production at Ford's plant, but he was also an expert in high-altitude flying. Additionally, he'd been testing and developing the fast and powerful Corsair—both the single- and the twin-engine versions. When he took them up for mock aerial battles, he "outguessed, outflew and outshot" pilots half his age, an eyewitness reported.

The US government needed him. Despite their earlier position, they asked him to travel to the South Pacific and inspect Corsair operating bases in the combat zone. The military had been receiving conflicting reports about the fighter planes' performance. Charles would gather facts and make recommendations for improvements in design. Although he'd go as a civilian (they were not reinstating his commission), he'd be required to wear a naval officer's uniform without any service rank or insignia. Under no circumstances would he be allowed to fight. And if he got captured, he would be a man without a country, protected by no international treaties.

Charles didn't care about any of that. This was his chance to get to the front and maybe go to war against that "yellow danger," the Japanese.

It was a happy Charles Lindbergh who finally headed into the combat zone on April 24, 1944. With him went a small canvas bag containing a waterproof flashlight, batteries, razor, soap, shoe polish, underwear, a spare uniform, and a pocket edition of the New Testament. "Since I can carry only one book—and a very small one—that is my choice. It would not have been a decade ago; but the more I learn and the more I read, the less competition it has."

The last thing Anne said to Charles as he headed out the front door to war was "Don't forget your lunch!"

Nevertheless, he went off, leaving it on the hall table.

Once he was gone, Anne became head of the household. She learned how to keep the accounts and deal with the gas cards and ration books. And when Land heard a strange noise one night, *she* investigated it. But with four children underfoot, she needed help. Luckily, there was Hilma, who scrubbed and vacuumed, as well as a cook who kept them all fed, because, remarked Anne, "I am very stupid at it." For a brief, nerve-wracking time, it seemed as if she would have to struggle on without a nurse for the children. But after hours spent writing and telephoning, a "cheerful and solid and ageless looking" woman named Miss Hanky arrived from Pittsburgh. Anne liked her immediately.

Freed from doing most of the housework and child care, and no longer confined to following Charles's plans, Anne made her own. She enrolled in sculpture classes and went to exhibitions and neighborhood parties, where she talked about music, art, books, and "politics sometimes." Out of her husband's shadow, she felt as if she'd found her "true self as I have never done [in] a group of people before." Most surprising, she exclaimed, "they like me!"

※

Forty-two-year-old Charles had begun flying combat missions in the South Pacific. (When he was done, he'd have flown fifty.) As a "civilian observer," his doing so was strictly against the rules, but the top brass looked the other way. Among fliers, the Lone Eagle remained a legend. And he was a brilliant, tireless pilot. Said his commanding officer, "He dive-bombed enemy positions, sank barges and patrolled our landing forces [on the ground]. He was shot at by almost every anti-aircraft gun the [Japanese] had in New Guinea." He also became an expert bombardier, although he hated it. "You press a button and death flies down," he said.

Ground crews soon noticed he always returned from missions with fuel in his tanks. His commanding officer asked how this was possible. Charles told him about his barnstorming days, and how he'd learned to get the best mileage out of every drop of fuel. Soon he was teaching these techniques to the younger pilots. Within weeks, the entire 475th Fighter Group was stretching their six-hour missions to ten hours, allowing them to penetrate deeper into enemy territory than the Japanese ever expected.

In August, Charles sent Anne a snapshot. Standing in his flak jacket beside four pilots half his age, he smiled broadly—as he seldom did—directly into the camera. It was like the old days, he wrote in the accompanying letter, the days of barnstorming and flying the airmail. Once again, he belonged to the "wild free fraternity of the air. . . ."

※

On June 6, 1944, forever known as D-Day, the combined power of British and American troops landed in Normandy on the coast of France. On their push eastward toward Berlin over the next weeks and months, they liberated Paris, Belgium, and Holland. Nazi Germany reeled toward total collapse.

In the South Pacific, Charles noted these events but kept his feelings about them to himself.

Meanwhile, in Bloomfield Hills, Anne was too busy to record her thoughts. That month she'd learned that their landlord would not be renewing their lease. The family would have to move again. Anne wrote to Charles, asking his advice. They had to be packed and out by September 1.

He could do nothing from New Guinea, he replied. She'd just have to find a place on her own. He knew she could do it. And it didn't have to be in the Detroit area. He wasn't returning to the Ford factory, so she was free to pick a home anywhere she wanted. "There is nothing I would rather do than spend a few months studying and writing in a beautiful and quiet place," he wrote.

With four children, Anne doubted the house would be very quiet, though she could probably find something beautiful. By August she'd rented a place in Darien, Connecticut, that "looks rather like us and has apple trees and a brook for the children and lots of room for Jon's goldfish and cocoons."

Planning. Packing. Train tickets. Busyness.

Goodbyes.

She regretted leaving all the friends she'd made—her *own* friends. She felt, she said, "snatched away."

One of the hardest leave-takings was from Evangeline. Charles's mother had enjoyed her time with the family. Now "frail and so gallant," she and "Brother" waved goodbye from the driveway. Anne felt she could hardly bear it.

In the middle of all this, at the end of August, Anne opened the newspaper to find a brief paragraph in the *Detroit Free Press*. That month, Paris had been liberated and the recently reinstated French government had turned the city's Palais des Sports into a detention camp for civilians accused of collaborating with the Germans. One of those arrested was Dr. Carrel.

SEPTEMBER 1944

The transport plane rose over the base in Honolulu and above broken cumulus clouds. Charles sat in the last seat in the tail. Reclining as much as possible, he folded his hands behind his head. In just a few days he'd be with his family again. Would Anne sense his disappointment at being back?

He longed to stay in the Pacific, flying with his fighter group, weaving through black puffs of smoke and strafing enemy barges, but he knew he couldn't. He wasn't enlisted in the military, and he certainly wasn't supposed to be flying missions. He'd carried out his assignment to survey aircraft thoroughly. Now he had no choice but to return to the countryside of Connecticut.

But oh, he wanted to stay!

And then he was back, joy "flooding everything," Anne wrote in her diary about his homecoming on the twentieth, "the house, the stream, the woods, the flowing fall weather . . . the children. [Ansy] tossed up in his arms. Scott, shy and round-eyed. The boys now at last free to vent their bursting energy . . . roughhousing with him, building a dam across the stream, or just throwing stones and trying their aim against his."

But where did she and Charles stand? She wasn't sure. Something had changed. "Both of us are groping and a little lost," she admitted, "but we are together."

PART NINE

FINAL FLIGHT

"After my death, the molecules of my being
will return to the earth and the sky."
—*Charles Lindbergh*

OUT OF THE ASHES

THE MORTAL SCIENTIST

There it was on page nineteen of the *New York Times:* **DR. ALEXIS CARREL DIES IN PARIS AT 71.** Charles read the brief article, struggling to take it in. A day earlier, on November 5, 1944, distressed over accusations that he was a Nazi collaborator, Dr. Carrel had had a fatal heart attack. To the very moment of his death, he had denied the charges.

Indignation surged through Charles. How dare the French suggest that Carrel had helped the Nazis? The scientist loathed the Germans and had often vented his disgust for them. He hadn't been a collaborator. The charges were completely baseless.

Sadness followed indignation. The father figure who'd shaped his thinking about race and civilization was no more. "I wanted to pick up the phone and call [him], to hear his voice at the other end, the precise French accent, the dignity, the warmth of welcome. But he is dead, killed by the unfairness of war, by the false accusations of men who never made a fraction of the sacrifice he did for his country." It was hard, Charles admitted, "to make myself realize he [was] gone."

ENDINGS AND BEGINNINGS

Charles was working as a test pilot again, this time for United Aircraft in Hartford, Connecticut. Absorbed in fighter designs and questions about fuel range, rate of climb, speed, and firepower, he spent little time with his family. He knew the end of the war in Europe was in sight. America's entry into the conflict, along with Britain's heroic efforts and the Russians' forcing Hitler to fight on two fronts, had turned the tide.

Now, as the spring of 1945 bloomed, so did hopes of an imminent German surrender. At the end of March, American and British troops marched into Germany's heartland. Moving eastward toward Berlin, they bombed cities and liberated concentration camps. What they found in those camps—gas chambers in which Jews, homosexuals, political opponents, and others had been murdered, ovens in which their bodies had been incinerated, piles of human ashes, stacks of corpses—sickened them. But it was the survivors who caused many battle-hardened men to break down and weep. Skeletal, starving, their heads shaved, some of the prisoners crowded around their liberators, kissing their arms and touching their jeeps to make sure it was true. Those who couldn't walk crawled toward the soldiers. Many hid in their barracks, too afraid to come out.

"I couldn't understand this," said Private Leon Ball, recalling the day his infantry unit arrived at Buchenwald, one of the largest concentration camps in Germany. "So I walked around . . . I wanted to . . . understand more. I went to a building where they stored body parts from 'medical experiments' in jars of formaldehyde. . . . I saw mounds of little children's clothing. Little children who didn't survive. . . . But I never saw a child. . . . If this could happen here, it could happen anywhere."

As camp after camp was liberated, a cold anger toward the Germans welled up among Allied troops. Those living in the nearby towns insisted they hadn't known about these atrocities. But the stench caused by overcrowded living conditions, as well as the odor of the crematories, wafted for miles over the countryside. It brought tears to the eyes of another Buchenwald liberator, Private Walter Lewis. "How," he wondered, "could [Hitler] give such an order, so cruel to human beings?"

News of these gruesome discoveries quickly made its way back to the United States. In Connecticut, an air of depression overtook Charles and Anne. "Obviously, this winter and spring [we] are going through profound disillusionments & despairs," she wrote to her mother in early April.

⌇⌇⌇

On Thursday evening, April 12, 1945, thirteen-year-old Jon and eight-year-old Land lay on the carpet in front of the radio listening to *The Adventures of Daniel Boone*. Suddenly, an announcer broke in. "We interrupt this program to bring you a special news bulletin. . . . President Franklin Roosevelt is dead. The president died of a cerebral hemorrhage. All we know so far is the president died at [his retreat in] Warm Springs at Georgia."

Neither Charles nor Anne mourned the president's passing. While most of the world felt they'd lost a great leader, Charles viewed the event differently. The American people, he believed, were lucky to finally be rid of the man who'd tricked them into war with Germany.

And Charles felt as if a load had been lifted from his back. Practically overnight, official attitudes toward him changed. "The vindictiveness in Washington [has] practically disappeared [where I am] concerned," he wrote an acquaintance from his America First days.

Indeed, Roosevelt had been dead just one week when military brass called Charles to the nation's capital. The Reich's surrender was expected any day. As soon as that happened, would Charles go to Germany to survey the Nazis' developments in high-speed aircraft and missiles, as well as interview their developers? As he had in the South Pacific, he would travel as a civilian consultant attached to the Naval Technical Expedition.

Charles eagerly accepted. "Some say the Germans would have held supremacy of the air if they had been a year farther ahead with their jet and rocket development," he wrote his mother. "It is important for us to find out what the real facts are, and that is my primary mission."

On April 30, with Russian troops just yards from his underground bunker, Adolf Hitler took a cyanide capsule, then put a pistol to his head and pulled the trigger. German troops struggled on for a few more days without their Führer. But on May 6, they laid down their arms. The next morning, they surrendered unconditionally. After six catastrophic years, the war in Europe was over. The Third Reich was no more.

～～

Five days later, Charles Lindbergh boarded a navy C-47 transport plane bound for Germany. Charles craned his neck and peered out of the porthole. Munich was coming into view. What he saw shocked him. Ruined walls. Piles of rubble. Blasted factories. "It is a city destroyed," he said.

When he'd last set foot in Germany seven years ago, the country was still "proud" and "virile." Now it felt like "hellish death." Anger surged through him. He'd warned against Western civilization fighting itself. He'd predicted it would lead to needless destruction. Now, here was proof. Western civilization, he wrote in his journal, "has reaped the whirlwind [it] caused."

The plane landed, then taxied over the rough runway with its gravel-filled bomb holes before coming to a stop beside the still-intact terminal. American soldiers occupied the building—"steel helmets, rifles, and khaki uniforms in the vestibule, jeeps and trucks parked all around outside."

One of those soldiers was Colonel George Gifford, a United States Marine who spoke fluent German and would act as Lindbergh's military escort. After introducing himself, Gifford led his guest to their jeep. Where did Charles want to go first? he asked. He expected Charles to say Dachau. The infamous concentration camp was just a few miles away and had become the place every GI and visiting dignitary went to see. The place, warned Gifford, was hard to take, but provided a clear reason for the fight.

"I prefer to miss Dachau," replied Charles. Instead, he wanted to see the Eagle's Nest, Hitler's former headquarters at Berchtesgaden in the Bavarian Alps.

With Gifford at the wheel, they drove along streets lined with mounds of rubble that had been pushed to the side to let traffic through. Block after block, Charles saw nothing but fallen walls, gutted interiors, collapsed ceilings. As they left the city, ruined buildings gave way to the burned and wrecked carcasses of German cars and trucks, hundreds of them, that had been strafed by low-flying Allied aircraft and bulldozed off the road as American troops advanced. Bomb craters dotted the surrounding hillside, and pine forests stood splintered and shattered. After turning up a winding, stone-paved road, they climbed into the mountains, around wreckage and rubble, until they arrived at the place where Hitler had lived, worked, and held many of his conferences.

Charles found himself standing in the Führer's debris-strewn office. Gazing out the picture window, with its shattered glass, to the most beautiful mountain view he'd ever seen, Charles imagined "the man Hitler, now the myth Hitler." Just a few weeks earlier, "he was here where I am standing, looking through that window, realizing the collapse of his dreams, still struggling desperately against overwhelming odds."

Charles couldn't grasp it. "Hitler, a man who controlled such power, who might have turned it to human good, who used it to such resulting evil: the best of his country dead; the cities destroyed;

the population homeless and hungry; Germany overrun by . . . the armies of Soviet Russia," he wrote in his journal later that day.

It was mild condemnation for a man who'd brought about the murder of some six million Jewish people, as well as countless others. But it was the closest Charles ever came to admitting he'd been wrong about Germany's dictator.

For the next five weeks, Charles toured the country, inspecting Nazi engine works, plane factories, and research facilities. More importantly, he searched out the men who'd headed these projects and recruited them to work for the United States government. With promises of expunged war crime records and lucrative jobs, Charles helped bring hundreds of former Nazi scientists and their families to America to assist in the development of the country's rocket and missile program. He particularly relished this part of the job, since every recruit meant one less scientist for the Soviets' rocket program.

As he "confiscated documents, interrogated engineers and scientists, and picked [his] way through litter in looted laboratories," Charles grew increasingly outraged at American treatment of the conquered Germans. At every turn, he saw old people hunting for scraps of food in army garbage pails, displaced families straggling along roadsides with carts and bundles, hungry children hanging around the Red Cross stand for bites of uneaten food. And while he conceded that Hitler and the Nazis had caused it, he placed most of the blame for their current misery on "well-fed [Americans]" who "stuffed themselves" while the German people suffered. "What right have we to damn the Nazi . . . while we carry on with such callousness and hatred in our hearts." It made him feel ashamed, he wrote in his journal. "We in America are supposed to stand for different things."

One morning, he and Gifford stopped to ask directions from a group of young German soldiers. In uniform but disarmed, they were plodding along a ruined road, apparently returning home from the war. They gave the Americans directions as best they could, "showing no trace of hatred or resentment, or of being whipped in battle," noted Charles. "They looked like farmers' sons." He would have given them a ride if it hadn't been against army regulations. Instead, he settled for sharing his rations.

But a few days later, when American officers asked him and Gifford to drive a Russian captain fifteen miles to Allied headquarters in Heidelberg, Charles balked. He didn't "like [the Russian's] face" or "the way he look[ed] at me." Convinced the officer was "capable of anything," Charles kept his right hand under his coat and on his gun. The exhausted captain soon fell asleep, but Charles remained on guard until they reached their destination.

THE MOUSERY

Toward the middle of June, Charles headed to Nordhausen in the Harz Mountains. He'd read reports of a V-2 rocket factory that had been built underground in a hill to avoid Allied bombing.

It was a pleasant drive. He and his new translator, Lieutenant E. H. Uellendahl, had spotted some canaries in the boughs of trees and stopped to taste the first strawberries of the season. As they neared the factory, however, they realized they could not reach its entrance without driving through the Dora-Mittelbau concentration camp.

Although American troops had liberated the camp in early April, some prisoners remained behind because they had nowhere else to go. Their families had been killed, their homes confiscated, their villages reduced to rubble. They'd been joined by hundreds of other newly released and homeless prisoners of the Nazis, mostly Russians, Poles, and Czechs. Camping out in the crude wooden barracks, they lived in overcrowded, squalid conditions.

As Charles rode through the camp, he noted that their clothes were filthy but "adequate for the season." And judging from their "faces and bodies," he determined that they were "not badly fed." But their odor! It assailed Charles's nostrils. And it pricked at his memory. Where had he smelled it before?

On the mountainside above the camp, the Americans noticed a "low, small, factory-like building with a brick smoke stack." None of their government reports had mentioned this structure. They turned, then headed up the hill to investigate.

The doors of the building stood wide open. The rodent smell was here, too, even stronger. The men stepped inside. On the concrete floor lay a corpse, carelessly covered with canvas. In another room stood two large cremation furnaces, "the steel stretchers for holding the bodies sticking out through the open doors," said Charles.

He'd heard the reports about the German atrocities, horrors beyond imagining. But he hadn't really believed them. How could something that evil be true? He'd put the worst rumors down as anti-German propaganda spread by the Jewish-controlled press.

But here, before his eyes, was terrible, terrible proof. "How could any reward in national progress even faintly justify [this]?" he asked himself in the pages of his journal.

A "man" wearing a prison costume shuffled into the room. "No," Charles corrected himself, "a boy." The uniform bagged around him. And as the boy moved closer, Charles saw he was a walking skeleton, "arms so thin that it seem[ed] only the skin is left to cover them."

Speaking in German, with Uellendahl translating, the boy told them he was seventeen and that he'd been at the camp for three years. He led them outside to what was once an oblong pit, eight feet long, six feet wide, and six feet deep. It was one of several such pits, each heaped with ash.

"Twenty-five thousand in a year and a half," the boy said. "And from each one there is only so much." He cupped his hands to show the measure. Then he walked over to a mound of ash yet to be dumped into the pit. Reaching inside, he pulled out something. Charles recognized it. It was a knee joint.

Charles remembered. The rodentlike smell that hung so heavily about the Nazi victims had also hung heavily in a place of science, *his* place of science, the laboratory where he'd worked beside Dr. Carrel. It was the smell of the mousery. The mousery—that living experiment in survival of the fittest—where the strong had dominated the weak through intimidation, violence, and death. He had believed it "represented real life and the struggle for existence," showed how "superior civilizations developed." But had it represented the truth?

A "strange sort of disturbance" came over him. Was science to blame for this abomination? Ever since his almost-fatal test flight at Willow Creek he'd been questioning its place in civilization. Was gaining knowledge for scientific power without considering deeper human values what had destroyed Germany? "The Germans had lost their balance," he decided. "Instead of balancing science with other fields of wisdom, they had let it dominate them, turned it loose in war and conquest. In their search for materialistic power, they had set science up as their god, and science had destroyed them."

For days . . . weeks . . . months after his return from Germany, Charles wrestled with these thoughts. Before the war, he'd regarded the fear of knowledge as ignorant superstition. But now he recalled his Bible reading. Hadn't God warned Adam and Eve not to eat from the tree of knowledge, for they would surely die? In Germany, he claimed, "he saw the danger [scientific] truth could bring. . . . [Scientific] truth unguided by moral principles . . . [and] unbalanced by the truths of religion." Germany's biggest mistake, he concluded, was having forgotten to bring together "the power of [its] science with the spiritual truths of [its] God."

This explanation—a sort of cloudy mysticism—was far more palatable to Charles than the alternative: admitting his own culpability. He had, after all, been committed to the idea of race betterment and had advocated for the propagation of "superior genetic material." He believed in the intrinsically racist theories of survival of the fittest and natural selection as they applied to human beings, and had stared with both fascination and awe into Dr. Carrel's mousery. Like scientists in Nazi Germany, he'd spent thousands of hours in the laboratory trying to scientifically advance the future of the white race. By discovering the key to immortality, he'd hoped to ensure the continued dominance of the "civilization-building white elite" over "faster-breeding racial inferiors."

And Charles Lindbergh was never one for self-doubt. He refused to see the connection between his own convictions and those of the Nazis. He could not acknowledge how his public admiration and support of the Third Reich might have contributed to the horrors of Dora-Mittelbau. He wasn't to blame. Science was. Its power, he claimed, had "hypnotized" him. It had forced him to "work for the idol of science" and "worship at its Godless temple."

His experience at the concentration camp drastically changed his views toward scientific advancement. But it did not seem to alter his opinions regarding race betterment. While much of the world had rejected eugenics after learning about the gruesome horrors involved in the Nazis' pursuit of a pure Aryan race, Charles remained a staunch defender of it. For the rest of his life he gave time and money to the American Eugenics Society. He even served as the organization's director from 1955 to 1959. And in 1967 he wrote to the secretary of AES, "I believe the simplest knowledge of eugenics, if taught in schools, would have a tremendous long-term effect."

〰️

On August 6, 1945, the first of two atomic bombs was dropped on Japan. By the fifteenth, war in the Pacific had ended, and Charles's ruminations about God and science had reached a crisis point. After realizing with sickening dismay that a plane—his life's work—had been the delivery system for mass killing, he wrote, "With the key to science, man has turned loose forces he cannot re-imprison." He began to obsess about intercontinental rockets armed with atomic warheads. What would keep mankind from blowing itself up?

Charles answered this question in a speech to the Washington, DC, Aero Club later that year, which he would expand into a little book called *Of Flight and Life,* published in 1948. He insisted that a moral force must take possession of nuclear power—and this force must follow "Christian ideals." Incredibly, the man who'd refused to have Bible verses read at his wedding was now advocating the formation of a worldwide organization possessing overwhelming military might but guided by Christian principles.

His idea sprang from the debate then raging about the creation of a new international body, the United Nations, to forge a lasting world peace. Of course, Charles was all for world peace; he just didn't agree with the idea of giving equal control to Russia, China, or India. "Leadership would pass from our western peoples, who have built this civilization, to the great masses of Asia," he said. "The high birth-rates of ignorance would outvote the low birth-rates of education, and the weapon of western science, from aircraft to atomic bomb, would be controlled by . . . the East." No, it should be America with its Christian morality that wielded world power. This, he argued, was the only way to save Western civilization from atomic annihilation. He also criticized the war trials just beginning at Nuremberg for their "vengeance" against Nazi perpetrators of the Holocaust.

The next morning, the press excoriated him. "[Charles Lindbergh] is saddened by the lack of Christian values in the postwar world as shown by . . . 'the court trials of our conquered enemies,' and in 'our attitude toward the famine-stricken peoples we have defeated,'" wrote the *New Republic.* "There is no similar concern for the victims of Nazism."

This criticism frustrated Charles. Didn't they see that universal equality among the world's peoples would be a "doctrine of death" for America? It was not "equality" but "quality" that mattered as Western civilization faced the new, postwar atomic world. And he seemed to find no contradiction between his idea of a "master race" and the teachings of Jesus Christ.

CHAPTER THIRTY-TWO

TOGETHER, YET APART

FATHER AT HOME

In 1946, Charles and Anne purchased a permanent home—their first since the Hopewell house. Located on Long Island Sound in Scott's Cove near Darien, Connecticut, it had nine bedrooms, six and a half bathrooms, and plenty of space for the family, which had grown in October 1945 with the birth of their second daughter, Reeve.

Anne envisioned them a settled family at last. No more moving every few years, no more glaring national spotlight. She and Charles would be together, peaceful, walking through the birch grove or open fields. He'd be home for good.

But Charles was incapable of staying still for long. It was as if he'd bought the house as a safe place to stow his family while he left and returned . . . left and returned . . . left and returned. Sometimes he didn't even come home for Christmas.

He packed his postwar schedule. He took a consultant job with Pan American World Airways and remained on constant call for various surveys and reports to the army. He became a special adviser to the chief of staff of the United States Army Air Forces, renamed from the earlier Army Air Corps and now its own separate branch of the military. He visited and reported on air bases in Alaska, Japan, Europe, and the Philippines. He flew the newest American jet fighters and accompanied bomber missions on polar flights. And he continued to adapt new equipment for commercial airlines.

His family never knew when or where he was going. They didn't know how long he'd be away, or even when he'd be returning. For the first hours after Father's leaving—they never called him Dad—there was a "deflated feeling in [the] house, as if the air had been let out of all its tires," recalled Reeve.

Soon, though, there came "a sense of release, an exhalation of long-held family breath." The house relaxed and grew noisy again. Ansy would play her records loudly. Scott and Land ran in and out, tracking mud and sneaking snakes and turtles into the house. Jon, now a teenager, spent hours out on his dinghy, setting up lines of lobster pots, while Reeve squished barefoot through the mud around the cove. At dinnertime, the children talked over each other, making jokes, sharing their day, teasing, laughing. Anne sat, listening for the most part. Charles's absences left her depressed, and little cheered her. Still, the children's antics amused her. She was not a stern disciplinarian. Certainly, the children followed a routine—they went to school and basketball practice or music lessons. They did their homework, brushed their teeth, had regular bedtimes. But Anne didn't lecture them if they left the rake out under the tree overnight or used a bath towel instead of a beach towel to go swimming.

Then Charles would walk through the front door, and everything "snapped . . . [to] military alertness." His presence sent waves of tension through the house. The boys would nervously shake his hand. The girls would hug him—but not too exuberantly. If they showed too much affection—giggling, hopping, flinging their arms around his neck—he would stop them with a stern "Now, now! Watch out for my hat!" He'd look around to make sure his house was shipshape.

He made sure his children were, too. That was why he made a checklist for each of them. Not long after his arrival, he would call them one by one into his study. Sometimes he simply wanted to chastise them for eating cookies or reading comic books, neither of which he allowed in the house. Other times, he felt they needed a lecture. His favorite topics were "Freedom and Responsibility," "Instinct and Intellect," and, of course, "Downfall of Civilization." When they were older he held forth about the importance of choosing a genetically appropriate mate. He forbade gum chewing, preached including fiber in their diets, and frequently said, "Don't . . . don't do this and don't do that."

He could be warm and playful. When he took his children for family hikes, the hidden "elves" never forgot to leave candies along the trail. He taught his children to climb trees, shoot, hike, and sail. When they were old enough, he taught them to drive. And on Saturdays, if he was home, he took them flying. In a single-engine, two-seat plane Charles rented (he no longer owned his own), he taught them to take off and land, dip and bank. But only Jon shared his enthusiasm. The others found flying loud, stomach-churning, and monotonous. Charles, however, insisted they take part in these family activities, even if they didn't want to. If his children grumbled, he pulled rank. "This is not a democracy," he liked to say. "It's a non-benevolent dictatorship."

Dinner was a serious occasion. A typical topic was nuclear war and what to do in case of one. Don't go to New York City, he warned. A big city would be a target. And don't drink the water, because the Soviets were sure to poison it.

Usually the children replied dutifully, "Yes, Father."

One day, while the rest of the family was having lunch, Reeve and Ansy pulled open the heavy front door to find a thin young man standing on the threshold. Reeve didn't hear what he said, but Ansy did. Crying out with fear, she slammed the door in the stranger's face.

Charles came on the run, his face tight and grim. What was the matter?

Ansy repeated what the stranger had said, and Charles's expression softened. Telling his daughters to stay put, he opened the door and stepped outside. To Reeve's amazement, he put his hand on the stranger's shoulder and, speaking gently, walked with him down the path. On Charles's face, Reeve recalled, was the same look of "open, loose-featured patience with which he approached nervous dogs or very small children. He didn't have the cold eyes and stern expression of the family disciplinarian. . . . Instead he looked the way I saw him look again once, years later . . . gazing quietly down upon a stray bird that had just flown at full speed into our kitchen windowpane, and lay stunned and twitching in my father's hand."

The young man, Reeve later learned, believed he was the Lindberghs' kidnapped baby. Through conspiracies and cover-ups, he'd been switched with another child and raised in the wrong family. But he was back now, he claimed. Charles's long-lost Buster.

His story came as a shock to the Lindbergh children. Not once had they heard their parents discuss the kidnapping. And while Anne sometimes talked about their first, lost child, Charles never did. Of course, the stranger's story wasn't true. In fact, over the years, more than a dozen such "pretenders," as Ansy came to call them, would make similar claims. Their stories must have caused Charles immeasurable pain. And yet he met their delusions with compassion, speaking with them logically, reasonably, and at length. He did so, believed Reeve, for his firstborn, his namesake. His little boy had not been forgotten. He was tenderly tucked away in his father's memories.

Inevitably, after being home for three or four days, Charles would pull out the calfskin briefcase he used as luggage. Then, he'd drop a comb, razor, and toothbrush into one of his socks, knot it, and put it in the pocket of his gray pinstripe suit. Into the briefcase went the other sock, a clean shirt, and underwear—he always traveled light. Another round of handshakes. Another round of hugs. Then he walked out the door again, "and left us [children] in peace," recalled Reeve.

And it would begin again, the waiting. Where was Father going? How long would he be gone? When would he be back?

ANNE ALONE

Charles had abandoned his faithful crewmate, leaving Anne feeling depressed and overwhelmed. Sometimes, she cried the whole day.

In hopes of finding solace, she retreated to her writing trailer behind the house. He'd installed it there as both encouragement and proof of his belief in her writing. But sometimes when she sat in it, her books and papers and pencils spread across the table, she felt guilty. She didn't feel like she was writing anything worthy. Since the move to Connecticut, she'd given up on two novels and stopped creating poetry.

It wasn't just because the children took up so much time and energy. She felt frozen with panic every time she tried to write something other than a diary entry or letter. She couldn't tell Charles this, though. She knew he'd just scold her for giving in to self-pity and not buckling down. "Will I ever feel creative again? With hands full?" she asked herself.

THE SPIRIT OF ST. LOUIS

Sometime in 1950, Charles handed Anne a manuscript. His manuscript. He'd been working on it everywhere—in planes, on ships, in taxis, in Papua New Guinea, in the Florida Keys, in Munich and Darien. For fourteen years it had been in the making—a memoir covering the first twenty-five years of his life, up to the end of his 1927 trans-Atlantic flight. It was ground he'd covered before in *We*, but he'd never been proud of that book. Since its publication, he'd longed to create a better, more accurate version. And so he'd written and rewritten his story—six drafts—without sharing a word of it with anyone. Until now. He looked forward to Anne's comments and suggestions.

Anger shot through her. All this time, as she'd been coping with the children with little time for "solitude [and] creative thinking," he had been writing. "*He* was being creative in these years; *I* was not—at least not in a way I could show." She felt he'd invaded her field, "the only field I had of my own." And after reading the manuscript, she recognized, with a flash of jealousy, that his book was brilliant.

Could he have written it without her? She believed not. "I know that he would not have told it—could not have told it that way if he had not married me. Twenty years of living with me have gone into that book—before the man who said to me when we were engaged: 'You like to *write* books?' (astonished and curiously condescending) 'I like to *live* them'—before that man absorbed my values about the written word."

But she pushed aside her feelings. "Keep your style, stay in character," she advised him. "'Your own style' is the style in which you speak. Imagine you are speaking to me, not writing at all."

When finished, the book—told almost entirely in the present tense—gave a sense of suspense to the flight that compelled readers—*lots* of readers.

Published in 1953, *The Spirit of St. Louis* became a huge success, selling hundreds of thousands of copies in its first year. Critics roundly praised it as a masterpiece and an American classic. "We have known Lindbergh the aviator, Lindbergh the scientist, and Lindbergh the man of action, but we had not known Lindbergh the artful rememberer of things past," raved the *New Yorker*. To both Charles's and Anne's amazement, the following spring the book won the Pulitzer Prize for biography.

"Boom days are here again," wrote Anne with a touch of sarcasm. "The Great Man—the Great Epic—the Great Author etc., etc. I am living in the aura of 1929 again. Only I am different. . . ."

GIFT FROM THE SEA

By 1954, Anne was writing again. Slowly, she'd come to grips with the marriage Charles had dictated—the not knowing, not talking, not sharing—and was rebuilding herself.

She did it on the page. "I cannot see what I have gone through until I write it down," she said. "I am blind without a pencil." Examining the stages of her life—wife, pilot, mother, victim of tragedy—she compared them with the different types of seashells she found on Captiva Island, Florida (a place she'd begun visiting in the 1940s). The Moon Shell. The Double Sunrise. The Argonauta.

It felt like the most courageous thing she'd ever done, this honest reflection of her life and marriage. And when she finished, she discovered she'd found her voice not only as an author, but also as a wife. After almost twenty-six years of marriage, she could separate herself from Charles. She no longer saw herself through his eyes, but through her own. Of course, that did not mean she'd stopped loving him, but she now understood she didn't have to give her life over to him.

Gift from the Sea is what she called her reflections. The book, published in 1955, touched a deep chord in women. Anne wrote honestly about the changing conditions of marriage and the "growing pains" of middle age. She sympathized with a woman's instinct to "spill herself away . . . the eternal nourisher of children, of men, of society." And she advised solitude as a way for women to rediscover their "inner spring." She encouraged them to find something "of one's own."

Her book became one of the greatest publication successes of the twentieth century, selling six hundred thousand copies in hardback that same year and remaining on the *New York Times* bestseller list for eighty weeks.

CHAPTER THIRTY-THREE

SORROWS AND SECRETS

DOUBLE LOSS

On September 7, 1954, after a decade of suffering from Parkinson's disease, Evangeline Lindbergh died at the age of seventy-eight. After hearing the news, Charles flew immediately to Detroit. Anne and the children, however, did not arrive for another four days. In that time, Charles and "Brother" struggled with details of Evangeline's funeral, choosing a casket and deciding on a gravesite.

Charles must have also struggled with his emotions, although he left no record of them. Throughout his mother's illness, he'd visited often. Toward the end of her life—bedridden, her voice weak and slurred—she still brightened at the sight of her son. A look would pass between them as Charles sat beside her in the old, dark and gloomy house—a look "so loving" that even eight-year-old Reeve could "feel the nature of it." Evangeline would smile, "the only time I can remember seeing any expression on her face at all," said Reeve. Then she'd try to speak. Only Charles understood her, "or pretended to."

The arrival of his family was a relief. Anne chose her mother-in-law's dress and picked out the Psalms to be read at her simple funeral service. They buried Evangeline quietly, without press, in an old country graveyard among her Land and Lodge kin.

Two months later, Anne and the children (Charles was traveling) went to Next Day Hill for Thanksgiving. Betty Morrow, lively as always at eighty-one, wore red to dinner and held a contest to see which of her grandchildren could guess the weight of the turkey. After the meal, Reeve, who'd recently celebrated her ninth birthday, put on her tutu and danced for everyone while fourteen-year-old Ansy reluctantly played her flute. The next morning, Friday, twelve-year-old Scott took a walk with his grandma Bee into the garden to cut the last of the roses. They talked about Christmas presents.

On Saturday, Betty put her hand to her head and said she felt odd. By the time the doctor arrived, she'd lost her speech and was partially paralyzed. A stroke, her physician diagnosed. He hoped she'd improve with time. But ten days later she suffered a second stroke and sank into a coma. For the next seven weeks, Anne stayed with her mother, holding her hand and reading her poetry, until Betty's death on January 24, 1955.

Exhausted and grieving, Anne sat down to write Charles with the news. She had no idea where he was or how to contact him. Instead, she sent the letter to his attention in care of the Pan Am office. She hoped it would reach him sooner rather than later.

Somehow, it did. Charles arrived home from Europe just in time for Betty's funeral.

SECRET FAMILIES, SECRET LIVES

In March 1958, on one of his numerous trips to Europe, Charles met the dark-haired Hesshaimer sisters—Brigitte and Marietta. It was at a small gathering in a Munich apartment, where he'd gone with his private secretary and translator, Valeska. Everyone at the get-together, of course, knew Valeska was also his girlfriend. The two had been having an affair for the past three years. But that didn't stop the sisters from admiring him. Brigitte noticed "his way of speaking, his beautiful hands, his smile . . . and the dimple on his chin."

Charles noticed her, too. And even though he'd come with his girlfriend, he asked Brigitte to show him around the city. She agreed, and two days later they spent the afternoon together. By dinnertime, he made a sudden confession. He loved her. The couple hurried back to her apartment. It was the start of a seventeen-year relationship that ended only with Charles's death.

Together, he and Brigitte had three children—Dyrk, born in 1958; Astrid, born in 1960; and David, born in 1967.

But that did not mean Charles gave up his relationship with Valeska. Instead, he started a third family with her, fathering a son in 1959 and a daughter in 1961. (Their identities, including Valeska's last name, remain secret.)

Incredibly, he also began a love affair with Brigitte's sister, Marietta. In 1962, Vago was born to them, followed by Christophe in 1967.

The secret families—two living in Germany and one (Marietta's) in Switzerland—knew about each other. They also knew about Charles's wife and five children in the United States. But Anne knew nothing. And Charles worked hard to keep it that way. Reminding the women of the need for "utmost secrecy," he supported them financially by sending large sums of cash rather than checks that could be easily traced. And he had them write to him at a post office box in Connecticut that he changed frequently.

He visited his families four times a year for a few days each time. Like his American children, they never knew when he might turn up. Sometimes he arrived only to have to leave immediately because of what he claimed was unexpected business. What did the children think their father did? Charles concocted a story with which their mothers went along. His name, he told them, was Careu Kent and he was a much-traveled American author, geologist, and ecologist. But *that* was nobody's business, he stressed. They were not to talk about him to anybody. If they did, he would never come back.

The children didn't whisper a word.

When Father visited, they went on outings and played games. He told them animal stories and whisked up omelets for breakfast. The houses were lively.

Even when he was away, they knew he cared about them. Hadn't he built houses for both Brigitte's and Marietta's family? Didn't he typically end all his letters with "my love to you and the children, all I can send"? Of course, he signed only his first initial, "C," and he wrote carefully, committing nothing to paper that would give away his identity should the letter fall into the wrong hands.

And it worked. All of it. No one ever knew Charles had three secret families. Even after his death, the women kept mum. It was Astrid, grown and searching for books written by her father, Careu Kent, who stumbled onto the truth. She showed a family photograph of him to a friend, who recognized him.

Was Charles Lindbergh her father? Astrid asked Brigitte, her mother.

Brigitte admitted he was but refused to let Astrid share the truth or her letters from him (150 in all) until after her death. Not until 2005 did Astrid and her brothers let others in on the secret, when DNA conclusively proved their parentage.

The news stunned those who'd known Charles. Three secret families? Seven more children? It seemed inconsistent with the chilly, exacting man who found physical displays of emotion embarrassing. Theories abounded as to why he did it. A eugenicist to the end, perhaps he wanted to spread what he believed was his superior genetic material. Or maybe it had something to do with his lifelong obsession with immortality. The only person who knew the truth, of course, was Charles, and he left no inkling. Said his daughter Reeve, "I don't know why he lived this way, and I don't think I will ever know, but what it means to me is that every intimate human connection my father had during his later years was fractured by secrecy."

AN AFRICAN STATE OF MIND

In 1962, Charles traveled to Kenya. "The vibrancy of nature in the wild, the stark rhythms of life and death, hunger and thirst" thrilled him, he wrote. Topi buck battling topi buck. A lioness sinking her teeth into the black-and-white-striped throat of a zebra. Hyenas fighting over a warthog carcass.

Even more thrilling were the weeks he spent in a Masai village. The freedom of these people, who lived off the land without schedules or technology, forced him to recognize the complications of his own life. He'd always thought of himself as a free man. But was he, really?

With the sun on his face and dust on his boots, in the prick of thorns and amid the yelling of hyenas and the bark of zebras, the sixty-year-old had yet another epiphany. At long last, he claimed, he understood the purpose of life. The man who'd spent so much of his time asking why people had to die now wrote, "When I watch wild animals on an African plain, my civilized [methods] of measuring time give way to a timeless vision in which life embraces the necessity of death in a miraculous plan of existence."

Death, he realized, *was* life. Another stage of existence. The "eternal life for which men during centuries have sought so blindly, not realizing that they had it as a birthright."

He now saw his experiments with Dr. Carrel as tampering. In trying to overcome death and maintain life artificially, they'd been dangerously meddling with something beyond their comprehension. Their scientific success would have separated man from his God-given right to immortality. "Only by dying," he concluded, "can we continue living."

Charles had come full circle. As a child, he'd drawn comfort and inspiration from the natural world. Now, recognizing that his latest insight had sprung from the wilderness, he resolved to help protect the world's natural places. "I did so casually," he later told a reporter.

After reading in the *New York Times* about the recent formation of the American chapter of the Switzerland-based World Wildlife Federation, he telephoned the organization's chairman, Ira Gabrielson, and offered to "build up conservation interest all over the world." Using his fame to get into the offices and boardrooms of political and business leaders, he spoke with them directly about saving endangered wildlife and habitats. Charles, who could be charming when he wanted to be, scored some big successes. He persuaded Indonesian officials to provide some protections for the Javanese rhino, and he lobbied President Ferdinand Marcos of the Philippines to create preserves for both the endangered monkey-eating eagle and the tamarau, a wild buffalo native to the island. He even sat down with businessmen in Peru to discuss protections for humpback and blue whales being caught off the coast of that country. So convincing was Charles, the board of directors decided to end the harpooning of endangered whales in that region.

As the 1960s gave way to the 1970s, Charles had cut down on his army and Pan Am commitments. But his appearances on behalf of the World Wildlife Federation (and other conservation groups) multiplied. The man who'd given up speaking after the war now returned to the podium on behalf of the bald eagle, the golden lion tamarin, the black rhino. He didn't claim to be an expert on conservation: "I just tell [people] how important it is," he said. Willingly, he gave interviews to newspapers and magazines. He lent his name to fundraising efforts. And he surprised people when he, the most famous aviator of the twentieth century, said, "I realized that if I had to choose, I would rather have birds than airplanes."

ONE LAST CHECKLIST

On a sparkling July afternoon in 1974, Charles lay naked in the sun on the rocks at Scott's Cove. The seventy-two-year-old felt content as he gazed up at the sky. He'd just returned to Connecticut after a string of tests and biopsies. His cancer was spreading.

Cancer. No one but Anne knew he had it. He'd sworn her to secrecy after he'd been diagnosed with lymphoma the previous October. But radiation therapy had caused him to drop thirty pounds from his lean frame, and for the first time he looked his age. Worried, his children had asked after his health. It was a virus he'd picked up on his travels, he'd told them. Nothing serious.

Still, they could see it was serious enough for him to return to living with Anne. It was the first time the couple had lived together for an extended period in decades. She'd been at his side when he grew anemic and suffered through a case of the shingles, and then a bout of the flu.

Just this past month, he'd spiked such a high fever he'd been hospitalized. Doctors began blood transfusions and a course of chemotherapy. And his children learned the truth. He played down the seriousness of his disease, of course. There was no need to tell *all* his private medical details. But he had no illusions. Charles was dying, and he knew it.

Now he let the sun warm his skin and listened to surf and seagulls. He wasn't concerned about death anymore. He saw that it was "no longer an ending, but an opening."

Charles had intended to go to Switzerland in August. This would have taken him close to his other families, and he might have hoped to say goodbye in person. But after a new round of tests, doctors told him the cancer had spread. It would be impossible to travel.

He understood.

And he had one last checklist.

First, he telephoned his publisher, William Jovanovich. Could

Bill come to the hospital to discuss a project? When Jovanovich arrived that same day, Charles pointed to a brown leather bag on the floor. It was his autobiography—four hundred pages he'd been working on for decades. There were more pages, too, locked away at Yale University, where he'd been depositing his personal papers since 1940. Charles asked the publisher to take the bag home, read it, and decide whether it was good enough to be published.

Jovanovich read what Charles had given him that night, and the next day they drew up a contract. Charles left the shaping and editing of the material to his publisher. It would be published posthumously in 1978 under the title *Autobiography of Values*.

Next, he wrote his families in Europe. They knew about his cancer—he had told them weeks ago. Now he bade them farewell. His letter to Brigitte read:

> *Dear Brigitte:*
>> *My strength is leaving every day, the situation is serious. It's very difficult just for me to write.*
>>> *My love to you and the children, all I can send.*
>>> *C.*
>
> *P.S. You will be getting word from a bank in Geneva asking you to come and see them. Go as soon as possible and personally. Hold the utmost secrecy.*

He said goodbye to his American family, too. Grown now, Ansy and Scott both flew in from France. Reeve drove in from Vermont. Jon came from Seattle and Land from Montana. For the first time in a long while, they were all together.

Finally, Charles reviewed his will. After making a few changes to the fourteen-page document, he turned to Anne and stunned her by saying, "I want to go home—to Maui."

In 1970, he'd built an A-frame structure on a hundred acres of grassland near the remote village of Kipahulu on the Hawaiian island of Maui. The place did not have a telephone or electricity. Propane motors powered the appliances and kerosene provided lighting. This was where he wanted to die.

Impossible, his doctors replied. He'd never get there alive. En route, he'd have a hemorrhage or experience a heart attack. But Charles told them he'd made up his mind.

"But you're abandoning science!" exclaimed one physician.

"No," replied Charles, "science abandoned me."

On August 18, his stretcher was carried into the first-class section—reserved entirely for him and Anne—of a plane bound for Honolulu. There they transferred to an ambulance plane that took them to Maui.

He and Anne settled into a friend's guesthouse in Hana. Without electricity or phone, Charles's A-frame was out of the question. Under Charles's watchful eye, the doctor installed the oxygen equipment in his room. Always fond of machines, Charles tested out the pump, face mask, and pressure regulators before falling asleep to the sound of the surf.

But his checklist wasn't done. As with all his important ventures—the flight across the Atlantic, choosing a wife, searching for a lost son—he left no detail to chance. His grave would be dug in traditional Hawaiian style (he'd already chosen and purchased the site), blessed by a local holy man and lined in lava rock. His coffin would be handmade from local trees and lined with cotton sheets and an old blanket he'd once given his mother, and his corpse would be dressed in a well-worn pair of gray cotton pants and a khaki shirt (no belt or shoes). Wanting a natural burial, Charles insisted his body not go to a mortuary for embalming, but straight from his deathbed to his grave. There would be a brief graveside service but no eulogy. As for hymns, "the music is alright, but the words are corny," he told Anne. He settled on Hawaiian ones. "Then nobody will know what they mean." Last, he chose the design of a simple headstone. Below his name should be the dates and places of his birth and death, along with this passage from Psalms: "If I take the wings of the morning / And dwell in the uttermost parts of the sea."

When he wasn't going over his checklist, Charles reminisced with Anne and his sons (Ansy and Reeve had stayed behind in Connecticut, where they waited for updates) about his childhood and his early flying days. He talked about America First, too. "Don't let your mother spend a lot of time defending me," he said to Land.

One night Anne asked him what it felt like to be dying.

The most surprising part, he answered, was the realization that "death is so close all the time—it's right there next to you." But it didn't frighten him. "It's harder on you watching than it is on me."

On the night of August 25, his breathing became labored. His physician brought him a larger oxygen mask.

"Now, Doctor," asked Charles, "is the caliber of the oxygen tube really large enough to supply me with the oxygen I need?" Hours later, he reached toward the respirator to adjust the valve. Then his hand dropped and he lapsed into a coma.

Anne and Land stayed with him through the night. His wife held his hand. His son, knowing how much Charles disliked being touched, laid his hand on the blanket covering his father's foot.

The sun peeked above the horizon on the morning of the twenty-sixth. The sky turned pink. Charles breathed in.

"I am form and I am formless," reads the last paragraph of his *Autobiography of Values*. "I am life and I am matter, mortal and immortal . . . [and] the molecules of my being will return to the earth and the sky. They came from the stars. I am of the stars."

Charles Lindbergh released his last breath.

BIBLIOGRAPHY

The following source material shows the path I took to researching and writing this book. As much as possible, I've let Charles and Anne Lindbergh speak for themselves in all their beauty . . . and their occasional ugliness. I also stuck as close as possible to original sources, seeking out newspaper articles and unpublished memoirs, delving into hundreds of pages of FBI documents related to both Charles and the America First Committee, reading countless court transcripts, speeches, letters, and diaries, and scouring microfilm at libraries and archives.

I owe a debt of gratitude to the biographers who have gone before me. David M. Friedman's book *The Immortalists* was crucial to my understanding of Lindbergh and Carrel's relationship. Invaluable, too, was Max Wallace's *The American Axis*. It provided original insights into Lindbergh's ties to Nazi Germany, while Frederick Lewis Allen's classic *Only Yesterday: An Informal History of the 1920s,* written just after the 1929 stock market crash, helped me to capture the zeitgeist of 1920s America. Of course, any research into the aviator's life must include A. Scott Berg's *Lindbergh*. Because Berg was given rare access to the family papers, his Pulitzer Prize–winning work includes material not found anywhere else. It is a treasure trove.

PRIMARY SOURCES

BOOKS

Bruno, Harry A. *Wings over America: The Inside Story of American Aviation.* New York: Robert M. McBride & Co., 1942.

Carlson, John Ray. *Under Cover: My Life in the Nazi Underworld.* New York: E. P. Dutton & Co. Inc., 1943.

Carrel, Alexis. *Reflections on Life.* Translated by Antonia White. New York: Hawthorn Books, Inc., 1952.

Carrel, Alexis. *Man, the Unknown.* New York: Harper & Brothers, 1935.

Carrel, Alexis. *Man, the Unknown.* Middlesex, England: Pelican Books, 1948.

Condon, John F. *Jafsie Tells All! Revealing the Inside Story of the Lindbergh-Hauptmann Case.* New York: Jonathan Lee Publishing Corp., 1936.

Coolidge, Calvin. *Foundations of the Republic: Speeches and Addresses by Calvin Coolidge.* New York: Scribner, 1926.

Drey, Elmer, with William Slocum. *The Tax Dodgers.* New York: Greenberg Publishing Co., 1948.

Fitzgerald, F. Scott. "Echoes of the Jazz Age," *Complete Works of F. Scott Fitzgerald.* Hastings, East Sussex: Delphi Classics, Series 2, 2015.

Keyhoe, Donald. *Flying with Lindbergh.* New York: Grosset & Dunlap, 1929.

Lindbergh, Anne Morrow. *Against Wind and Tide: Letters and Journals, 1947–1986.* New York: Pantheon Books, 2012.

Lindbergh, Anne Morrow. *Bring Me a Unicorn: Diaries and Letters of Anne Morrow Lindbergh, 1922–1928.* New York: Harcourt Brace Jovanovich, Inc., 1972.

Lindbergh, Anne Morrow. *The Flower and the Nettle: Diaries and Letters of Anne Morrow Lindbergh, 1936–1939.* New York: Harcourt Brace & Company, 1976.

Lindbergh, Anne Morrow. *Gift from the Sea: An Answer to the Conflicts in Our Lives.* New York: Pantheon, 1955.

Lindbergh, Anne Morrow. *Hour of Gold, Hour of Lead: Diaries and Letters of Anne Morrow Lindbergh, 1929–1932.* New York: Harcourt Brace Jovanovich, Publishers, 1973.

Lindbergh, Anne Morrow. *Locked Rooms and Open Doors: Diaries and Letters of Anne Morrow Lindbergh, 1933–1935.* New York: Harcourt Brace & Company, 1974.

Lindbergh, Anne Morrow. *War Within and Without: Diaries of Anne Morrow Lindbergh, 1939–1944.* New York: Harcourt Brace Jovanovich, 1980.

Lindbergh, Anne Morrow. *The Wave of the Future: A Confession of Faith.* Harcourt Brace & Co., 1940.

Lindbergh, Charles A. *Autobiography of Values.* New York: Harcourt Brace Jovanovich, 1977.

Lindbergh, Charles A. *Boyhood on the Upper Mississippi: A Reminiscent Letter.* St. Paul: Minnesota Historical Society, 1972.

Lindbergh, Charles A. *Of Flight and Life.* New York: Charles Scribner's Sons, 1948.

Lindbergh, Charles A. *The Spirit of St. Louis.* New York: Scribner, 2003.

Lindbergh, Charles A. *The Wartime Journals of Charles A. Lindbergh.* New York: Harcourt Brace Jovanovich, Inc., 1970.

Lindbergh, Charles A. *"WE."* New York: G. P. Putnam's Sons, 1927.

Lindbergh, Reeve. *Under a Wing: A Memoir.* New York: Simon & Schuster, 1998.
Newton, James. *Uncommon Friends: Life with Thomas Edison, Henry Ford, Harvey Firestone, Alexis Carrel & Charles Lindbergh.* New York: Harcourt, Inc., 1987.
Nicolson, Harold. *The Harold Nicolson Diaries 1907–1964.* Edited by Nigel Nicolson. London: Phoenix Books, 2004.
Smith, Truman, Col. USA (ret.). *Berlin Report: The Memoirs and Reports of Truman Smith.* Edited by Robert Hesse. Stanford, CA: Hoover Institution Press, 1984.
Whipple, Sidney B. *The Lindbergh Crime.* New York: Blue Ribbon Books, 1935.

MAGAZINE ARTICLES

Butterfield, Roger. "Lindbergh: A Stubborn Young Man of Strange Ideas Becomes a Leader of Wartime Opposition." *Life.* August 11, 1941.
Calhoun, Fill. "How Isolationist Is the Midwest?" *Life.* December 1, 1941.
Fulton, John F. "Can Science Save Society?" *Saturday Review.* September 21, 1935.
Gill, Brendan. "The Doom of Heroes." *The New Yorker.* September 19, 1953.
Lindbergh, Charles A. "Aviation, Geography and Race." *Reader's Digest.* November 1939.
Lindbergh, Charles A. "What Substitute for War?" *Atlantic Monthly.* March 1940.
"The Lindy Hop." *Life.* August 23, 1943.
Long, J. C. "Dwight W. Morrow, the End of an Era." *Scribner's Magazine.* September 1935.
Lyman, Lauren D. "How Lindbergh Wrote a Book." *The Beehive.* Summer 1954.
Muller, H. J. "The Dominance of Economics over Eugenics." *The Scientific Monthly,* Vol. 37, July 7, 1933.
Post, August. "Columbus of the Air." *North American Review.* September–October 1927.
Walsh, Harry W., as told to E. Collins. "Hunt for the Kidnappers: The Inside Story of the Lindbergh Case." *Jersey Journal.* November 17, 1932.
White, E. B. Talk of the Town. *The New Yorker.* November 26, 1938.
Whittemore, Reed. "The Flyer and the Yahoos." *The New Republic.* October 3, 1970.

NEWSPAPER ARTICLES

THE NEW YORK TIMES
"Flight to Paris Lures Noted Pilots of the Air." March 20, 1927.
"Wife Betrays Paramour." March 22, 1927.
"May Start Tomorrow." May 13, 1927.
"40,000 Join in Prayer That Lindbergh Wins." May 21, 1927.
"Mother of Flier Sure He Will Win." May 21, 1927.
"Other Flyers Wish Lindbergh All Luck." May 21, 1927.
"Lindbergh Talks to Mother by Phone." May 22, 1927.
"Shaves Himself While Sitting Atop Flagpole." June 19, 1927.
"Kidnapping Holds First Place on Radio." March 4, 1932.
"Father on Impulse Looks at Dead Son." May 14, 1932.
"Five Men and Woman Believed Identified as Slayers of Baby." May 16, 1932.
"Second Son Is Born to the Lindberghs at the Morrow Home in Englewood." August 17, 1932.
"Nazi Convicted of World Crimes by 20,000 in Rally." March 8, 1934.

"Colonel and Mrs. Lindbergh on Stand." January 4, 1935.

"Testimony by Lindbergh on Second Day on Stand." January 5, 1935.

"Hauptmann Admits Lying and Says Wilentz Lies Too; Still Protests Innocence." January 29, 1935.

"Hauptmann's Guilt Overwhelmingly Proved, Declared Hauck for Prosecution." February 12, 1935.

"Carrel, Lindbergh Develop Device to Keep Organs Alive Outside Body." June 21, 1935.

"Everybody Has Telepathic Powers, Dr. Carrel Says After Research." September 18, 1935.

Lyman, Lauren D. "Lindbergh Family Sails for England to Seek a Safe, Secluded Residence; Threats on Son's Life Force Decision." December 23, 1935.

"Hoffman Defends Granting Reprieve." January 18, 1936.

"Lindbergh Ends Stay in Germany." August 3, 1936.

"Lindbergh Shows the Robot Heart." August 12, 1936.

"Lindbergh Said to Plan to Move to Berlin." November 16, 1938.

Krock, Arthur. "The Invaluable Contribution of Colonel Lindbergh." February 1, 1939.

"Carrel Explains Mechanical Heart." May 16, 1939.

"British Host Gives Lindbergh Excuse." October 22, 1939.

"British Seeks Another A.E.F., Lindbergh Tells 10,000 Here." April 24, 1941.

"President Defines Lindbergh's Niche." April 26, 1941.

"Lindbergh Joins Wheeler Plea to U.S. to Shun War." May 24, 1941.

"Lindbergh Views Hotly Assailed." August 8, 1941.

"Text of Lindbergh's Address at America First Rally in Madison Square Garden." October 31, 1941.

"Dr. Alexis Carrel Dies at Age 71." November 5, 1944.

Whitman, Alden. "Lindbergh Traveling Widely as Conservationist." June 23, 1969.

OTHER NEWSPAPERS

"Red Hot Cuties of Atlantic City." *New York Daily News.* August 15, 1925.

"I Know Who Killed My Brother." *New York Daily News.* October 16, 1926.

"Colonel Expresses Doubt to Admiral Burrage as Escort Comes." *Washington Post.* June 11, 1927.

"Anne Morrow Lindbergh Rides 'The Wave of the Future.'" *Columbus Daily Spectator.* January 19, 1941.

McNamee, Graham. "Lindbergh's Homecoming," Discography of American Historical Recordings, UC Santa Barbara, 2019.

SPEECHES

Churchill, Winston. "Blood, Toil, Tears and Sweat." International Churchill Society. winstonchurchill.org/resources/speeches/1940-the-finest-hour/blood-toil-tears-and-sweat-2.

Coolidge, Calvin. "Lindbergh: Welcoming Home Speech." June 11, 1927. coolidgefoundation.org/resources/speeches-as-president-1923-1929-8.

King George VI of Great Britain. "There May Be Days Ahead." Radio address, September 3, 1939. *Vital Speeches of the Day,* vol. 5, October 1939.

Lindbergh, Charles A. "Let Us Look to Our Own Defense." Radio address, September 15, 1939. *Vital Speeches of the Day,* vol. 5, October 1939.

Lindbergh, Charles A. "Our Policy Must Be Our Bond with Europe." Radio address, October 13, 1939. *Vital Speeches of the Day,* vol. 6, November 1939.

Lindbergh, Charles A. "Let Us Turn Our Eyes to Our Own Nation." Radio address, May 19, 1940. *Vital Speeches of the Day,* vol. 6, June 1940.

Lindbergh, Charles A. "Our Drift Toward War." Radio address, June 15, 1940. *Vital Speeches of the Day,* vol. 6, July 1940.

Lindbergh, Charles A. "We Are Weakening Our Defense Position." Delivered in New York City, April 23, 1941. *Vital Speeches of the Day,* vol. 7, May 1941.

Lindbergh, Charles A. "We Lack Leadership That Places America First." Delivered at Madison Square Garden, New York, rally, May 23, 1941. *Vital Speeches of the Day,* vol. 7, June 1941.

Lindbergh, Charles A. "Des Moines Speech: Delivered in Des Moines, Iowa, September 11, 1941." charleslindbergh.com/americanfirst/speech.asp.

Roosevelt, Franklin D. "Address to Congress Requesting a Declaration of War with Japan, December 8, 1941." Franklin D. Roosevelt Presidential Library and Museum, Hyde Park, NY. FDR Library, docs.fdrlibrary.marist.edu/tmirhdee.html.

OTHER DOCUMENTS

"America First Committee." FBI File, National Archives and Records Administration.

"First and second ransom notes." New Jersey State Archives. nj.gov/state/archives/images/slcsp001/SLCSP001_11.jpg.

Holmes, Oliver Wendell, and Supreme Court of the United States. *U.S. Reports: Buck v. Bell, 274 U.S. 200,* 1926. Library of Congress, loc.gov/item/usrep274200.

Laughlin, Harry H. "Testimony Before the House Committee on Immigration and Naturalization." Papers C-2-66, Harry H. Laughlin Papers, Truman State University.

Lindbergh, Charles A., to Henry Breckinridge, June 30, 1936. Lindbergh Papers, Series I, Manuscripts and Archives, Yale University Library.

Lindbergh, Charles A., to Harry Davidson, January 23, 1936. Lindbergh Papers, Series I, Manuscripts and Archives, Yale University Library.

Lindbergh, Charles A., to Leon Klink, April 24, 1924. Charles A. Lindbergh and Family Papers, box 16, folder 10, Minnesota Historical Society.

Lindbergh, Charles A., to Evangeline Lindbergh, June 8, 1926. Charles A. Lindbergh and Family Papers, box 18, folder 4, Minnesota Historical Society.

Lindbergh, Charles A., to Evangeline Lindbergh, August 28, 1926. Charles A. Lindbergh and Family Papers, box 18, folder 4, Minnesota Historical Society.

Lindbergh, Charles A., to Frederick Osborn, May 10, 1967. American Eugenics Society Records, Series I, American Philosophical Society Library.

Lindbergh, Charles A., to Truman Smith, May 23, 1940. Lindbergh Papers, Series I, Manuscripts and Archives, Yale University Library.

Lindbergh, Evangeline, to Charles A. Lindbergh, April 17, 1923. Charles A. Lindbergh and Family Papers, box 16, folder 10, Minnesota Historical Society.

Lindbergh, Evangeline, to Charles A. Lindbergh, May 26, 1924. Charles A. Lindbergh and Family Papers, box 18, folder 1, Minnesota Historical Society.

Mitchell, Charles. "Report on Unknown Baby." 1935. New Jersey State Police Museum, West Trenton, NJ. In *New Jersey's Lindbergh Kidnapping and Trial,* by Mark W. Falzini and James Davidson, Charleston, SC: Arcadia Publishing, 2012. 57. Print.

Morgenthau, Henry, Jr. Diaries of Henry Morgenthau Jr., April 27, 1933–July 27,

1945. Henry Morgenthau Jr. Papers, Presidential Diary, Volume 3, May 16, 1940–February 28, 1941, Franklin D. Roosevelt Presidential Library and Museum.

Roosevelt, Franklin D. "Franklin Roosevelt's Press Conference," December 17, 1940. Series I, Press Conferences of President Franklin D. Roosevelt, November 29, 1940–December 31, 1940, Franklin D. Roosevelt Presidential Library and Museum.

Roosevelt, Franklin D. "Fireside Chat 16: On the 'Arsenal of Democracy.'" Transcript, Presidential Speeches, Miller Center, University of Virginia.

Smith, Katherine. *My Life—Berlin, 1935–1939.* Unpublished autobiography, Truman Smith Papers, box 3, folder 3, Herbert Hoover Presidential Library and Museum.

Smith, Truman, Col. USA (ret.). "Air Intelligence Activities Office of the Military Attaché American Embassy, Berlin, Germany, August 1935–April 1939, with Special Reference to the Services of Colonel Charles A. Lindbergh Air Corp (res.)." 1953. Truman Smith Papers, box 1, folder 1, Manuscript Collection, Herbert Hoover Presidential Library and Museum.

Smith, Truman, Col. USA (ret.), to Charles A. Lindbergh, May 25, 1936. Truman Smith Papers, box 3, folder 1, Herbert Hoover Presidential Library and Museum.

Sordillo, Ralph to Charles A. Lindbergh, August 1, 1931. Lindbergh Papers, Series I, Manuscripts and Archives, Yale University.

"Yea I Have a Goodly Heritage." eugenicsarchive.org/eugenics/image_header.p|?id =1564&detailed=1.

SECONDARY SOURCES

BOOKS

Bak, Richard. *The Big Jump.* New York: Wiley, 2011.

Baker, Nicholson. *Human Smoke: The Beginnings of World War II, the End of Civilization.* New York: Simon & Schuster, 2008.

Bekker, Cajus. *Luftwaffe Air Diaries: The German Air Force in World War II.* London: MacDonald, 1967.

Berg, A. Scott. *Lindbergh.* New York: G. P. Putnam's Sons, 1998.

Bernard, Claude. *An Introduction to the Study of Experimental Medicine.* Translated by Henry Copley Green. New York: Dover Publications, Inc., 1957.

Clifford, J. Garry, and Samuel R. Spencer Jr. *The First Peacetime Draft.* Lawrence: University Press of Kansas, 1986.

Cole, Wayne S. *Charles A. Lindbergh and the Battle Against American Intervention in World War II.* New York: Harcourt Brace Jovanovich, 1974.

Davis, Kenneth S. *The Hero: Charles A. Lindbergh and the American Dream.* New York: Doubleday & Company, 1959.

Dunn, Susan. *1940: FDR, Willkie, Lindbergh, Hitler—the Election amid the Storm.* New Haven: Yale University Press, 2013.

Durkin, Joseph T., S.J., *Hope for Our Time: Alexis Carrel on Man and Society.* New York: Harper & Row, 1965.

Fisher, Jim. *The Lindbergh Case.* New Brunswick, NJ: Rutgers University Press, 1987.

Fleming, Candace. *Amelia Lost: The Life and Disappearance of Amelia Earhart.* New York: Schwartz & Wade, 2011.

Friedman, David M. *The Immortalists: Charles Lindbergh, Dr. Alexis Carrel, and Their Daring Quest to Live Forever.* New York: Ecco, 2007.

Gill, Brendan. *Lindbergh Alone.* St. Paul: Minnesota Historical Society Press, 2002.

Groom, Winston. *The Aviators: Eddie Rickenbacker, Jimmy Doolittle, Charles Lindbergh, and the Epic Age of Flight.* Washington, DC: National Geographic Books, 2013.

Grover, Warren. *Nazis in Newark.* New York: Routledge, 2017.

Haines, Lynn, and Dora B. Haines. *The Lindberghs.* New York: Vanguard Press, 1931.

Hamilton, David. *The First Transplant Surgeon: The Flawed Genius of Nobel Prize Winner, Alexis Carrel.* London: World Scientific Publishing Co., 2017.

Hertog, Susan. *Anne Morrow Lindbergh: Her Life.* New York: Anchor Books, 2010.

Kessner, Thomas. *The Flight of the Century: Charles Lindbergh and the Rise of American Aviation.* New York: Oxford University Press, 2010.

Ketchum, Richard M. *The Borrowed Years, 1939–1941: America on the Road to War.* New York: Random House, 1989.

Lardner, John. "The Lindbergh Legends." In *The Aspirin Age 1919–1941,* edited by Isabel Leighton. New York: Simon & Schuster, 1949.

Larson, Bruce Llewellyn. *Lindbergh of Minnesota: A Political Biography.* New York: Harcourt Brace Jovanovich, 1973.

Manchester, William. *The Last Lion: William Spencer Churchill.* Vol 2, *Alone, 1932–1940.* Boston: Little, Brown and Company, 1988.

Milton, Joyce. *Loss of Eden: A Biography of Charles and Anne Morrow Lindbergh.* New York: Open Road Media, 2013.

Mosley, Leonard. *Lindbergh: A Biography.* Mineola, NY: Dover Publications, 2000.

Murray, Williamson. *Strategy for Defeat: The Luftwaffe.* Baltimore: Nautical & Aviation Publishing Company of America, 1985.

Norwood, Stephen H. *Anti-Semitism and the American Far Left.* New York: Cambridge University Press, 2013.

Olson, Lynne. *Those Angry Days: Roosevelt, Lindbergh, and America's Fight over World War II, 1939–1941.* New York: Random House, 2013.

Reggiani, Andrés Horacio. *God's Eugenicist and the Sociobiology of Decline.* New York: Berghahn Books, 2007.

Ross, Walter S. *The Last Hero: Charles A. Lindbergh.* New York: Harper & Row, 1964.

Rudel, Anthony. *Hello, Everybody! The Dawn of American Radio.* New York: Harcourt Inc., 2008.

Sarles, Ruth A. *A Story of America First: The Men and Women Who Opposed U.S. Intervention in World War II.* Westport, CT: Praeger, 2003.

Schröck, Rudolf. *Das Doppelleben des Charles A. Lindbergh.* Translated by Katrin Tiernan. Munich: Random House, 2005.

Shirer, William L. *20th Century Journey: A Memoir on Life and the Times.* vol. 2, *The Nightmare Years, 1930–1940.* Boston: Little, Brown and Company, 1984.

Shirer, William L. *The Rise and Fall of the Third Reich: A History of Nazi Germany.* New York: Rosetta Books LLC, 2011.

Soupault, Robert. *Alexis Carrel.* Paris: Les Sept Couleurs, 1972.

Suchenwirth, Richard. *Development of the German Air Force, 1919–1939.* New York: Arno Press, 1968.

Wallace, Max. *The American Axis: Henry Ford, Charles Lindbergh, and the Rise of the Third Reich.* New York: St. Martin's Press, 2004.

Waller, George. *Kidnap: The Story of the Lindbergh Case.* New York: Dial Press, 1961.

MAGAZINE AND JOURNAL ARTICLES

"Charles Lindbergh." Spartacus Educational, spartacus.educational.com /USAlindbergh.htm.

Correll, John T. "The Cloud over Lindbergh." *Air Force Magazine.* August 2014.

DenHoed, Andrea. "The Forgotten Lessons of the American Eugenics Movement." *The New Yorker.* April 27, 2016.

Dunn, Susan. "The Debate Behind U.S. Intervention in World War II." *The Atlantic.* July 8, 2013, theatlantic.com/archive/2013/07/the-debate-behind-us-intervention -in-world-war-ii/277572/.

Escobar, Natalie. "What Was the Inspiration for 'The Murder on the Orient Express'?" Smithsonian.com. November 22, 2017. smithsonianmag.com/history/what-was -inspiration-murder-orient-express-180967305.

Hansen, Lauren. "When Nazi Germany Hosted the Summer Olympics." *The Week Online.* August 6, 2001. theweek.com/captured/640037/when-nazi-germany-hosted -summer-olympics.

Klein, Gil. "The Day Charles Lindbergh Spoke to the National Press Club." Press.org. press.org/news-multimedia/news/day-charles-lindbergh-spoke-national-press -club.

"Lindbergh's Double Life." Minnesota Historical Society, MNHS.org. mnhs.org /lindbergh/learn/family/double-life.

Lombardo, Paul. "Eugenics Laws Restricting Immigration." Image Archive on the American Eugenics Movement, February 2000. *Eugenics Archive.* eugenicsarchive .org/html/eugenics/essay9text.html.

"Oh, No, It Can't Be." Holocaust Teacher Resource Center. holocaust-trc.org/the -holocaust-education-program-guide/oh-no-it-cant-be-questions.com.

Schiff, Barry. "The Spirit Flies On." charleslindbergh.com/plane/spirit.asp.

Trenholm, Sandra. "Food Conservation During World War I: 'Food Will Win the War.'" Gilder Lehrman Institute of American History. gilderlehrman.org/content/food -conservation-during-wwi-food-will-win-war.

"Two Historic Speeches: October 13, 1939 & August 4, 1940." charleslindbergh.com /americanfirst/speech3.asp.

DVD AND VIDEO

"Kristallnacht—The Night of Broken Glass." From "America and the Holocaust." *American Experience,* 2013. PBS. pbs.org/newshour/extra/app/uploads/2013/11 /Kristallnacht-Text-American-Experience.pdf.

"We interrupt this program." From 1945 Philco News Reports FDR's Death. youtube .com/watch?v=c_FohJgLrvA.

SOURCE NOTES

PROLOGUE: THE RALLY

AID TO FRANCE: "British Seek Another A.E.F., Lindbergh Tells 10,000 Here," *New York Times,* April 24, 1941, 12.

"MAINTAIN THE BRITISH BLOCKADE": ibid.

"Nazis!" a protestor retorted: Lynne Olson, *Those Angry Days: Roosevelt, Lindbergh, and America's Fight over World War II, 1939–1941,* New York: Random House, 2013, loc. 5753.

"Contemptible" and "Dishonest parasites": America First Committee, FBI File, FOIA.

"dangerous elements": ibid.

"ramparts" and "alien blood": Charles A. Lindbergh, "Aviation, Geography and Race," *Reader's Digest,* November 1939, 66.

"preserve our American way of life": "Lindbergh Joins Wheeler Plea to U.S. to Shun War," *New York Times,* May 24, 1941, 6.

"Throw him out!": ibid.

"the rumbles of revolution": Anne Morrow Lindbergh Diary, May, 23, 1941, Anne Morrow Lindbergh, *War Within and Without: Diaries of Anne Morrow Lindbergh, 1939–1944,* New York: Harcourt Brace Jovanovich, 1980, 189.

"a deep-throated, unearthly, savage roar": John Ray Carlson, *Under Cover: My Life in the Nazi Underworld,* New York: E. P. Dutton & Co. Inc., 1943, 250.

"Give it to them!": Anne Morrow Lindbergh Diary, May 9, 1941, *War Within and Without,* 177.

"For six full minutes": Carlson, 250.

"We are assembled": Charles A. Lindbergh, "We Lack Leadership That Places America First," delivered at Madison Square Garden, New York, rally, May 23, 1941, *Vital Speeches of the Day,* vol. 7, 482.

"Lindbergh! Lindbergh! Lindbergh!": Roger Butterfield, "Lindbergh: A Stubborn Young Man of Strange Ideas Becomes a Leader of Wartime Opposition," *Life,* August 11, 1941, 67.

PART ONE: GROWING UP

"A sound individual:" Charles A. Lindbergh, *Autobiography of Values,* New York: Harcourt Brace Jovanovich, 1977, 43.

CHAPTER ONE: IN THE BEGINNING

"You have been a good friend to me": Charles A. Lindbergh, *The Spirit of St. Louis,* New York: Scribner, 2003, 222.

"genetic composition": Charles A. Lindbergh, *Autobiography of Values,* New York: Harcourt Brace Jovanovich, 1977, 308.

"I was born a child of man": Charles A. Lindbergh, *Autobiography of Values,* New York: Harcourt Brace Jovanovich, 1977, 3.

"Is it a boy?": A. Scott Berg, *Lindbergh,* New York: G. P. Putnam's Sons, 1998, 26.

"It is": ibid.

"Are you sure?": ibid.

"Dead sure!": ibid.

"curv[ing] upward in their courses": Charles A. Lindbergh, *The Spirit of St. Louis,* 333.

"Charles!": ibid., 372.

"Father will build us a new house": ibid.

But my toys: ibid., 374.

"It was a dreary winter": Charles A. Lindbergh, *The Spirit of St. Louis,* 373.

"hours on end in dry, heated rooms": ibid., 374.

"experiment[ing] . . . in strange new fields": ibid.

"Why can't I hold ten marbles": ibid.

"How long can a cream-filled chocolate last": ibid.

"I don't tell people when I'm pleased": Lynn and Dora B. Haines, *The Lindberghs,* New York: Vanguard Press, 1931, 246.

"I was in close contact with sun": Charles A. Lindbergh, *Boyhood on the Upper Mississippi: A Reminiscent Letter,* St. Paul: Minnesota Historical Society, 1972, 8–9.

"I am not happy": Berg, 34.

"But you have to be grownup to understand": Charles A. Lindbergh, *The Spirit of St. Louis,* 309.

"If there were no God": ibid., 309–310.

"certain changes in life for me": ibid., 311.

CHAPTER TWO: ROOTLESS

"I never had a dull moment": Berg, 40.

"taking inventory of himself": ibid, 34.

"There are the steps": Charles A. Lindbergh, *The Spirit of St. Louis,* 317.

"There were drills of all sizes": ibid., 40.

"you must have patience": ibid.

"hum in my ears like a church sermon": Charles A. Lindbergh, *The Spirit of St. Louis,* 318.

"science is a key to all mystery": ibid., 319.

"My Grandfather is as wise as he is old": ibid., 318.

Is there something within one's body that doesn't age: ibid., 320.

"throb[bed] in my mind": ibid.

"explore the mysteries of life and death": ibid.

"For me, the city formed a prison": Charles A. Lindbergh, *The Spirit of St. Louis,* 311.

"Surrounded by strange adults": Berg, 42.

"One of the planes took off": Charles A. Lindbergh, *The Spirit of St. Louis,* 314.

"I like my mother": Berg, 41.

"sit still in a strange room": ibid.

"I did not find much friendship": ibid., 42.

"Limburger or simply Cheese": ibid.

"It was always too hot": Charles A. Lindbergh, *The Spirit of St. Louis,* 312.

"who are no smarter than the rest of us": Bruce Llewellyn Larson, *Lindbergh of Minnesota: A Political Biography,* New York: Harcourt Brace Jovanovich, 1973, 110.

"Money Trust": Charles A. Lindbergh, *The Spirit of St. Louis,* 392.

"undermined free speech": ibid.

"It is better to speak the truth": Larson, 116.

"L-l-l-ittle-e-e Fa-a-a-l-l-l-s!": Charles A. Lindbergh, *The Spirit of St. Louis,* 333.

"Winter's school is over": ibid.

"There's the maidenhair patch to visit": ibid., 334–335.

"The difference between life and death": Charles A. Lindbergh, *Autobiography of Values,* 129.

"Why does [God] make you die?" ibid, 5.

"When you die, you go to God": ibid.

If God was so good: ibid.

"There was nothing good about death": ibid.

"Those clouds, how far away were they?": Charles A. Lindbergh, *The Spirit of St. Louis,* 244.

"Suppose the engine stopped": ibid., 245.

"Swoop[ing] down off our roof": ibid.

"Danger was a part of life": ibid., 245–246.

"foot-pedal gearshift": Charles A. Lindbergh, *Boyhood on the Upper Mississippi,* 25.

"Age seemed to make no difference": Charles A. Lindbergh, *The Spirit of St. Louis,* 377.

"[The] kid . . . loved machinery": Kenneth S. Davis, *The Hero: Charles A. Lindbergh and the American Dream,* New York: Doubleday & Company, 1959, 62.

"Nobody recalls [him] ever having attended a social function": Berg, 50.

"a grubby youth": Joyce Milton, *Loss of Eden: A Biography of Charles and Anne Morrow Lindbergh,* New York: Open Road Media, 2013, loc. 821.

CHAPTER THREE: CHANGES

"buncoed the citizens": Larson, 211.

"While I wanted very much to have my father win": Charles A. Lindbergh, *Boyhood on the Upper Mississippi,* 29.

"the trouble with war": Charles A. Lindbergh, *The Spirit of St. Louis,* 392.

"The thing has been done": Larson, 205.

"Food Will Win the War": Sandra Trenholm, "Food Conservation During World War I: 'Food Will Win the War,'" www.gilderlehrman.org.

"We'll make our hundred and twenty acres": Charles A. Lindbergh, *The Spirit of St. Louis,* 381.

"a gesture": ibid.

"I was rescued by World War I": Charles A. Lindbergh, *Boyhood on the Upper Mississippi,* 33.

"Farm work enabled me": Charles A. Lindbergh, *Autobiography of Values,* 62.

"too rusty to keep up?": Charles A. Lindbergh, *The Spirit of St. Louis,* 384.

"I loved . . . our Minnesota home": ibid.

"probably more because of its nearby lakes": Charles A. Lindbergh, *Boyhood on the Upper Mississippi,* 45.

"I knew that day that childhood was gone": Berg, 72.

PART TWO: AIRBORNE

"I tasted": Charles A. Lindbergh, *The Spirit of St. Louis,* 262.

CHAPTER FOUR: SCHOOLED

"going hedonistic": F. Scott Fitzgerald, "Echoes of the Jazz Age," *Complete Works of F. Scott Fitzgerald,* Hastings, East Sussex: Delphi Classics, Series 2, 2015, 3.

"who went home every night": Berg, 56.

"Why should one spend hours": Charles A. Lindbergh, *The Spirit of St. Louis,* 403.

"vagabond[ing] in the air": Candace Fleming, *Amelia Lost: The Life and Disappearance of Amelia Earhart,* New York: Schwartz & Wade, 2011, 64.

"All right," she finally said: Charles A. Lindbergh, *The Spirit of St. Louis,* 231.

"Welcome . . . to school": Charles A. Lindbergh, *The Spirit of St. Louis,* 248.

"CONTACT!" hollered the pilot: ibid.

"Now! The ground recedes": ibid., 249.

"I lose all conscious connection": ibid.

"The air's too turbulent": Charles A. Lindbergh, *The Spirit of St. Louis,* 251.

"Slim, it was just too rough": ibid.

"You can get up and down all right": ibid., 253.

CHAPTER FIVE: DAREDEVIL LINDBERGH

"I tasted a wine of the gods": Charles A. Lindbergh, *The Spirit of St. Louis,* 262.

"brand-new Curtiss OX-5 engine": ibid., 436.

"Well, she's ready": ibid., 437.

"What an exhibition I'd made!": ibid., 438.

"Why don't you let me": ibid., 439.

"Why don't we make a few rounds": ibid., 439.

"far different from all other flights": ibid., 440.

"This is sure a great life": Berg, 67.

"I'd go with you": Evangeline Lindbergh to Charles A. Lindbergh, April 17, 1923, Charles A. Lindbergh and Family Papers, Minnesota Historical Society.

CHAPTER SIX: SILVER WINGS

"to view the show": Charles A. Lindbergh, *The Spirit of St. Louis,* 272.

"I couldn't stay on the ground": ibid., 274.

"I felt highly professional": ibid.

"I'd been used to flying": ibid.

"God Almighty!" he sputtered: ibid.

"like a forty-acre farmer": ibid., 275.

"Now you fellows are going to think": Charles A. Lindbergh, *The Spirit of St. Louis,* 418.

"Photography, motors, map-making": ibid., 420.

"I studied after classes": ibid., 419.

"school and life became": Berg, 74.

"able to blend into any environment": ibid., 77.

"I may be 'washed out'": Charles A. Lindbergh to Leon Klink, April 24, 1924, Charles A. Lindbergh and Family Papers, Minnesota Historical Society.

"Later," wrote Evangeline, "when you come": Evangeline Lindbergh to Charles A.

Lindbergh, May 26, 1924, Charles A. Lindbergh and Family Papers, Minnesota Historical Society.

"compartmentalized existence": Berg, 79.

"St. Louis is a city of winds": Charles A. Lindbergh, *The Spirit of St. Louis,* 278.

"There was never another like him": Davis, 128.

"Ploughing through storms": Charles A. Lindbergh, *The Spirit of St. Louis,* 4.

"Whether the mail compartment contains ten letters": ibid.

"fly . . . where the wind blows": Charles A. Lindbergh to Evangeline Lindbergh, June 8, 1926, Charles A. Lindbergh and Family Papers, Minnesota Historical Society.

"The monotony of [it] is terrible": Charles A. Lindbergh to Evangeline Lindbergh, August 28, 1926, Charles A. Lindbergh and Family Papers, Minnesota Historical Society.

"Unless something new turns up": ibid.

"fly on forever through space": Charles A. Lindbergh, *The Spirit of St. Louis,* 12.

"roundabout method": ibid., 13.

If only I had a Bellanca: ibid., 14.

"set a dozen marks": ibid.

"I could fly nonstop between New York and Paris": ibid.

PART THREE: NEW YORK TO PARIS

"The greatest feat": Thomas Kessner, *The Flight of the Century: Charles Lindbergh and the Rise of American Aviation,* New York: Oxford University Press, 2010, 201.

CHAPTER SEVEN: PLANS AND FRUSTRATIONS

New York to Paris: Charles A. Lindbergh, *The Spirit of St. Louis,* 14.

I'm almost twenty-five: ibid., 15.

RED HOT CUTIES: "Red Hot Cuties of Atlantic City," *New York Daily News,* August 15, 1925, 1.

I KNOW WHO KILLED MY BROTHER: "I Know Who Killed My Brother," *New York Daily News,* October 16, 1926, 1.

"WIFE BETRAYS PARAMOUR": "Wife Betrays Paramour," *New York Times,* March 22, 1927, 1.

"[MAN] SHAVES HIMSELF": "Shaves Himself While Sitting Atop Flagpole," *New York Times,* June 19, 1927, 15.

"Somebody *will* fly from New York to Paris": "Flight to Paris Lures Noted Pilots of the Air," *New York Times,* March 20, 1927, Special Features, XXS.

"It would show people what airplanes can do": Berg, 92.

"From now on . . .": Charles A. Lindbergh, *The Spirit of St. Louis,* 67.

"What would you think of naming [the plane]": ibid., 74.

The Spirit of St. Louis: ibid.

"I expected at least some interest": ibid., 68.

"We will sell our plane": ibid., 75.

"I'm afraid there's been a misunderstanding": ibid.

"The Columbia Aircraft Corporation cannot afford": ibid.

"There's no use thinking it over": ibid., 75–76.

"You are making a mistake": ibid., 76.

"Our company would not be interested": ibid., 28.

"CAN YOU CONSTRUCT A WHIRLWIND ENGINE PLANE": ibid., 69.

Two months: ibid., 70.

"You don't plan on making that flight alone": ibid., 83.

"That would cost almost twenty pounds": ibid., 88.

"Atlantic Fever": Richard Bak, *The Big Jump,* New York: Wiley, 2011, 175.

"the most spectacular race ever held": "May Start Tomorrow," *New York Times,* May 13, 1927, 1.

"the most advanced . . . navigational devices": Charles A. Lindbergh, *The Spirit of St. Louis,* 90.

"If I get to Paris": Walter S. Ross, *The Last Hero: Charles A. Lindbergh,* New York: Harper & Row, 1964, 91.

There's no use blinding myself to reality: Charles A. Lindbergh, *The Spirit of St. Louis,* 107.

"My God!" exclaimed Charles: ibid., 119.

"flying in a box with fabric walls": ibid., 191.

"The Spirit is high-strung": Barry Schiff, "The Spirit Flies On," charleslindbergh.com/plane/spirit.asp.

"Send us a wire when you get to Paris": Charles A. Lindbergh, *The Spirit of St. Louis,* 134.

CHAPTER EIGHT: THE FLYING KID

"The chief business of the American people": Calvin Coolidge, *Foundations of the Republic: Speeches and Addresses by Calvin Coolidge,* New York: Scribner, 1926, 187.

"a widespread neurosis": Fitzgerald, 7.

"In the spring of '27": ibid.

"When are you going to take off": Charles A. Lindbergh, *The Spirit of St. Louis,* 154.

"My engine needs servicing": ibid.

"How's about letting the camera boys get a picture": ibid., 151.

"flying kid": Ross, 100.

"Lucky Lindy": Bak, 172.

"this fellow will never make it": ibid., 175.

"When you get back, look me up": Charles A. Lindbergh, *Autobiography of Values,* 80.

"He was happy as a kid": Harry A. Bruno, *Wings over America: The Inside Story of American Aviation,* New York: Robert M. McBride & Co., 1942, 173.

"Get me out of here": ibid.

"What's your favorite pie?" Charles A. Lindbergh, *The Spirit of St. Louis,* 152.

"Well, son, good-bye and good luck": Berg, 108.

"But accuracy means something to me": Charles A. Lindbergh, *The Spirit of St. Louis,* 166–167.

"My problems are already shifting": ibid., 162.

"Weather over the Atlantic is clearing!": ibid., 171.

a pilot should be fresh: ibid., 173–174.

"Slim, what am I going to do when you're gone?": ibid., 175.

"Good Lord!": ibid.

Wind, weather, power, load: ibid., 183.

"I'll start at daybreak": ibid., 178.

TAKEOFF

"It's the weather!": Charles A. Lindbergh, *The Spirit of St. Louis,* 182.

"five miles an hour *tail*!": ibid., 181.

Nothing about my plane has the magic quality: ibid., 186.

"the load shifting from wheels to wings": ibid.

Is there still time, still space?: ibid.

"taut, alive, straining": ibid.

"My heart was in my throat": Davis, 192.

"*willed* his plane into the air": ibid., 190.

"God be with him": "Other Flyers Wish Lindbergh All Luck," *New York Times,* May 21, 1927, 4.

"My heart and soul is with my boy": "Mother of Flier Sure He Will Win," *New York Times,* May 21, 1927, 2.

CHAPTER NINE: 33 HOURS, 30 MINUTES, 29.8 SECONDS

"But I mustn't feel sleepy": Charles A. Lindbergh, *The Spirit of St. Louis,* 201.

"the last point on the last island": ibid., 295.

"No attempt at jokes today": Davis, 196.

"Captain Lindbergh we're with you": ibid, 195.

"Rise to your feet": "40,000 Join in Prayer That Lindbergh Wins," *New York Times,* May 21, 1927, 13.

The stars have always been there: Charles A. Lindbergh, *The Spirit of St. Louis,* 303.

"an automaton, flying mechanically": ibid., 353.

"Vaguely outlined forms": ibid., 389.

"a gathering of family and friends": ibid., 390.

"solid walls of bone": ibid.

"immortal existence that lies outside": ibid.

"Death no longer seems the final end": ibid., 390–391.

"wide, empty sea": Davis, 196.

"defiant and pathetic": ibid.

For twenty-five years I've lived: Davis, 463.

"I [didn't] want the litter from a sandwich": ibid., 485.

"Cette fois ça va!": Berg, 129.

"Are there any mechanics here?": Charles A. Lindbergh, *The Spirit of St. Louis,* 495.

"It was like drowning in a human sea": ibid., 496.

"Come! They will smother him!": ibid., 497.

"There is Lindbergh!": ibid.

"Young man, I'm going to take you home": Davis, 210.

CHAPTER TEN: THE MOST FAMOUS MAN IN THE WORLD

"We just went dippy with joy": Bak, 200.

"I am proud to be the mother of such a boy": "Lindbergh Talks to Mother by Phone," *New York Times,* May 22, 1927, 3.

"Lindy's done it!": "The Lindy Hop," *Life,* August 23, 1943, 22.

"one of those shared national experiences": Bak, 201.

"the greatest feat of solitary man": Thomas Kessner, *The Flight of the Century: Charles Lindbergh and the Rise of American Aviation,* New York: Oxford University Press, 2010, 201.

"the long-awaited joy of humanity": August Post, "Columbus of the Air," *North American Review,* September–October 1927, 357.

"We are proud": Calvin Coolidge, "Lindbergh: Welcoming Home Speech," June 11, 1927, coolidgefoundation.org/resources/speeches-as-president-1923-1929-8.

"a victory for the entire human race": Bak, 207.

"The victory of Lindbergh": ibid.

"While everyone else jockeyed for money and publicity": Davis, 213.

"[Like Lindbergh,] it is necessary for us all": ibid.

"set down their glasses": Fitzgerald, 7.

"I wonder if I really deserve all this?": "Colonel Expresses Doubt to Admiral Burrage as Escort Comes," *Washington Post,* June 11, 1927, 1.

"Now tell me, Captain Lindbergh": Berg, 148.

"From the moment I woke in the morning": Charles A. Lindbergh, *Autobiography of Values,* 314.

"Once more I stand, America abreast the world": Davis, 244.

"Here comes the boy!": Gil Klein, "The Day Charles Lindbergh Spoke to the National Press Club," National Press Club, Press.org.

"On the evening of May twenty-first": Anthony Rudel, *Hello, Everybody!: The Dawn of American Radio,* New York: Harcourt Inc., 2008, 171–172.

"came long applause": Charles A. Lindbergh, *"WE,"* New York: G. P. Putnam's Sons, 1927, 281.

"Is it true, Colonel": Donald Keyhoe, *Flying with Lindbergh,* New York: Grosset & Dunlap, 1929, 17.

"If you can show me what that has to do with aviation": ibid.

"dumb, Midwestern hayseed": Milton, loc. 2767.

"I wish the public would just remember": Keyhoe, 289.

"You are a public figure": ibid.

"I can either be in public life": ibid, 290.

"I'd like to be free to work": ibid.

If [man] could learn to fly: Charles A. Lindbergh, *Autobiography of Values,* 130.

PART FOUR: COPILOT

"[He] has swept out of sight": Anne Morrow Lindbergh, *Bring Me a Unicorn: Diaries and Letters of Anne Morrow Lindbergh, 1922–1928,* New York: Harcourt Brace Jovanovich, Inc., 1972, 99.

CHAPTER ELEVEN: CHARLES AND ANNE

"a regular newspaper hero": Anne Morrow Diary, December 21, 1927, Anne Morrow Lindbergh, *Bring Me a Unicorn,* 81.

"worship[ping] Lindy": ibid.

"a tall slim boy . . .": ibid.

"very confused and overwhelmed": ibid.

"Why is it that attractive men": ibid., 82.

"swept out of sight all the other men": Anne Morrow Diary, December 28, 1927, ibid., 99.

"God, let me be *conscious* of it": Anne Morrow Diary, December 25, 1927, ibid., 95.

"*real* and intense *consciousness* of flying": ibid., 96.

"Oh, to go on and on": ibid., 97.

"He was so perfectly at home": ibid., 96.

"I will not be happy": ibid., 97.

"[It] was time to meet girls": Charles A. Lindbergh, *Autobiography of Values,* 118.

"[G]ood health, good form": ibid., 119.

an "attitude of mind," . . . "not a mass of knowledge," . . . a "mental attractiveness":
    ibid., 120.

"My experience in breeding animals": ibid., 118.

"When you saw the mothers and fathers": ibid., 119.

"mating [was] the most important choice": ibid., 16.

"conducive to evolutionary progress": Berg, 192.

"YEA I HAVE A GOODLY HERITAGE": "Yea I Have a Goodly Heritage," eugenicsarchive
    .org/eugenics/image_header.pl?id=1564&detailed=1.

"the central mission of all politics is race hygiene": Andrea DenHoed, "The Forgotten
    Lessons of the American Eugenics Movement," *The New Yorker,* April 27, 2016.

"feeblemindedness, insanity": "Harry H. Laughlin Testimony Before the House
    Committee on Immigration and Naturalization," Harry H. Laughlin Papers, Truman
    State University.

"America must remain American": Paul Lombardo, "Eugenics Laws Restricting
    Immigration," Image Archive, American Eugenics Movement.

"It is better for the world": Oliver Wendell Holmes and Supreme Court of the United
    States, *U.S. Reports: Buck v. Bell, 274 U.S. 200,* 1926, Library of Congress.

"Girls were everywhere": Charles A. Lindbergh, *Autobiography of Values,* 122.

"resting in [her] shadow": ibid., 123.

"noticed her [only] casually": ibid.

"achieving my objective with the girl": ibid.

"to approach Anne": ibid.

"Hello—hello": Anne Morrow Lindbergh Diary, October 8, 1928, *Bring Me a Unicorn,* 179.

"Hello. This is Lindbergh speaking": ibid.

"T-tomorrow?" she stammered: ibid.

"Well, *what time* tomorrow afternoon?": ibid., 180.

"Any time after three?": ibid.

"Well, tomorrow at four, shall we say?": ibid.

"a small boy": Anne Morrow to Constance Morrow, October 12, 1928, ibid., 180.

"tall and thin": ibid., 182.

"Now, *really,* please": Anne Morrow to Constance Morrow, October 16, 1928, ibid., 188.

"It's no bother at all": ibid.

"push[ing] open the great carved door": ibid., 193.

"He's just *terribly* kind": ibid., 194.

"gatehouses and towers": ibid., 193.

"I can't describe the flying": ibid., 195.

"link[ed] up through aviation": Anne Morrow to Constance Morrow, October 26, 1928,
    ibid., 205.

"You like to *write* books?": Anne Morrow Lindbergh Diary, July 27, 1953, Anne Morrow
    Lindbergh, *Against Wind and Tide: Letters and Journals, 1947–1986,* New York:
    Pantheon Books, 2012, 85.

"You must be kidding!" Susan Hertog, *Anne Morrow Lindbergh: Her Life,* New York:
    Anchor Books, 2010, 79.

"Oh, I do know": ibid.

"a knight in shining armor": Anne Morrow Lindbergh, *Hour of Gold, Hour of Lead: Diaries and Letters of Anne Morrow Lindbergh, 1929–1932,* New York: Harcourt Brace Jovanovich, Publishers, 1973, 4.

CHAPTER TWELVE: I DO

"Ambassador and Mrs. Morrow announce the engagement": Berg, 198.

"Unlike most brides-to-be": Anne Morrow Lindbergh, *Hour of Gold, Hour of Lead,* 3.

"Never say anything": ibid., 6.

"The lid of caution": ibid.

"in the privacy of a plane": ibid.

"lovely, warm group": Anne Morrow Lindbergh to Betty Morrow, May 27, 1928, *Hour of Gold, Hour of Lead,* 41.

"I had never before navigated a vessel": Charles A. Lindbergh, *Autobiography of Values,* 128.

"It took a whole day": Anne Morrow Lindbergh to Betty Morrow, May 31, 1928, *Hour of Gold, Hour of Lead,* 43.

"The soap powder": ibid., 44.

"But it takes most of the day": ibid., 43.

"Is this Colonel Lindbergh's boat?": Anne Morrow Lindbergh to Betty Morrow, June 7, 1928, *Hour of Gold, Hour of Lead,* 45.

CHAPTER THIRTEEN: SETTLING DOWN

"We avoid[ed] all personal questions": Anne Morrow Lindbergh, *Hour of Gold, Hour of Lead,* 9.

"And there he is—darn it all": Anne Morrow Lindbergh to Corliss Lamont, undated, *Bring Me a Unicorn,* 228.

"nonpilot than a poor pilot": Leonard Mosley, *Lindbergh: A Biography,* Mineola, NY, Dover Publications, 200, 145.

"Not good. Take her up again": ibid.

"For the first time": Anne Morrow Lindbergh, *Hour of Gold, Hour of Lead,* 4.

"the first couple of the air": John T. Correll, "The Cloud over Lindbergh," *Air Force Magazine,* August 2014, 78.

ADVISE PURCHASING PROPERTY: Anne Morrow Lindbergh to Evangeline Lindbergh, June 10, 1930, *Hour of Gold, Hour of Lead,* 137.

ADVISE ACCEPT TERMS OF CONTRACT: ibid.

Oh, dear, it's going to look like me: Anne Morrow Lindbergh to Evangeline Lindbergh, June 23–24, 1930, ibid., 138.

"Congratulations to the Happy Lindberghs": Berg, 217.

"Surely a hero": Ralph Sordillo to Charles A. Lindbergh, August 1, 1931. Lindbergh Papers, Yale University.

"There is something about too much prosperity": J. C. Long, "Dwight W. Morrow, the End of an Era," *Scribner's Magazine,* September 1935, 131.

"It will furnish a fine test": ibid.

"terribly dear:" Anne Morrow Lindbergh to Constance Morrow, January 28, 1931, *Hour of Gold, Hour of Lead,* 152.

"fat lamb": Anne Morrow Lindbergh to Constance Morrow, November 10, 1930, ibid.,147.

CHAPTER FOURTEEN: IMMORTAL

"brain waves controlling the facial muscles": David M. Friedman, *The Immortalists: Charles Lindbergh, Dr. Alexis Carrel, and Their Daring Quest to Live Forever,* New York: Ecco, 2007, 4.

"linked by strong psychic bonds": Davis, 344.

"had to be kept circulating": Charles A. Lindbergh, *Autobiography of Values,* 132.

"quite simple to design a mechanical pump": Berg, 221.

Could it be that no one: Charles A. Lindbergh, *Autobiography of Values,* 132.

Why could not a part of the body be kept alive: ibid.

"blood soon coagulates": Berg, 223.

"If you like, I will show you": Davis, 344.

"metaphysical researches": Alexis Carrel, *Man, the Unknown,* Middlesex, England: Pelican Books, 1948, 122.

"medieval alchemy and the weird experiments": Davis, 347.

"To learn how man and animals live": Claude Bernard, *An Introduction to the Study of Experimental Medicine,* trans. Henry Copley Green, New York: Dover Publications, Inc., 1957, 15.

"to re-create real life": David Hamilton, *The First Transplant Surgeon: The Flawed Genius of Nobel Prize Winner, Alexis Carrel,* London: World Scientific Publishing Co., 2017, 330.

"the pure mechanism of natural selection": ibid.

"removed from the body": Davis, 347.

"improve on them": Charles A. Lindbergh, *Autobiography of Values,* 133.

"Science is a key": Charles A. Lindbergh, *The Spirit of St. Louis,* 319.

"for contemplating . . . the phenomenon and rationality of death": Charles A. Lindbergh, *Autobiography of Values,* 133–134.

"Young and pulsing": ibid., 135.

"[E]ach one of them myself": ibid., 392.

"the mystical and": ibid., 134.

"The animal on the operating table": ibid., 135.

"If I could design": ibid.

"original in his ideas": Davis, 345.

"difficulty of teaching a camel": Berg, 225.

"relative intelligence of dogs and monkeys": ibid.

"[French] peasant hypnotizing animals": Joseph T. Durkin, S.J., *Hope for Our Time: Alexis Carrel on Man and Society,* New York: Harper & Row, 1965, 115.

"The white race is drowning": Robert Soupault, *Alexis Carrel,* Paris: Les Sept Couleurs, 1972, 148.

"There is no escaping that men [are] definitely *not* created equal": "Everybody Has Telepathic Powers, Dr. Carrel Says After Research," *New York Times,* September 18, 1935, 25.

"Instead of encouraging": Alexis Carrel, *Reflections on Life,* translated by Antonia White, New York: Hawthorn Books, Inc., 16.

"We must not forget": Alexis Carrel, *Man, the Unknown,* New York: Harper & Brothers, 1935, 213–214.

"Perhaps it would be effective": "Everybody Has Telepathic Powers, Dr. Carrel Says After Research," *New York Times,* September 18, 1935, 25.

"Those who have murdered": Carrel, *Man, the Unknown* 1935, 318.

"Why preserve useless and harmful human beings?": ibid.

"like puppies": ibid., 296.

"I would have been content to stay home": Berg, 227.

"Oh, how she loved her Lindy!": ibid.

"strangles [it] affectionately": Anne Morrow Lindbergh to Evangeline Lindbergh, April [n.d.], 1931, *Hour of Gold, Hour of Lead,* 159.

"such joy as this with Charlie": Anne Morrow Lindbergh to Betty Morrow, April 4, 1931, ibid., 160.

"Charles [Sr.] begins to be interested in him": Anne Morrow Lindbergh to Evangeline Lindbergh, ibid., 162.

"bouquets, cameras, reporters, crowds": Berg, 229.

"such poor sportsmanship": ibid.

"snip of gold": ibid, 227.

"*When* will we get home?": Anne Morrow Lindbergh to Betty Morrow, October [n.d.], 1931, *Hour of Gold, Hour of Lead,* 202.

"And oh, the baby!": Anne Morrow Lindbergh to Evangeline Land, November 12, 1931, ibid., 204.

"He began to take such an interest": ibid.

"ceiling flying": Anne Morrow Lindbergh to Constance Morrow, November 10, 1930, ibid., 147.

"Den!" ("Again!"), screeched the toddler: Anne Morrow Lindbergh to Evangeline Lindbergh, November 12, 1931, ibid., 204.

"good looking" and "pretty interesting": ibid.

"Hi, Buster," he would call: Anne Morrow Lindbergh to Evangeline Lindbergh, December [n.d.], 1931, ibid., 207.

PART FIVE: KIDNAPPED

"He was twenty": Charles A. Lindbergh, *Autobiography of Values,* 139.

CHAPTER FIFTEEN: "THEY HAVE STOLEN OUR BABY"

"What was that?": George Waller, *Kidnap: The Story of the Lindbergh Case,* New York: Dial Press, 1961, 8.

"Colonel Lindbergh, have you got the baby?": Jim Fisher, *The Lindbergh Case,* New Brunswick, NJ: Rutgers University Press, 5–6.

"Isn't he in his crib?": ibid., 6.

"No!": ibid.

"Anne, they have stolen our baby": Berg, 240.

"Only a cat": Fisher, 6.

"Dear Sir": New Jersey State Archives, nj.gov/state/archives/images/slcsp001/SLCSP001_11.jpg.

"The world dropped": "Kidnapping Holds First Place on Radio," *New York Times,* March 4, 1932, 8.

"Little Lindy was everybody's other baby": Natalie Escobar. "What Was the Inspiration for 'The Murder on the Orient Express'?" Smithsonian.com, November 22, 2017, smithsonianmag.com/history/what-was-inspiration-murder-orient-express-180967305.

"a general managing his forces": Anne Morrow Lindbergh to Evangeline Lindbergh, March 8, 1932, *Hour of Gold, Hour of Lead,* 233.

"Capone doesn't know who has the child": Elmer Irey with William Slocum, *The Tax Dodgers,* New York: Greenberg Publishing Co., 1948, 68.

"New Jersey bootlegger": Berg, 248.

"ready to open up negotiations": Waller, 28.

"just a little more time": Sidney B. Whipple, *The Lindbergh Crime,* New York: Blue Ribbon Books, 1935, 55.

"We have warned you": Berg, 252.

"keep the baby for a longer time": ibid.

"*gut* health": ibid.

"The first two days": Anne Morrow Lindbergh to Evangeline Lindbergh, March 5, 1932, *Hour of Gold, Hour of Lead,* 231.

"buoyant and alive": Anne Morrow Lindbergh to Evangeline Lindbergh, March 7, 1932, ibid., 232.

"mak[e] the right moves": Berg, 253.

CHAPTER SIXTEEN: "JAFSIE" AND CEMETERY JOHN

"so a loving mother may again have her child": John F. Condon, *Jafsie Tells All! Revealing the Inside Story of the Lindbergh-Hauptmann Case,* New York: Jonathan Lee Publishing Corp., 1936, 18.

"Kindly open [the letter]": ibid., 26.

"Dear Sir, Mr. Condon may act as go-between": ibid.

"Is it important?": Waller, 34.

"money is ready": Condon, 48.

"You have no business": Fisher, 43–44.

"Did you got it, the money?": Waller, 53.

"Come back here!": Condon, 76.

"[W]hat if the baby is dead?": ibid., 78.

"The baby is all right": ibid., 79.

"the sleeping suit from the baby": ibid., 93.

"Baby is alive": ibid., 90.

"Cemetery John:" Harry W. Walsh as told to E. Collins, "Hunt for the Kidnappers: The Inside Story of the Lindbergh Case," *Jersey Journal,* November 17, 1932, 10.

"was pulled by an independent": John Lardner, "The Lindbergh Legends," in *The Aspirin Age 1919–1941,* ed. Isabel Leighton, New York: Simon & Schuster, 1949, 205.

MONEY IS READY: Berg, 261.

"I ACCEPT. MONEY IS READY": ibid.

"It looks like my son's garment": Berg, 262.

"I have a sustained feeling": Anne Morrow Lindbergh to Elizabeth Morrow, March 18, 1932, *Hour of Gold, Hour of Lead,* 237.

CHAPTER SEVENTEEN: THE RANSOM

"so many false clues": Waller, 69.

"[Mr. Lindbergh] knows we are right party": ibid.

"I ACCEPT. MONEY IS READY": ibid.

"Colonel Lindbergh, unless you comply with our suggestions": Irey, 75.
"I am just desperately anxious": ibid.
"YES. EVERYTHING O.K. JAFSIE": Waller, 73.
"Hey, Doctor! Here, Doctor!": Berg, 303.
"Don't open that note [yet]": Condon, 156.
"The baby—where is the baby?": Berg, 266.
"We'll keep our end of the bargain": Condon, 157.
"To be, or not to be": Drey, 71.
"When [Jafsie] wasn't reciting": ibid.
"I'm sorry": Fisher, 82.

CHAPTER EIGHTEEN: SEARCH'S END
"All the newspapers here lately say": Anne Morrow Lindbergh to Evangeline
    Lindbergh, April 8, 1932, *Hour of Gold, Hour of Lead,* 238–239.
"With a worse start": Anne Morrow Lindbergh to Evangeline Lindbergh, April 10, 1932,
    ibid., 241.
"I have, of course, great confidence": Anne Morrow Lindbergh to Evangeline
    Lindbergh, May 7, 1932, ibid., 246.
"It really wasn't a grave": Fisher, 106.
"The baby is with [your] Daddy": Berg, 272.
"Colonel, I have a message for you": Waller, 104.
"Found—?" cried Charles: ibid.
"He is dead": ibid.
"I'm going home": Fisher, 115.
"fractured skull": Charles Mitchell, "Report on Unknown Baby," 1935, New Jersey State
    Police Museum, West Trenton, NJ, in *New Jersey's Lindbergh Kidnapping and Trial,*
    by Mark W. Falzini and James Davidson, Charleston, SC: Arcadia Publishing,
    2012, 57.
"every incident, every act, every word": Anne Morrow Lindbergh Diary, May 14, 1932,
    Hour of Gold, Hour of Lead, 251.
"His terrible patience": Anne Morrow Lindbergh Diary, May 13, 1932, ibid., 250.
"I hoped so I would bring that baby back": Anne Morrow Lindbergh Diary, May 17,
    1932, ibid., 254.
"the truest and the most intimate measure": Reeve Lindbergh, *Under a Wing: A
    Memoir,* New York: Simon & Schuster, 1998, 92.
"I am perfectly satisfied": "Father on Impulse Looks at Dead Son," *New York Times,*
    May 14, 1932, 2.

PART SIX: BLOWN OFF COURSE

"We are starting": Berg, 278.

CHAPTER NINETEEN: REBUILDING
"I went through it [once]": Anne Morrow Lindbergh Diary, February 5, 1933, Anne
    Morrow Lindbergh, *Locked Rooms and Open Doors: Diaries and Letters of Anne
    Morrow Lindbergh, 1933–1935,* New York: Harcourt Brace & Company, 1974, 13.
"They talk and talk": Anne Morrow Lindbergh Diary, May 18, 1932, *Hour of Gold, Hour
    of Lead,* 254–255.

"insane on the subject": Fisher, 127.

"[I] had every reason to believe": "Five Men and Woman Believed Identified as Slayers of Baby," *New York Times,* May 16, 1932, 2.

"death and horror": Anne Morrow Lindbergh to Elizabeth Morrow, June 10, 1932, *Hour of Gold, Hour of Lead,* 272.

"Oh, what a terrible train": ibid.

"[He] has hold of things": ibid.

"just like Grandma Morrow": Anne Morrow Lindbergh Diary, August 16, 1932, ibid., 302.

"my little rabbit": Anne Morrow Lindbergh Diary, August 19, 1932, ibid., 304.

"stretching his mouth": ibid.

"to lead the lives of normal Americans": "Second Son Is Born to the Lindberghs at the Morrow Home in Englewood," *New York Times,* August 17, 1932, 1.

"I don't believe I can ever live in [that] house": Anne Morrow Lindbergh Diary, June 30, 1932, *Hour of Gold, Hour of Lead,* 284.

"never be able to go away to work": Anne Morrow Lindbergh to Evangeline Lindbergh, June 10, 1932, ibid., 271.

"I want to know": Anne Morrow Lindbergh, *Locked Rooms and Open Doors,* 13.

"Horrible horrible-looking people": Anne Morrow Lindbergh Diary, January 6, 1933, ibid., 4.

"terrified of a smashup": ibid.

"I will never accept it": Anne Morrow Lindbergh Diary, September 25, 1932, *Hour of Gold, Hour of Lead,* 318.

"cut her free": Hertog, 232.

"My time is my own": Berg, 288.

CHAPTER TWENTY: ORDEAL BY TRIAL

"Oh, God! It's starting . . . again.": Berg., 296.

"but they've got him at last": ibid.

"2974 Decatur"; Fisher, 218.

"Hey, Doctor! Here, Doctor!": Berg, 303.

"Lindy" ice cream sundaes and "Lamb Chops Jafsie": Berg, 310.

"disappoint [Charles] at the Trial": Anne Morrow Lindbergh Diary, December 30, 1934, *Locked Rooms and Open Doors,* 232.

"The grief of Mrs. Lindbergh": "Colonel and Mrs. Lindbergh on Stand," *New York Times,* January 4, 1935, 2.

"very clearly coming from the cemetery": "Testimony by Lindbergh on Second Day on Stand," *New York Times,* January 5, 1935, 9.

"Whose voice was it, Colonel?": ibid.

"That was Hauptmann's voice": ibid.

his expression "stone-cold": Berg, 314.

"day and night": Fisher, 337.

"just looked them over casually": ibid., 337–338.

"Where are they getting these witnesses?": ibid, 334.

"You're having a lot of fun with me": "Hauptmann Admits Lying and Says Wilentz Lies Too; Still Protests Innocence," *New York Times,* January 29, 1935, 1.

"No. Should I cry?": ibid.

"You think you are bigger than everybody": ibid.

"No, but I know I am innocent": ibid.

"We have shown conclusively": "Hauptmann's Guilt Overwhelmingly Proved, Declared Hauck for Prosecution," *New York Times,* February 12, 1935, 12.

"weak, less, irretrievably broken": Berg, 330.

"Charles isn't capable of understanding": ibid.

"I must not talk. I must not cry": Anne Morrow Lindbergh Diary, January 20, 1935, *Locked Rooms and Open Doors,* 240–241.

"Kill Hauptmann!" Davis, 356.

"Thus there were jokes and jazz": Harold Nicolson to Vita Sackville-West, February 14, 1935, *The Harold Nicolson Diaries 1907–1964,* ed. Nigel Nicolson, London: Phoenix Books, 2004, 138.

"Hauptmann has been condemned to death": ibid.

"You have heard the verdict": ibid.

"There is no doubt Hauptmann did the thing": ibid., 139.

"Turn that off": ibid., 138.

"The trial is over": Anne Morrow Lindbergh Diary, February 14, 1935, *Locked Rooms and Open Doors,* 249.

CHAPTER TWENTY-ONE: LOST FAITH

"succumbed to ochlocracy": Milton, loc 6976.

"higher council of learning": Andrés Horacio Reggiani, *God's Eugenicist and the Sociobiology of Decline,* New York: Berghahn Books, 2007, 70.

"the salvation of the white race": John F. Fulton, "Can Science Save Society?" *Saturday Review,* September 21, 1935, 11.

"immortal brain": Reggiani, 68.

"robot heart": "Lindbergh Shows the Robot Heart," *New York Times,* August 12, 1936, 21.

"A new era has opened": Berg, 336.

"the artificial heart": "Carrel, Lindbergh Develop Device to Keep Organs Alive Outside Body," *New York Times,* June 21, 1935, 1.

"most sensational [discovery]": ibid.

"a big wire entanglement": Mosley, 193.

"I carried a Colt thirty-eight caliber revolver": Charles A. Lindbergh, *Autobiography of Values,* 142.

"No arrests were made": ibid., 144.

"Mother's little girl": Anne Morrow Lindbergh Diary, January 28, 1936, Anne Morrow Lindbergh, *The Flower and the Nettle: Diaries and Letters of Anne Morrow Lindbergh 1936–1939,* New York: Harcourt Brace & Company, 1976, 16.

"flying in a fog": Lauren D. Lyman, "Lindbergh Family Sails for England to Seek a Safe, Secluded Residence; Threats on Son's Life Force Decision," *New York Times,* December 23, 1935, 1.

"The English have greater regard": ibid.

PART SEVEN: LOSING ALTITUDE

"Hitler, I am beginning": Anne Morrow Lindbergh to Betty Morrow, August 5, 1936, *The Flower and the Nettle,* 100.

CHAPTER TWENTY-TWO: SPRING 1936

"Crooked, rambling [with] tipsy floors and slanting walls": Anne Morrow Lindbergh
 Diary, February 20, 1936, *The Flower and the Nettle*, 25.

The Lindberghs "laugh[ed] for joy": ibid.

"It'll do": ibid.

"carnations, gilt door handles": Anne Morrow Lindbergh Diary, January 27, 1935,
 ibid., 13.

"When you get to the country": Anne Morrow Lindbergh Diary, February 4, 1936,
 ibid., 18.

"We have been bothered very little": Berg, 346.

"Merry-go-round!" . . . "A darn fast one": Anne Morrow Lindbergh Diary, May 13–14,
 1936, *The Flower and the Nettle*, 53.

"Heil Hitler!": William L. Shirer, *The Rise and Fall of the Third Reich: A History of Nazi
 Germany,* New York: Rosetta Books LLC, 2011, loc. 6732.

"Men of the Reichstag": ibid.

"Their hands raised in slavish salute": ibid., loc. 6743.

"[I] swear to yield to no force whatever": ibid.

WOULD LIKE TO OFFER: Berg, 352.

"I am worried": "Hoffman Defends Granting Reprieve," *New York Times,* January 18,
 1936, 2.

"There has never been any question": Berg, 352.

"What is it—a mouse?": Anne Morrow Lindbergh Diary, March 23, 1936, *The Flower
 and the Nettle,* 36.

"There is an air of discouragement and neglect": Charles Lindbergh to Henry
 Breckinridge, June 30, 1936, Lindbergh Papers, Series I, Manuscripts and Archive,
 Yale University Library.

"inefficient by American standards": ibid.

"mechanical designs were behind the times": ibid.

"What amazed me was the fact that": ibid.

"the symbol of conquest of the world": Max Wallace, *The American Axis: Henry Ford,
 Charles Lindbergh, and the Rise of the Third Reich,* New York: St. Martin's Press,
 2004, 99.

"It was [my] impression": Truman Smith, Col. USA (ret.), "Air Intelligence Activities
 Office of the Military Attaché American Embassy, Berlin, Germany, August 1935–
 April 1939, with Special Reference to the Services of Colonel Charles A. Lindbergh
 Air Corp (res.)," 1953. Truman Smith Papers, Manuscript Collection, Herbert
 Hoover Presidential Library and Museum.

"I consider that your visit here": Colonel Truman Smith to Charles Lindbergh, May 25,
 1936. Truman Smith Papers, Herbert Hoover Presidential Library and Museum.

"crimes against civilization": "Nazi Convicted of World Crimes by 20,000 in Rally," *New
 York Times,* March 8, 1934, 1.

"I AM CONVINCED": Berg, 358.

"give aid to anti-Semitism?": ibid., 359.

CHAPTER TWENTY-THREE: "HITLER IS UNDOUBTEDLY A GREAT MAN"

"neatness, order, trimness, cleanliness": Anne Morrow Lindbergh Diary, July 22, 1936,
 The Flower and the Nettle, 83.

JEWS NOT WELCOME signs: Lauren Hansen, "When Nazi Germany Hosted the Summer Olympics," *The Week Online,* August 6, 2001.

"perfectly normal place": Wallace, 104.

"a naïve political thinker": Katherine Smith, *My Life—Berlin, 1935–1939,* unpublished autobiography, Truman Smith Papers, Herbert Hoover Presidential Library, unpaged.

"an empty void": ibid.

"a spirit in Germany": Charles Lindbergh to Henry Breckinridge, September 23, 1936, Lindbergh Papers, Series I, Manuscripts and Archives, Yale University Library.

"dictatorships are of necessity wrong": Anne Morrow Lindbergh to Betty Morrow, August 5, 1936, *The Flower and the Nettle,* 100.

"no question of the power": ibid.

"The organized vitality of Germany": Charles A. Lindbergh, *Autobiography of Values,* 147.

"science and technology harnessed": Hertog, 324.

"strong central leadership": ibid.

"Look, Charles! Look!": Katherine Smith, *My Life—Berlin, 1935–1939* unpaged.

"intensely pleased": "Lindbergh Ends Stay in Germany," *New York Times,* August 3, 1936, 2.

"making Lindbergh 'understand' Nazi Germany": William Shirer, *20th Century Journey: A Memoir of a Life and the Times,* Vol. 2, *The Nightmare Years 1930–1940,* Boston: Little, Brown and Company, 1984, 236–237.

"thrilling . . . Hitler is a very great man": Susan Dunn, 1940: *FDR, Willkie, Lindbergh, Hitler—the Election Amid the Storm,* New Haven: Yale University Press, 2013, 50.

"Hitler is undoubtedly a great man": Charles Lindbergh to Harry Davidson, January 23, 1936, Lindbergh Papers, Series I, Manuscripts and Archives, Yale University Library.

"a very distorted and incomplete picture": Wayne S. Cole, *Charles A. Lindbergh and the Battle Against American Intervention in World War II,* New York: Harcourt Brace Jovanovich, 1974, 35.

"stablizing factor": ibid.

Are we deluding ourselves: Warren Grover, *Nazis in Newark,* New York: Routledge, 2017, 299.

"the only hope for restoring a moral world": Hertog, 324.

Nazi "virility" and "efficiency": Davis, 375.

the British people's "softness" and "stupidity": ibid.

"the early symptoms of the breakup": Charles A. Lindbergh, *Autobiography of Values,* 148.

"The Greek city-states": ibid., 149.

"ragged, hungry people": Charles A. Lindbergh, *Autobiography of Values,* 148.

"a civilization of art and architecture and religion": ibid.

"distant white men's frontiers": ibid., 154.

"secure beyond the need of questioning": ibid., 152.

"We whites [were] so accustomed to dominating": ibid.

Germany's "magnificent spirit": ibid., 156.

"Grandma Morrow's nose": Anne Morrow Lindbergh Diary, May 20, 1937, *The Flower and the Nettle,* 162.

"As we couldn't agree": Anne Morrow Lindbergh to Betty Morrow, June 22, 1937, ibid., 168.

"when I was thinking of all my other birthdays": ibid., 169.

"once more a world power in the air": Winston Groom, *The Aviators: Eddie Rickenbacker, Jimmy Doolittle, Charles Lindbergh, and the Epic Age of Flight,* Washington, DC: National Geographic Books, 2013, 280.

Lindbergh's "willing self-deception": Richard Suchenwirth, *Development of the German Air Force, 1919–1939,* New York: Arno Press, 1968, 190.

The Germans' "sense of decency": Grover, 299.

"The whole idea seems a little effeminate": Olson, loc. 412.

"[It] is ten times superior": Harold Nicolson Diary, May 26, 1938, *The Harold Nicolson Diaries,* 188.

"crumbling, backward England": Berg, 365.

"as if it were mine": Anne Morrow Lindbergh Diary, May 16, 1938, *The Flower and the Nettle,* 268.

CHAPTER TWENTY-FOUR: LINDBERGH REPORTS

"only too well": Charles Lindbergh Journal, March 31, 1938, Charles Lindbergh, *The Wartime Journals of Charles A. Lindbergh,* New York: Harcourt Brace Jovanovich, Inc., 1970, 10.

"degeneration": Reggiani, 95.

"construction of civilized men": ibid., 90.

"suited to *their* needs": ibid.

"a new social order": ibid., 91.

"the problems of civilization and survival": Charles A. Lindbergh, *Autobiography of Values,* 373.

"see enough of Europe to be able to think intelligently": Charles Lindbergh Journal, August 15, 1938, *Wartime Journals,* 44.

I must go: Anne Morrow Lindbergh Diary, August 6, 1938, *The Flower and the Nettle,* 336.

"secret trials and executions": Charles A. Lindbergh, *Autobiography of Values,* 167.

"infusion of Mongol blood" . . . "yellow race": Olson, loc. 1357.

"Asia presses towards us": Charles A. Lindbergh, "Aviation, Geography, and Race," 65.

"There is still hope": Anne Morrow Lindbergh Diary, September 14, 1938, *The Flower and the Nettle,* 405.

"Nothing is desperate": ibid.

"But not for long": Anne Morrow Lindbergh Diary, September 20, 1938, ibid., 408.

"When will that be?": ibid.

"Without doubt the German air fleet is now stronger": Truman Smith, *Berlin Report: The Memoirs and Reports of Truman Smith,* edited by Robert Hessen, Stanford, CA: Hoover Institution Press, 1984, 154–155.

"There's some good news coming in": Charles Lindbergh Journal, September 28, 1938, *Wartime Journals,* 78.

"not surprised [by the outcome]": ibid.

"the Führer [has] found a most convenient ambassador": Cole, 53.

"due to German propaganda": ibid., 55.

"with a pinch of salt": ibid.

"pin pricks": Williamson Murray, *Strategy for Defeat: The Luftwaffe,* Baltimore: Nautical & Aviation Publishing Company of America, 1985, 18.

"Do not let us deceive ourselves": Cajus Bekker, *Luftwaffe Air Diaries: The German Air Force in World War II,* London: MacDonald, 1967, 24.

CHAPTER TWENTY-FIVE: NO PLACE LIKE HOME

"some groundwork on homes": Anne Morrow Lindbergh to Betty Morrow, September 24, 1938, *The Flower and the Nettle,* 413.

JEWRY IS CRIMINAL and JEWS NOT WANTED: Anne Morrow Lindbergh Diary, October 11, 1938, ibid., 428.

"The shops [are] luxurious": ibid.

"It would break to pieces": Anne Morrow Lindbergh Diary, October 13, 1938, ibid., 432.

"creepers" and "parasites": ibid.

"expelled to Madagascar": ibid.

"I was depressed": ibid.

JEWS ARE NOT WANTED HERE: Anne Morrow Lindbergh Diary, October 27, 1938, ibid., 439.

"depressed": ibid.

"It would be an excellent place": Charles A. Lindbergh Journal, October 28, 1938, *Wartime Journals,* 111.

"There seemed to be something strange": Charles A. Lindbergh Journal, October 29, 1938, ibid.

"Jewish Problem": Nicholson Baker, *Human Smoke: The Beginnings of World War II, the End of Civilization,* New York: Simon & Schuster, 2008, 110.

"obtained the ownership of a large percentage of property": Charles Lindbergh Journal, December 22, 1938, *Wartime Journals,* 131.

"by order of the Führer": William Manchester, *The Last Lion: William Spencer Churchill,* Vol. 2, *Alone, 1932–1940,* Boston: Little, Brown and Company, 1988, 317.

"I want to thank you especially": Wallace, 170.

"Judenschwein!": "Kristallnacht—The Night of Broken Glass," from "America and the Holocaust," *American Experience,* 2013, PBS.org.

"We shed not a tear": ibid.

"I do not understand these riots": Charles A. Lindbergh Journal, November 11, 1938, *Wartime Journals,* 115.

"How *can* we go there to live?": Anne Morrow Lindbergh Diary, November 12, 1938, *The Flower and the Nettle,* 450.

"plan to move to Berlin": "Lindbergh Said to Plan to Move to Berlin," *New York Times,* November 16, 1938.

"With confused emotions": E. B. White, Talk of the Town, *The New Yorker,* November 26, 1938, 14.

"unfair labeling": Anne Morrow Lindbergh Diary, December 10, 1938, *The Flower and the Nettle,* 470.

"not and never has been Anti-Semitic": ibid.

"marvelously untouched": ibid.

"air of discipline and precision": Charles A. Lindbergh Journal, December 16, 1938, *Wartime Journals,* 126.

"moved a little faster": Charles A. Lindbergh Journal, April 2, 1939, ibid., 173.

"It is time to turn from our quarrels": Charles A. Lindbergh, "Aviation, Geography and Race," 66.

"shortsightedness and vacillation": Charles A. Lindbergh Journal, April 2, 1939, *Wartime Journals,* 173.

PART EIGHT: AMERICA FIRST

"We [must] band together": Charles A. Lindbergh, "Aviation, Geography and Race," 66.

CHAPTER TWENTY-SIX: AN INFLUENTIAL CITIZEN

"Where does freedom end": Charles A. Lindbergh Journal, April 14, 1939, *Wartime Journals,* 182.

"The steward tells me": Berg, 386.

"Imagine the United States": ibid.

a "barbaric" return to his country: Charles A. Lindbergh Journal, April 14, 1939, *Wartime Journals,* 183.

"Air-Mail Fiasco:" Berg, 296.

"flashed [his] familiar": ibid., 294.

"Roosevelt judges his man quickly": Charles A. Lindbergh Journal, April 20, 1939, *Wartime Journals,* 187.

"handles better than the [Germans']": Charles A. Lindbergh Journal, April 24, 1939, ibid., 190.

"[C]riticism of any of his activities": Arthur Krock, "The Invaluable Contribution of Colonel Lindbergh," *New York Times,* February 1, 1939, 16.

"superior in the air:" Friedman, 164.

"vibrant, new [Nazi-infused] spirit": ibid.

"imperative for the sake": ibid, 165.

"Asiatic hordes": Mosley, 250.

"The first laboratory approach": "Carrel Explains Mechanical Heart," *New York Times,* May 16, 1939, 7.

"The hours spent arranging what nights are free": Anne Morrow Lindbergh Diary, May 22, 1939, *War Within and Without,* 8.

"It isn't like Illiec": Anne Morrow Lindbergh Diary, June 23, 1939, ibid., 15.

"keep this place as peaceful as it seems": ibid.

CHAPTER TWENTY-SEVEN: THE HERO SPEAKS

Why did England and France: Charles A. Lindbergh Journal, September 1, 1939, *Wartime Journals,* 249.

Somebody blundered and *This war will change*: ibid.

"I saw them tortured": Anne Morrow Lindbergh Diary, September 3, 1939, *War Within and Without,* 48–49.

"Anne, what *is* it?": ibid, 49.

"Just the war": ibid.

"You see it all too clearly": ibid.

"In this grave hour": King George VI of Great Britain, "There May Be Days Ahead," radio address, September 3, 1939, *Vital Speeches of the Day,* vol. 5, p. 713.

"I speak tonight": Charles A. Lindbergh, "Let Us Look to Our Own Defense," radio address, September 15, 1939, *Vital Speeches of the Day,* vol. 5, p. 751.

Oh, how can *they understand?:* Anne Morrow Lindbergh Diary, September 15, 1939, *War Within and Without,* 57.

"answered a real need": Berg, 397.

"The speech became a national sensation": Olson, loc. 1369.

"Our bond with Europe": Charles A. Lindbergh, "Our Policy Must Be Our Bond with Europe," radio address, October 13, 1939, *Vital Speeches of the Day,* vol. 6, p. 57.

"somber cretin" . . . "a man without feeling": Berg, 397.

"a pro-Nazi recipient of a German medal": ibid.

"Charles Lindbergh . . . is and always will be": "British Host Gives Lindbergh Excuse," *New York Times,* October 22, 1939, 4.

the "backwash" from his speeches: Anne Morrow Lindbergh Diary, October 28, 1939, *War Within and Without,* 64.

"Bitter criticism": ibid., 64–65.

"The phony war": Wallace, 195–196.

"The Germans are meeting with amazing success": Charles A. Lindbergh to Truman Smith, May 23, 1940, Lindbergh Papers, Series I, Manuscripts and Archives, Yale University Library.

"blood, toil, tears and sweat": Winston Churchill, "Blood, Toil, Tears and Sweat" speech, International Churchill Society, Winston Churchill.org.

"Poor people, poor people": ibid.

"There is near hysteria": J. Garry Clifford and Samuel R. Spencer Jr., *The First Peacetime Draft,* Lawrence: University Press of Kansas, 1986, 10.

NAZIS SMASH THROUGH BELGIUM: Susan Dunn, "The Debate Behind U.S. Intervention in World War II," *The Atlantic,* July 8, 2013, theatlantic.com.

"Regardless of which side wins": Charles A. Lindbergh, "Let Us Turn Our Eyes to Our Own Nation," radio address, May 19, 1940, *Vital Speeches of the Day,* vol. 6, pp. 484–485.

"I am absolutely convinced": Henry Morgenthau Jr. Diary, May 20, 1940, Henry Morgenthau Jr. Papers, Presidential Diaries, vol. 3, May 16, 1940–February 28, 1941, Franklin D. Roosevelt Presidential Library and Museum.

"natural right" and "desire[d] to enjoy rather than acquire": Charles A. Lindbergh, "What Substitute for War?" *Atlantic Monthly,* March 1940, 304.

"Asiatic barbarians": ibid.

"the West's great protector": Friedman, 180.

"two very unequal classes": ibid.

"the saving of Western civilization": ibid.

"Carrel is still able to discuss the war": Charles A. Lindbergh Journal, May 28, 1940, *Wartime Journals,* 351.

"friendly reference to France?": Charles A. Lindbergh Journal, June 15, 1940, *Wartime Journals,* 358.

"I [do not] see how I could": ibid.

"But it is the Nazis who are destroying Western civilization!": Milton, loc. 7796.

"being irrational": ibid.

"the minority" who were trying: Charles A. Lindbergh, "Our Drift Toward War," radio address, June 15, 1940, *Vital Speeches of the Day,* vol. 6, p. 550.

"Germany has demonstrated an ability": Charles A. Lindbergh to Truman Smith, May 23, 1940, Lindbergh Papers, Series I, Manuscripts and Archives, Yale University Library.

"In England," he told the crowd: "Two Historic Speeches: October 13, 1939 & August 4, 1940," charleslindbergh.com/americanfirst/speech3.asp.

"You have let America down": Anne Morrow Lindbergh Diary, August 13, 1940, *War Within and Without,* 136.

"You stand for the atrocities of Hitler": ibid.

"I just can't talk about him anymore": Butterfield, 75.

"He who spreads the gospel of defeatism": Dunn, 391.

"The giving up of all contacts": Anne Morrow Lindbergh Diary, May 24, 1940, *War Within and Without,* 88.

"a *moral* argument for isolationism": Anne Morrow Lindbergh to Betty Morrow, September 4, 1940, ibid., 143.

CHAPTER TWENTY-EIGHT: "THE BUBONIC PLAGUE AMONG WRITERS"

"so spontaneous" . . . "pushed": Anne Morrow Lindbergh to Betty Morrow, September 4, 1940, ibid., 142.

"faith" . . . "not seen, but felt": Anne Morrow Lindbergh, *The Wave of the Future: A Confession of Faith,* Harcourt Brace & Co., 1940, 7.

"energetic and dynamic": Dunn, *1940,* 242.

"inefficient and exhausted": ibid.

"Democracies" . . . "decay, weakness and blindness": Anne Morrow Lindbergh, *The Wave of the Future,* 11.

"a new conception of humanity": ibid.

"Because we [in democratic nations] are blind": ibid.

"but the greatness [of Nazism]": ibid.

"scum on the wave of the future": ibid., 19.

"such as blindness": ibid., 11.

"crisp, clear, tart, sunny, and crimson": ibid., 26.

"simply skim off the scum of Nazism": Dunn, *1940,* 243.

"Lindbergh's mouthpiece" and "Satan's little wife": Hertog, 383.

"poisonous": Olson, loc. 4336.

"an outright apology for fascism": "Anne Morrow Lindbergh Rides 'The Wave of the Future,'" *Columbus Daily Spectator,* January 19, 1941, 2.

"the Bible of": Dunn, 244.

"I am hurt": Anne Morrow Lindbergh Diary, October 27, 1940, *War Within and Without,* 148.

"I am now": Anne Morrow Lindbergh Diary, January [n.d.] 1941, ibid., 161.

"You see?": "Franklin Roosevelt's Press Conference," December 17, 1940, Series I, Press Conferences of President Franklin D. Roosevelt, November 29, 1940–December 31, 1940, Franklin D. Roosevelt Presidential Library and Museum.

"in a position to bring": "Fireside Chat 16: On the 'Arsenal of Democracy,'" transcript, Presidential Speeches, Miller Center, University of Virginia.

"There is far less chance": ibid.

"I feel sure": Charles A. Lindbergh Journal, January 7, 1941, *Wartime Journals,* 437.

"The pall of war": Wallace, 238.

"a little too late" . . . "a little too hot": Charles A. Lindbergh Journal, February 2, 1941, *Wartime Journals,* 450.

"uninspired drabness of everyday life": Charles A. Lindbergh Journal, February 24, 1941, ibid.

CHAPTER TWENTY-NINE: CRASH LANDING

"hodge-podge of sincere citizens": Fill Calhoun, "How Isolationist Is the Midwest?" *Life,* December 1, 1941, 40.

"Jews or their appointees": Ruth A. Sarles, *A Story of America First: The Men and Women Who Opposed U.S. Intervention in World War II,* Westport, CT: Praeger, 2003, 43.

"Jewish" . . . "half-Jew": ibid., 39.

"When we get through with the Jews in America": Richard M. Ketchum, *The Borrowed Years, 1939–1941: America on the Road to War,* New York: Random House, 1989, 124.

"United States cannot win this war for England": Charles A. Lindbergh, "We Are Weakening Our Defense Position," delivered in New York City, April 23, 1941, *Vital Speeches of the Day,* vol. 7, p. 424.

"curl inside with shock": Anne Morrow Lindbergh Diary, May 9, 1941, *War Within and Without,* 178.

"great strength and power": ibid.

just "dumb" . . . "Are you talking about Colonel Lindbergh?" . . . "Yes": "President Defines Lindbergh's Niche," *New York Times,* April 26, 1941, 5.

"My Dear Mr. President": Dunn, *1940,* 292.

"no hesitation about sending back to the president": ibid., 311.

a "little revulsion": Olson, loc. 2379.

"I always understood": Mosley, 263.

"personal neutrality": Olson, loc. 2379.

"Hang Roosevelt": Charles A. Lindbergh Journal, October 30, 1941, *Wartime Journals,* 551.

"Lindbergh is Hitler's puppet-agent": "Lindbergh Views Hotly Assailed," *New York Times,* August 8, 1941, 18.

began chanting "Nazi-lover": Milton, loc. 7814.

"It is a perfect base for German invasion": Olson, loc. 5786.

"What is being done to guard this island?": ibid.

"with a fine-tooth comb": Charles A. Lindbergh Journal, August 9, 1941, *Wartime Journals,* 524.

"x-rayed the furniture": ibid.

"Lindbergh for president!" . . . "Nazi-lover": Butterfield, 67.

"public enemy No. 1": Olson, loc. 6836.

"Hang Roosevelt!": Charles A. Lindbergh Journal, October 30, 1941, *Wartime Journals,* 551.

"Go back to Germany!": Butterfield, 67.

"the naked facts": Charles A. Lindbergh, "Des Moines Speech: Delivered in Des Moines, Iowa, on September 11, 1941," charleslindbergh.com/americanfirst/speech.asp.

"make bitter enemies of any race": ibid.

"The Jewish races . . . for reasons which are not American": ibid.

"and I decided if I waited any longer": Milton, loc. 8045.

"It sounds like Charles A. Lindbergh": Dunn, *1940,* 302.

"The voice is the voice of Lindbergh": ibid.

"intemperate," "intolerant," and "repugnant": Stephen H. Norwood, *Anti-Semitism and the American Far Left,* New York: Cambridge University Press, 2013, 67.

"the most dangerous man in America": Berg, 428.

"the most un-American talk": ibid.

"I felt I had worded my Des Moines speech": Charles A. Lindbergh Journal, September 15, 1941, *Wartime Journals,* 539.

"one last desperate plan remaining": "Text of Lindbergh's Address at America First Rally in Madison Square Garden," *New York Times,* October 31, 1941, 4.

"All . . . are now in dark war paint": Charles A. Lindbergh Journal, November 30, 1941, *Wartime Journals,* 559.

CHAPTER THIRTY: THE LINDBERGHS' WAR

"How did the [Japanese] get close enough": Charles A. Lindbergh Journal, December 8, 1941, ibid., 560.

"And the Angel said": Anne Morrow Lindbergh Diary, December 8, 1941, *War Within and Without,* 241.

"Yesterday, December 7, 1941": Franklin D. Roosevelt, "Address to Congress Requesting a Declaration of War with Japan, December 8, 1941," Franklin D. Roosevelt Presidential Library.

"And more and more angels came": Anne Morrow Lindbergh Diary, December 8, 1941, *War Within and Without,* 242.

"no misgivings about an all-out war against Japan": Butterfield, 67.

"I want to do my part": Charles A. Lindbergh Journal, December 12, 1941, *Wartime Journals,* 566.

"You can't have an officer leading men": Dunn, *1940,* 311.

"Obstacles have been put in our way": Charles A. Lindbergh Journal, January 1, 1942, *Wartime Journals,* 588.

"loaded with dynamite": Charles A. Lindbergh Journal, February 25, 1942, ibid., 597.

"Henry Ford wants to talk to [you]": Charles A. Lindbergh Journal, March 21, 1942, ibid., 607.

"Very Hollywood!": Anne Morrow Lindbergh Diary, July 18, 1942, *War Within and Without,* 273.

"in the quiet of an afternoon": Anne Morrow Lindbergh Diary, August 4, 1942, ibid., 284.

"To others he is only a dead dog": ibid.

"It's all right": ibid.

"There is a great empty, lonely feeling": Charles A. Lindbergh Journal, August 4, 1942, *Wartime Journals,* 689.

"It is a boy" . . . "A *boy!?*": Anne Morrow Lindbergh Diary, August 12, 1942, *War Within and Without,* 294.

"We'll never be able to name it": ibid.

"A letter from me might have been used": Friedman, 220

"It *is* the loss of civilizations": Anne Morrow Lindbergh Diary, December 12, 1942, *War Within and Without,* 310.

"pain and hurt and wrong of my book": Anne Morrow Lindbergh Diary, August 27, 1944, ibid., 450.

"point of light from a burning-glass": Anne Morrow Lindbergh Diary, October 8, 1944, ibid., 446.

"I want to be forgiven": Anne Morrow Lindbergh Diary, December 12, 1942, ibid., 309.

"For what? And by whom?": ibid.

"I don't know [by whom]": ibid.

"Help me to live": Anne Morrow Lindbergh Diary, December 12, 1942, ibid., 311.

"Russian dominated Europe": Reed Whittemore, "The Flyer and the Yahoos," *The New Republic,* October 3, 1970, 12.

"a vagueness of mind": Charles A. Lindbergh, *Of Flight and Life,* New York: Charles Scribner's Sons, 1948, 6.

"I'm blind . . . I can't see the [dials]": ibid., 7.

"pure joy of existence": ibid., 8.

"a part of all things": ibid., 7–8.

"a sudden revulsion": ibid., 8.

"a terrible giant's womb": ibid., 9.

"a temple of the god of science": ibid.

"in worshipping science": ibid., 10.

"outguessed, outflew and outshot": Berg, 448.

"yellow danger": "Charles Lindbergh," Spartacus Educational, spartacus-educational .com/USAlindbergh.htm.

"Since I can carry only one book": Charles A. Lindbergh Journal, April 3. 1944, *Wartime Journals,* 775.

"Don't forget your lunch!": Anne Morrow Lindbergh Diary, April 5, 1944, *War Within and Without,* 424.

"I am very stupid at it": Anne Morrow Lindbergh Diary, May 26, 1947, *Against Wind and Tide,* 27.

"cheerful and solid": Anne Morrow Lindbergh Diary, April 5, 1944, *War Within and Without,* 423.

"politics sometimes": Anne Morrow Lindbergh Diary, June 20, 1944, ibid., 427.

"true self as I have never done": ibid.

"they like me!": ibid.

"He dive-bombed enemy positions": Berg, 451.

"You press a button and death flies down": Charles A. Lindbergh Journals, May 29, 1941, *Wartime Journals,* 835.

"wild free fraternity of the air": Davis, 422.

"There is nothing I would rather do": Berg, 456.

"looks like us and has apple trees and a brook": Anne Morrow Lindbergh to Margot Morrow, September 7, 1944, *War Within and Without,* 438.

"snatched away": Anne Morrow Lindbergh Diary, October 8, 1944, ibid., 445.

"frail and so gallant": ibid., 446.

"flooding everything": Anne Morrow Lindbergh Diary, October 27, 1944, *War Within and Without,* 451.

"Both of us are groping": ibid., 452.

PART NINE: FINAL FLIGHT

"After my death": Charles A. Lindbergh, *Autobiography of Values,* 402.

CHAPTER THIRTY-ONE: OUT OF THE ASHES

DR. ALEXIS CARREL DIES IN PARIS: "Dr. Alexis Carrel Dies at Age 71," *New York Times,* November 5, 1944, 19.

"I wanted to pick up the phone": Charles A. Lindbergh Journal, May 13, 1945, *Wartime Journals,* 936.

"to make myself realize he [was] gone": Friedman, 220.

"I couldn't understand this": "Oh, No, It Can't Be," Holocaust Teacher Resource

Center, holocaust-trc.org/the-holocaust-education-program-resource-guide/oh-no
-it-cant-be-questions.

"How," he wondered, "could [Hitler] give such an order": ibid.

"Obviously, this winter": Berg, 463.

"We interrupt this program": 1945 Philco News Reports FDR's Death, youtube.com/
watch?v=c_FohJgLrvA.

"The vindictiveness in Washington": Berg, 463.

"Some say the Germans": ibid.

"It is a city destroyed": Charles A. Lindbergh Journal, May 17, 1945, *Wartime Journals,* 944.

"proud" and "virile": ibid., 943.

"has reaped the whirlwind [it] caused": ibid.

"steel helmets, rifles, and khaki uniforms": ibid., 944.

"I prefer to miss Dachau": Mosley, 330.

"the man Hitler, now the myth Hitler": Charles A. Lindbergh Journal, May 18, 1945,
Wartime Journals, 949.

"he was here where I am standing": ibid.

"Hitler, a man who controlled such power": ibid.

"confiscated documents": Berg, 466.

"well-fed [Americans]" who "stuffed themselves": Charles A. Lindbergh Journal,
May 23, 1945, *Wartime Journals,* 961.

"What right have we to damn the Nazi": ibid.

"We in America are supposed to stand": ibid.

"showing no trace of hatred or resentment": Charles A. Lindbergh Journal, May 18,
1945, ibid., 948.

"like [the Russian's] face": Charles A. Lindbergh Journal, May 24, 1945, ibid., 961.

"the way he look[ed] at me": ibid., 962.

"capable of anything": ibid.

"adequate for the season": Charles A. Lindbergh Journal, June 10, 1945, ibid,. 992.

"low, small, factory-like building": Charles A. Lindbergh Journal, June 11, 1945, ibid.,
995.

"the steel stretchers for holding the bodies": ibid., 994–995.

"How could any reward": ibid., 995.

A "man" . . . "No," Charles corrected himself, "a boy": ibid., 995.

"arms so thin": ibid.

"Twenty-five thousand in a year and a half": ibid.

"represented real life": Reggiani, 67.

"strange sort of disturbance": Charles A. Lindbergh Journal, June 11, 1945, *Wartime
Journals,* 996.

"The Germans had lost their balance": Charles A. Lindbergh, *Of Flight and Life,* 19.

"he saw the danger": ibid, 20.

"the power of [its] science": ibid.

"superior genetic material": H. J. Muller, "The Dominance of Economics over
Eugenics," *The Scientific Monthly,* Vol. 37, issue 1, July 7, 1933, 41.

"Civilization-building white elite" over "faster-breeding racial inferiors": Friedman,
242–249.

Its power, he claimed, had "hypnotized" him: ibid., 28.

"work for the idol of science": ibid.

"worship at its Godless temple": ibid., 9.

"I believe the simplest knowledge of eugenics": Charles A. Lindbergh to Frederick
    Osborn, May 10, 1967, American Eugenics Society Records, Series I, American
    Philosophical Society Library.

"With the key to science": Charles A. Lindbergh, *Of Flight and Life,* 28.

"Christian ideals": ibid., 35.

"Leadership would pass from our western peoples": ibid., 34–35.

"vengeance": Davis, 426.

"[Charles Lindbergh] is saddened": ibid., 426.

"doctrine of death": Charles A. Lindbergh, *Of Flight and Life,* 35.

"equality" but "quality": ibid.

CHAPTER THIRTY-TWO: TOGETHER, YET APART

"deflated feeling in [the] house": Reeve Lindbergh, 61.

"a sense of release": ibid.

"snapped . . . [to] military alertness": ibid., 41.

"Now, now! Watch out for my hat!": ibid., 40.

"Freedom and Responsibility," "Instinct and Intellect," and, of course, "Downfall of
    Civilization": ibid., 38.

"Don't . . . Don't do this": Ross, 350.

"elves": Berg, 479.

"This is not a democracy": Reeve Lindbergh, 45.

"Yes, Father": ibid., 47.

"open, loose-featured patience": ibid., 78.

more than a dozen such "pretenders": ibid.

"and left us [children] in peace": ibid., 41.

"Will I ever feel creative again?": Anne Morrow Lindbergh Diary, July 14, 1951, *Against
    Wind and Tide,* 78.

"solitude [and] creative thinking": Anne Morrow Lindbergh Diary, July 27, 1953,
    Against Wind and Tide, 86.

"the only field I had of my own": ibid.

"I know that he would not have told it": ibid., 85.

"Keep your style": Lauren D. Lyman, "How Lindbergh Wrote a Book," *The Beehive,*
    Summer 1954, 19.

"We have known Lindbergh the aviator": Brendan Gill, "The Doom of Heroes," *The
    New Yorker,* September 19, 1953, 110.

"Boom days are here again": Berg, 490.

"I cannot see what I have gone through": Anne Morrow Lindbergh Diary, July 3, 1956,
    Against Wind and Tide, 152.

"growing pains": Anne Morrow Lindbergh, *Gift from the Sea: An Answer to the Conflicts
    in Our Lives,* New York: Pantheon, 1955, 87.

"spill herself away": ibid., 45.

"inner spring": ibid., 44.

"of one's own": ibid., 51.

CHAPTER THIRTY-THREE: SORROWS AND SECRETS

a look "so loving" . . . "feel the nature of it": Reeve Lindbergh, 117.

"the only time I can remember": ibid.

"or pretended to": ibid.

"his way of speaking": Rudolf Schröck, *Das Doppelleben des Charles A. Lindbergh*, trans. Katrin Tiernan for the author, Munich: Random House, 2005, 35.

"utmost secrecy": ibid., 117.

"my love to you and the children": ibid., 176.

he only signed his first initial, "C": ibid.

"I don't know why he lived this way": "Lindbergh's Double Life," Minnesota Historical Society, mnhs.org.

"When I watch wild animals": Charles A. Lindbergh, *Autobiography of Values*, 36.

"eternal life for which men during centuries have sought": ibid.

"Only by dying": ibid.

"I did so casually": Alden Whitman, "Lindbergh Traveling Widely as Conservationist," *New York Times*, June 23, 1969, 26.

"build up conservation": ibid.

"I just tell [people] how important it is": ibid.

"I realized that if I had to choose": ibid.

"no longer an ending": James Newton, *Uncommon Friends: Life with Thomas Edison, Henry Ford, Harvey Firestone, Alexis Carrel & Charles Lindbergh*, New York: Harcourt, Inc., 1987, 337.

"Dear Brigitte": Schröck, 177.

"I want to go home": Berg, 553.

"But you're abandoning science!": Brendan Gill, *Lindbergh Alone*, St. Paul: Minnesota Historical Society Press, 2002, 174.

"No, science abandoned me": ibid.

"the music is alright": Berg, 558.

"If I take the wings of the morning": ibid., 557.

"Don't let your mother spend a lot of time": ibid., 559.

"death is so close all the time": ibid.

"Now, Doctor": ibid., 560.

"I am form and I am formless": Charles A. Lindbergh, *Autobiography of Values*, 402.

INDEX

475th Fighter Group, 287, 289

Acosta, Bert, 72
Adventures of Daniel Boone, The (radio show), 295
Air Service Reserve Corps, 24, 56, 149; *see also* U.S. Army Air Corps
airmail, 57–59, 69, 77, 80, 126, 249, 287
  stamps featuring Charles, 97–98
Alcock, John, 63–64
Allen, William, 171
America First, 269–271, 273–277, 296, 321; *see also* isolationism
  anti-Semitism and, 270, 275–277
  founding principles, 269
  protests against, 1–3, 277
  rallies, 1–4, 271, 273–276
American Breeders Association, 110
American Eugenics Society, 111–112, 302
American Federation of Labor (AFL), 149–150
American Importer (ship), 202
American Legion (plane), 72–73
Anschluss, 228–229, 230–231
appeasement, 236–237, 244, 253
Aquitania (ship), 247
Arc de Triomphe, 93, 261
Arlington National Cemetery, 24
Arnold, Henry H., 248, 279
"Atlantic Fever," 66, 71, 76; *see also* Orteig Prize
Atlantic Monthly, The, 259–260
atomic bombs, 302–304, 307
Autobiography of Values (C. Lindbergh), 319, 321

aviation
  Charles's advocacy, 100–102, 116, 215–216, 248
  commercial, 24, 35, 43, 56–57, 58, 67, 96–97, 100–101, 124–125, 202, 279, 305
  dangers, 30–31, 43, 72–73
  exploration and, 59
  high-altitude, 35, 281–282, 284–285
  military, 24–25, 34–35, 52, 289, 305
  records broken in, 72, 127
  seediness, 43
  technological advances in, 34–35, 52, 95, 124

B-24 bomber planes, 280, 283
Badge of a Knight of the Order of Leopold, 97
Bak, Richard, 95
Ball, Leon, 294
barnstorming, 47–51, 52, 56, 58, 63, 111, 118, 287
Belgium, 97, 99, 211, 243
  liberation of, 288
  surrender to Germany, 257, 258
Bellanca planes, 59–60, 64, 66, 67, 68, 72, 78
Berchtesgaden, 297
Biffle, Ira ("Biff"), 45–46, 53
Bitz, Irving, 154, 160
Bixby, Harold, 67
Blitzkrieg, 258
Bloomfield Hills, Michigan, 280, 288
Blythe, Dick, 78, 79–80, 83
Boeing planes, 67, 69
Bonnie Laddies, 87
Booster (dog), 55
Boughton, Willis A., 98